Praise

"Arlen Payne writes with a pastor's heart, a theologian's pen, and a worshipper's passion in *Consider His Word*. I believe that Christians will benefit from his insights and devotional style that will cause them to reflect on the word of God. This book is the result of a lifetime that has been spent with God in His Word."

Tom Messer, Pastor
Trinity Baptist Church, Jacksonville, FL

"I have known and admired Arlen Payne for over twenty-five years. His deep and real love for Jesus, for God's word, and his family have made him a man easy to admire. His love for the 'first Floridians,' the Seminole and Miccosukee tribes, has long inspired me to see beyond the glare of modern South Florida and see the deep roots of special lives long lived in Florida's wilderness. Arlen's words have deep roots as well and are worth listening to."

Bud McCord
Abide Brazil Ministries, Brazil, S.A.

"Arlen Payne has exemplified a man whose heart is after God while serving for many years among the Seminole Tribe of Florida. His faithfulness to service is evident in churches established and his dedication to the Word of God is evident in this devotional. No doubt this book will help the individual read through the Bible and 'consider' what God has to say."

Dr. Jon Konnerup, Mission Director
Baptist Bible Fellowship International, Springfield, Missouri

"This devotional book has been a refreshing new way to read through my Bible this year. The comments highlighting a portion of each day's reading are a stimulus to be faithful as well as to consider carefully what one is reading. Because of its helpfulness, I highly recommend *Consider His Word*."

Gary Tomberlin
Baptist Bible Fellowship Int., Missionary to Brazil

"Dr. Arlen Payne makes spending time in God's Word a wonderful experience. His daily devotion takes you on a journey through the whole Bible in just one year. Brother Arlen makes it like taking a walk with an old friend."

Roland Lawson, Evangelist
Intercession City, Florida

CONSIDER HIS

CONSIDER HIS WORD

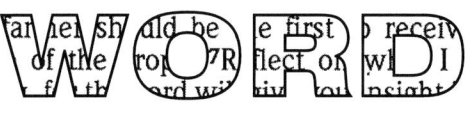

A Daily Devotional

Arlen J. Payne

TATE PUBLISHING & *Enterprises*

Consider His Word
Copyright © 2009 by Arlen J. Payne. All rights reserved.

No part of this publication may be reproduced, stored in a retrieval system or transmitted in any way by any means, electronic, mechanical, photocopy, recording or otherwise without the prior permission of the author except as provided by USA copyright law.

Scripture quotations are taken from the Holy Bible, King James Version, Cambridge, 1769. Used by permission. All rights reserved.

The opinions expressed by the author are not necessarily those of Tate Publishing, LLC.

Published by Tate Publishing & Enterprises, LLC
127 E. Trade Center Terrace | Mustang, Oklahoma 73064 USA
1.888.361.9473 | www.tatepublishing.com

Tate Publishing is committed to excellence in the publishing industry. The company reflects the philosophy established by the founders, based on Psalm 68:11,
"The Lord gave the word and great was the company of those who published it."

Book design copyright © 2009 by Tate Publishing, LLC. All rights reserved.
Cover design by Stephanie Woloszyn
Interior design by Janae J. Glass

Published in the United States of America

ISBN: 978-1-60604-558-9
1. Religion: Christian Life: Devotional
09.07.15

TO

my lovely wife, Lana, who completes me in every way;

my children, Sara, Rachel, and James, who have brought more joy to my life than they will ever know;

my granddaughter, Kaylana, who just makes me laugh;

my late grandfather, Roy Taylor, who taught me to be a gentleman;

the Lord Jesus Christ who loved me, saved me, and keeps me in the palm of his hand

I humbly dedicate this book.

Acknowledgements

I am grateful to the staff and editors at Tate Publishing for putting the finishing touches to this project and for making a dream become a reality.

I appreciate the help my wife, Lana, and mother-in-law, Lois Ryerson, who helped correct my bad spelling and poor grammar.

I am thankful to the people of the Seminole Tribe of Florida for loving my wife and me and allowing us to minister amongst them.

I also appreciate the churches and individuals who have supported us, prayed for us, and encouraged us in our ministry on the Seminole reservations.

Most of all I am forever grateful to the Lord who blessed me more abundantly than I will ever deserve.

Foreword

> This book of the law shall not depart out of thy mouth; but thou shalt meditate therein day and night, that thou mayest observe to do according to all that is written therein: for then thou shalt make thy way prosperous, and then thou shalt have good success. Joshua 1:8

Arlen Payne, missionary to the Seminole Indians, has written an excellent devotional book based on the Word of God. Every child of God should want to be successful and prosper spiritually. God's Word explains fully how this can be experienced in our daily walk with him. Your spiritual well-being and growth depends on spiritual nourishment (Matthew 4:4).

Every Christian needs a daily appointment with God. The most vital time in the life of a child of God is the time spent in fellowship with him. If one wants to grow spiritually, this is a requirement established by God. This book is not the Bible but will point you to the Word of God, which is forever settled in heaven and will endure forever (1 Peter 1:25).

My prayer is that you will read, study, and meditate on a daily basis, and *Consider His Word*. Then, you will make thy way prosperous and have good success.

Bob Baird, Mission Director Emeritus
Baptist Bible Fellowship International

Introduction

Today our churches are filled with weak and immature believers. This, in turn, makes our churches weak and anemic. The problem lies in the fact that the majority of people who profess Christ as their Lord and Savior spend little or no time reading and studying the Word of God. Bibles are frequently purchased and given as gifts or awards, and they are rarely opened. In order for there to be genuine spiritual growth in our churches and individual lives, we must open God's Word and consider what he is saying to us. The Bible is relevant for our modern society and culture. Its message is still true and life changing.

Consider His Word was written to encourage readers to consider the truth of the Bible, God's Holy Word. The devotional message written for each day of the year is short and to the point, giving the reader more time to spend reading the Word of God. A recommended reading is given each day, leading the reader to completely read through the Bible in one year. The daily scripture and devotional thought is then taken from that daily reading.

Following each daily devotion space has been provided where the readers may add their own thoughts and feelings concerning the daily verse of Scripture. Space has also been provided for writing down daily praise offerings and prayer requests.

As you *Consider His Word* each day, take time to *meditate* on what you have read. Before Joshua lead the children of Israel across the Jordan river, God gave him this promise: "This book of the law shall not depart out of thy mouth; but thou shalt meditate therein day and night, that thou mayest observe to do according to all that is written therein: for then thou shalt make thy way prosperous, and then thou shalt have good success" (Joshua 1:8). In this verse is recorded the only promise in the whole Bible that God gave us for success. Notice that God told Joshua to meditate in his Word, and then "do according to all that is written therein." The Bible was not just written for our entertainment. To just read the Bible and then set is aside is of little value. One must take time to absorb its message then practice what it says.

May God bless and encourage you as you read, absorb, and obey his Word.

January 1
Genesis 1–4

"In the beginning God created the heaven and the earth" (Genesis 1:1).

Imagine when the world was brand new. Everything was absolutely perfect; there was no pollution, no toxic waste, and no smog. The water was clean, the soil perfect, and the sky was clear. Adam enjoyed a perfect environment. As you begin this new year, it is also unstained. What will you do with it? In the Garden of Eden, Adam enjoyed a close walk and fellowship with his heavenly Father. God wants to have a relationship with you just like he did with Adam in the Garden of Eden. That is why he gave his only Son, Jesus Christ, to reconcile you to him. Sin has separated you from God. Have you received his offer of reconciliation? If not, you can be reconciled with God today. Pray this prayer from your heart:

> Dear Lord, I know that I have sinned against you, please forgive all my sin and come into my life that I may walk close to you. Reconcile me to yourself through the shed blood of Jesus Christ, in his name, amen.

Perhaps you have received the Lord and have experienced the joy of walking with him. Make a new commitment today to walk with him more closely than you have before. He is waiting to hear from you.

Ponderings

Praise

Petitions

January 2
Genesis 5–8

"But Noah found grace in the eyes of the Lord" (Genesis 6:8).

Grace is God's unmerited, undeserved favor for man. It was by grace that Noah and his family were spared the wrath of God's judgment upon the earth. What did Noah do to deserve God's grace? My suspicion is that it was exactly the same thing we do today to deserve God's grace—nothing. Neither Noah nor anyone else deserves to receive God's grace. It comes because God, in his infinite love and mercy, extends his grace to us. Just like Noah was saved by grace, so are we saved by the grace of God. We did nothing to earn or deserve it. God simply extended his grace toward us because he loved us. There is nothing we did or can do to deserve such a gift. Maybe that is why they call it amazing grace.

> Amazing grace, how sweet the sound that saved a wretch like me! I once was lost, but now I'm found, was blind but now I see.
>
> —John Newton, 1725–1807

Ponderings
_____
_____
_____

Praise
_____
_____
_____

Petitions
_____
_____
_____

January 3
Genesis 9–12

"I do set my bow in the cloud" (Genesis 9:13).

Many myths surround the meaning and significance of a rainbow. Some say that at its end there is a pot of gold, or that the sighting of a rainbow brings good luck. God told us exactly why he set the rainbow in the clouds. It is a reminder of his judgment and his grace. It reminds us of the judgment that came to the earth because "every imagination of the thoughts of his heart was only evil continually" (Genesis 6:5), but then, "Noah found grace in the eyes of the Lord" (Genesis 6:8).

The rainbow not only reminds us of God's judgment but also of his grace. In his divine attributes, God is perfectly just and perfectly gracious. The rainbow is a reminder of both. It is also representative of a promise that God made to man: "The waters shall no more become a flood to destroy all flesh" (Genesis 9:15b). Next time you see a rainbow, think of God's judgment, God's grace, and God's unbroken promises.

Ponderings

Praise

Petitions

January 4
Genesis 13–17

"And Lot chose him all the plain of Jordan" (Genesis 13:11).

Choices. We make them every day. Some are of great significance and require much thought and wisdom; others seem to be made with little thought or effort. We make many choices every day of our lives. Every choice bears its own consequences. Lot chose the plain of Jordan and his life was forever changed. What if he had chosen Canaan instead? Lot's choice of the Jordan seems to have come from what he could physically see and what he wanted at that moment. He did not see the consequences of living in Sodom and Gomorrah.

How do you make the right choices? Look what Abram (Abraham) did. "Abram called on the name of the Lord" (Genesis 13:4). Making the right choice requires the wisdom of someone who can see the things we cannot see. Making the right choice requires that we call on the One who knows what the right choice is. To help you make the right choices, pray. God will give you the wisdom to make the right choices. "If any of you lack wisdom, let him ask of God, that giveth to all men liberally, and upbraideth not; and it shall be given him" (James 1:5).

Ponderings

Praise

Petitions

January 5
Genesis 18–20

"Therefore Sarah laughed within herself" (Genesis 18:12).

Sarah laughed at the promise of God when she heard that she would bear a child in her old age. She laughed because she thought that it would be impossible. How many times have we laughed at God's promises to us? He has never broken one of his promises, so why do we laugh as Sarah did? Most likely it is just a lack of faith in God's ability and power. God asked Abraham "Is anything too hard for the Lord?" (Genesis 18:14a). Well, how about it? Is there anything too hard for him? Why do we worry when he has promised to meet all of our needs? Is it too hard for God who owns everything to supply what you need today? Rather than laughing at God's promises, we should be more faithful like Abraham. Oh! Did you know that Abraham laughed too? Both Sarah and Abraham saw firsthand that nothing was too hard for the Lord. You'll find the same is true in your life. *Is anything too hard for the Lord?*

Ponderings

Praise

Petitions

January 6
Genesis 21–23

"And Abraham rose up early in the morning" (Genesis 22:3a).

I wonder if Abraham slept very well the night before he was to take his son, Isaac, and offer him as a burnt offering before the Lord. From what Scripture tells us about Abraham, he probably slept pretty well. Abraham had complete trust in the Lord. Abraham trusted God so completely, he was willing to do anything or go anywhere that God told him. Even as his son, Isaac, asked about the materials they were taking up on one of the mountains of Moriah, Abraham was confident that God would provide a lamb for a burnt offering.

Do you have that kind of trust? Do you lose sleep worrying over the troubles of life? Are there too many bills or problems at work? Take all your burdens and cares to the One who promised to take care of you. Peter said it this way, "Casting all your cares upon him; for he careth for you" (1 Peter 5:7). Now do it! Take your burdens and cares to the Lord, put your complete trust in him, and get a good night's sleep.

Ponderings

Praise

Petitions

January 7
Genesis 24–25

"And the man wondering at her held his peace, to wit whether the Lord had made his journey prosperous or not" (Genesis 24:21).

Abraham had sent his servant to find a wife for his son, Isaac. As he stopped at the Well of Nahor, he prayed that God would, in a very specific manner, show him the young lady that God intended to be Isaac's bride. God soon answered in exactly the way the servant had prayed. But still he wondered, *Is this really the one? Had God really answered my prayer?*

How often have we made exactly the same error? We ask God specifically for an answer to prayer, and when God answers we stand looking at the answer, wondering if God has really answered our prayer.

After watching his answer to prayer—the woman giving water to the camels—the servant finally came to the conclusion that "The Lord hath prospered my way" (Genesis 24:56). There was no doubt that God had specifically answered a specific prayer. Yes, God does answer prayer, so when he does answer, don't just stand there wondering about it. Thank him and give him glory for working in your life.

Ponderings

Praise

Petitions

January 8
Genesis 26–28

"And, behold, I am with thee, and will keep thee in all places whither thou goest" (Genesis 28:15).

Jacob had been exiled to Padan-aram because of his and his mother's scheme to take the blessing of his father from Esau, his brother. Here we see him finding a place to sleep, using a stone for a pillow. As he fell asleep, God came to him in a dream, giving him the same promise that he had given to his father. Jacob realized that he was not alone but that God was there and intended to use him to carry on his plan: to continue in him a great nation. God has great plans for you as well. You may not discover them all at once. God may choose to reveal his plan for you a little at a time. Do not fail to follow him. When you feel all alone or that you have no purpose in life, remember that you have a heavenly Father who loves you very much and has a great plan for your life. He is with you and "will keep you in all places, wither thou goest" (Genesis 28:15).

Ponderings

Praise

Petitions

January 9
Genesis 29–31

"God hath seen my affliction and the labor of my hands" (Genesis 31:42b).

Jacob was in a dispute with his father-in-law, Laban, over his family and his livestock. God had greatly blessed Jacob and now he was on his way home. Before confronting Jacob, Laban had been told in a dream, "Take heed that thou speak not to Jacob either good or bad" (Genesis 31:24b). When Laban came to Jacob there was the potential for a big fight. But rather than engage in battle, both men were careful to listen to the voice of God. Jacob knew that his blessings were from God and had followed his direction in dealing with Laban. Jacob's position was simply that "God knows." In a day when so many want to claim and proclaim their *rights*, wouldn't it be much more peaceful if we would just rely on God? If, when the disputes arise, we take the position of Jacob—"God knows." Yes, he knows what you are going through, he knows your afflictions and labor, and he has promised: "your labor is not in vain in the Lord" (1 Corinthians 15:58).

Ponderings

Praise

Petitions

January 10
Genesis 32–35

"I will surely do thee good" (Genesis 32:12).

Jacob had confidence that God's intentions for him were good. Though he feared Esau, his fear was unfounded; Esau had no intention of harming him. When he finally met with his older brother, rather than the retaliation that he anticipated, he found grace and mercy. How often have we been afraid to approach God for fear of his wrath and judgment? Yet when we finally turn to him, we find his abundant grace and great mercy. God's plan for you is only good. It may seem that you are going through difficult trials and that life has dealt you a tough blow. Even so, God still loves you very much and desires only good for you. God's will for you is perfect and good. Allow him to reveal his will to you day by day. Just trust him and surely he will "do thee good."

Ponderings

Praise

Petitions

January 11
Genesis 36–38

"Thus his father wept for him" (Genesis 37:35).

Jacob had sent his favorite son, Joseph, on a simple assignment to see how his brothers were faring. Yet the news returned that Jacob's favorite son had been attacked by wild animals and killed (it was a lie). Jacob's heart was broken. He would mourn for a lifetime, all because of a lie. How careful we must be to speak the truth. A plot had been devised to deceive Jacob and cover up the truth! Why? Because of simple jealousy. The other ten brothers had grown jealous of the *dreamer* and their father's favoritism toward Joseph. Now they had done away with Joseph for good, or so they thought. Though the brothers had no idea that they were in the midst of it, God had a plan. The weeping of Jacob would some day be turned to joy. In your darkest hour, isn't it comforting to know that the heavenly Father has a plan? Though you may be weeping, though you may be hurting, just lean on the Lord for he has a plan for you as well. Trust him.

Ponderings
_____
_____
_____

Praise
_____
_____
_____

Petitions
_____
_____
_____

January 12
Genesis 39–41

"And it came to pass, as she spake to Joseph day by day, that he hearkened not unto her, to lie by her, or to be with her" (Genesis 39:10).

Joseph had been taken to Egypt and was now a servant/slave in Potiphar's house. While Potiphar was away on a trip, his wife repeatedly approached Joseph with evil intentions. In our lives there will always be the temptation to join the crowd. "Come lie with me," the world begs. Like Joseph, we should take our stand and resist the world and its temptation to sin. Joseph never gave in, and neither should we. The temptations of the world are often inviting and appear to promise happiness, but the happiness is only temporary. Keep your eyes on the Savior and "love not the things of the world" (1 John 2:15). It is always better to obey the Word of God than give in to the temptations that come before us. Though the temptations may be strong, God will give us strength to bear any temptation that the world or Satan will try to throw at us. Take your stand against the world and its temptations. Submit to the Lord and faithfully obey his Word.

Ponderings

Praise

Petitions

January 13
Genesis 42–43

"We are verily guilty concerning our brother...therefore is this distress come upon us" (Genesis 42:21).

As Joseph and his brothers were being reunited, they were all thinking similar thoughts. Joseph was remembering the dreams he had as a young man that pointed to this very day. The brothers were remembering how they had mistreated their brother and were reaping the consequences of their sinful scheme. When they sold Joseph into slavery, the ten sons of Jacob could not have foreseen that this day was coming.

There are always consequences to sin. Oh, if we could only get a glimpse of the consequences of our own sin, perhaps it would keep us from making foolish and wicked choices. You cannot sin and get away with it. There will always be consequences to follow. "Be not deceived; God is not mocked: for whatsoever a man soweth, that shall he also reap" (Galatians 6:7).

Ponderings

Praise

Petitions

January 14
Genesis 44–46

"…for God did send me before you to preserve life" (Genesis 45:5).

Joseph, who had been abused and sold into slavery by his brothers and served as a servant/slave in Potiphar's house, had been seduced and falsely accused by his owner's wife. Joseph was sent to prison, forgotten, and then elevated to the second-highest position in a foreign land. He saw his life in the hands of an Almighty God. It was God who had taken Joseph through all these experiences, both good and bad. God had ultimately used Joseph to save his own family from starvation. We often do not clearly see what God is doing in our lives at any given moment. But we can be assured that God is working out his plan for our lives to the good. Do you suppose Joseph thought about God's plan during those years he spent in prison? Do you consider that in whatever trials you face, God is working his plan in your life? Hang in there—God is not finished with you yet. "And we know that all things work together for good to them that love God, to them who are the called according to his purpose" (Romans 8:28). God is preparing you for great things yet to come.

Ponderings

Praise

Petitions

January 15
Genesis 47–50

"Fear not: for am I in the place of God?" (Genesis 50:19).

After everything that Joseph had gone through and after his family had settled in the land of Goshen in Egypt, Joseph was able to see God's plan for his life. After Jacob had died, Joseph's brothers came to him in fear that he would seek some kind of retaliation against them. Joseph was not interested in retaliation or revenge. Through his faith and loyalty to God, he could see that in the end, they were together and God had abundantly blessed them. He had no interest in passing judgment on his brethren for their deeds of evil against him. He understood that, and even though they had thought evil against him, Joseph said to his brothers, "But as for you, ye thought evil against me; but God meant it unto good, to bring to pass, as it is this day, to save much people alive" (Genesis 50:20). Because Joseph could see himself used by God, rather then seek revenge, he encouraged his brothers and promised to take care of them and their children. Joseph was content to allow God to use him to do his work. He continually committed everything to God and to his glory and just left it at that. Why can't we follow his example and do the same when we have been wronged? Look at the example Jesus left us: "Who, when he was reviled, reviled not again; when he suffered, he threatened not; but committed himself to him that judgeth righteously" (1 Peter 2:23). A life committed to the Lord is never out of place.

Ponderings

Praise

Petitions

January 16
Exodus 1–4

"And the Lord said unto him, what is that in thine hand?" (Exodus 4:2).

When God appeared to Moses in the burning bush, he gave Moses a big job to do. As Moses began making excuses for why he could not do the work, God began taking away all of Moses' reasons for refusing to go to Egypt. Notice that God used what Moses had in his hand and provided for him what he did not have. God always equips us to do the task that he calls us to do. First, he uses what we do have, then he equips us with the gifts and talents that we do not have. God used the rod that was in Moses' hand to be a sign that he was sent from God. When Moses began to use his apparent speech impediment as an excuse, God sent his brother, Aaron, to help. God will use what you have if you will just yield yourself completely to him. When the job seems more than you can bear, God will provide what is necessary to complete the task he has given you to do. Now, what do you have that God can use? Yield it to him. What help do you need? Ask the Lord and he will provide just what you need or he will send someone to help.

Ponderings

Praise

Petitions

January 17
Exodus 5–7

"And the Egyptians shall know that I am the Lord" (Exodus 7:5). God was about to show Pharaoh and all the Egyptians that he was the Lord. The Egyptians believed that their pharaoh was god, that he had certain powers and privileges that only a god could have. As God began to free the children of Israel from the Egyptian bondage, he was going to show the Egyptians who he really was. Often God works in our lives through trials and miracles just to let us know who he is—that he is Almighty God! Have you seen his work? Have you seen him heal someone in such a way that you know it was only God who could work such a miracle? When all human endeavors have failed and all that is left is prayer and faith in an all-powerful God, he will reveal himself and show you his power. Jesus said, "The things which are impossible with men are possible with God" (Luke 18:27). It seemed impossible that Pharaoh would let the children of Israel go, but he did, and all the Egyptians knew that it was the Lord who made it happen. Now, what can he do for you?

Ponderings

Praise

Petitions

January 18
Exodus 8–10

"…that thou mayest know that there is none like me in all the earth" (Exodus 9:14).

God had sent Pharaoh and the Egyptians ten horrible plagues. The people of Egypt and Pharaoh believed and served many gods. Each of the ten plagues was a demonstration of God's power over the gods of Egypt. For example, the Egyptians believed that the Nile River possesssed powers of deity. Through Moses, God turned their river into blood. God was attempting to show Pharaoh and all the Egyptians that he was—and still is!—Lord. At one point, it seemed that Pharaoh was getting the message. Pharaoh called for Moses and said, "I have sinned against the Lord your God, and against you. Now therefore forgive, I pray thee, my sin only this once, and entreat the Lord your God, that he may take away from me this death only (Exodus 10:16)." It was apparently an empty confession because Pharaoh continued to harden his heart. Look around you today; how is God making himself known to you? What will it take for God to get your attention?

Ponderings

Praise

Petitions

January 19
Exodus 11-13

"…it is the Lord's Passover" (Exodus 12:11).

The Passover was the last plague that God brought to the Egyptians and the last night that the Israelite slaves spent in Egypt. Imagine the furor as each father found that perfect lamb to kill in order to place its blood around the door of his home. Imagine the anticipation as they waited for the Lord to pass over their houses. Imagine the wailing of the Egyptians as they awoke to find that their firstborn children had mysteriously died in the night. The Passover is a beautiful picture of the death of Jesus Christ on Calvary's cross. There his blood was shed for us, an innocent one dying for the guilty. As God's judgment passes over us, he will declare, "When I see the blood, I will pass over you" (Exodus 12:13). Each year the Passover is to be remembered and relived as a celebration of God's deliverance. Each day should be a celebration for the believer who has been delivered by the shed blood of the Lamb of God. Have a great celebration today!

Ponderings

Praise

Petitions

January 20
Exodus 14–16

"Thy right hand, O Lord, is become glorious in power" (Exodus 15:6).

The children of Israel had seen the hand of God in delivering them from Egypt. They had seen the ten plagues brought upon Pharaoh and the Egyptians. They had seen the power of God in the Passover; they had also seen his grace in sparing their own firstborn because of the blood placed upon the doorposts. They had seen the Red Sea open up to allow them to pass through on dry ground. They had seen the mighty power of God. They were now on their way to the Promised Land. It would not be long until they had a hard time finding food and good water. They started to murmur against the Lord. How quickly they had forgotten his power. We say that God is omnipotent (all-powerful), but do we really believe it? When faced with a problem that seems so big we cannot overcome it, do not forget that the Lord is *glorious in power* and that nothing is too hard for him. What problem can he solve for you today by his almighty power?

Ponderings

Praise

Petitions

January 21
Exodus 17–20

"Fear not: For God is come to prove you, and that his fear may be before your faces, that ye sin not" (Exodus 20:20).

At Mount Sinai, Moses and the people received the Ten Commandments of God. Paul said in Galatians 3:24 that the law is our *schoolmaster* and that it will teach us how to recognize sin. Here in Exodus, God laid down the Law. The violation of any one of these commandments would be sin in God's sight. These laws were to be obeyed. When one of the commandments was broken, all of the Law was violated. God gave the Law so that his people would know how to recognize sin and avoid it. Yet, man being under the curse of sin found it very difficult to live without breaking his Law. Concerning the Law, Paul continued to say that it was given to eventually bring us to Christ, that we might be justified by faith in him. God would one day send his Son to pay the price of our sin for us. Have you put your faith in the Son of God? "The wages of sin is death, but the gift of God is eternal life through Jesus Christ our Lord" (Romans 6:23).

Ponderings

Praise

Petitions

January 22
Exodus 21–23

"Thou shalt not follow a multitude to do evil" (Exodus 23:2).

How easy it is to follow the crowd. To *go with the flow*. God is looking for people who will take a stand for what is right, even when the rest of the world is bent toward doing evil. We often speak of peer pressure among our young people and how it may lead them to do wrong. Peer pressure is not just a phenomena reserved for the young. We are all capable of following a crowd to do evil. To stand up against the wrong direction of a crowd takes commitment and courage; commitment that you are going to obey God and his righteousness at all cost to your convenience and comfort. We must also have courage to stand alone. We are so often drawn into sin by following the crowd, by declaring, "Everybody else is doing it." Our choices should not be made on the basis of what everybody else is doing, but in the clear teaching of the Word of God. Take your stand; make a commitment to do right no matter what everyone else is doing. You are called to follow Jesus, not the crowd. After all, Jesus said, "Follow me," not follow them.

Ponderings

Praise

Petitions

January 23
Exodus 24–27

"And let them make me a sanctuary; that I may dwell among them" (Exodus 25:8).

A sanctuary is a holy place. God wanted a place where he could come and dwell with his people. It would later be called the Tabernacle, or *dwelling place*. The plans were very elaborate and precise. The Tabernacle was to be constructed of the finest materials. When God told the people to move, it would be taken down and moved with them. It would be the place where God could meet with his people. So where is the Tabernacle now? Where is God's dwelling place? It has to be a holy place, a pure place, a sanctuary. Once Jesus took our sin upon himself and gave us his righteousness, the believer would become that holy place—the dwelling place of God. The Lord found his dwelling place in the believer's heart, the place where he could be closer to you than anyone else could be. The believer in Christ has become his dwelling place. "What? Know ye not that your body is the temple of the Holy Ghost which is in you, which ye have of God, and ye are not your own? For ye are bought with a price: therefore glorify God in your body, and in your spirit, which are God's" (1 Corinthians 6:19–20).

Ponderings

Praise

Petitions

January 24
Exodus 28–30

"And I will dwell among the children of Israel, and will be their God"(Exodus 29:45).

The children of Israel had lived in Egypt for hundreds of years and had been exposed to the many gods of Egypt; some of them had even embraced these foreign gods. The Lord had rescued the children of Israel and delivered them from a life of slavery and oppression. As he gave them instructions on how he wanted to be worshiped and honored, he declared that now he "will be their God." They were to abandon the old Egyptian gods they had served on the other side of the Red Sea and serve the Lord God only. He instructed them to construct a Tabernacle, a dwelling place where he could meet with them. He was setting in order a system of priests, offering, and sacrifices. He wanted the people to know that he was different from the Egyptian gods, that he would not be cold and uncaring but instead loving and forgiving. He dwells in you and will never leave you. He is a jealous God who wants to dwell with you and be the only God that you worship and serve.

Ponderings

Praise

Petitions

January 25
Exodus 31–34

"For thou shalt worship no other god: for the Lord, whose name is Jealous, is a jealous God" (Exodus 34:14).

There is a universal need among all people groups to worship something or someone. Moses had been gone for over a month, and it seemed no one knew where he was. The people had been used to worshiping idols and animals. They needed a god to worship and honor for bringing them out of Egypt. Aaron was quick to collect their earrings and molded a calf for the people to worship. Had they already forgotten the God who had actually delivered them from slavery in Egypt? To this new god, a golden calf, they built an altar, offered sacrifices, and attributed to it their newfound freedom. God was angry; were it not for the interceding of Moses, he would have destroyed them. It is so easy to attribute our good fortunes to so many other sources than to the God who gave them to us. The psalmist knew this and reminded us, "Give unto the Lord the glory that is due unto his name; worship the Lord in the beauty of holiness" (Psalms 29:2). Give credit where credit is due... unto the Lord.

Ponderings

Praise

Petitions

January 26
Exodus 35–37

"And every wisehearted among you shall come, and make all that the Lord hath commanded" (Exodus 35:10).

The call had gone out for offerings and workers to build the sanctuary. In the above verse, the word *wise* means to be skillful or to have a particular skill. God had prepared the hands and hearts of a number of people to build his house. Scripture specifically mentions Bezalel as one of the men that God had given special skills to do the work on the Tabernacle. Many women were given the skill to make materials of all kinds and colors. When God calls us to do a particular work, he also gives us the ability or skill to do the work. Each person was given a job to do according to the skill that God had given him or her. God is still calling and equipping people to build his church. He calls out people for special tasks then gives them the skill to do it. You possesss a skill that God has given you. You must now yield to him so that he can use you to do his work. What is God calling and enabling you to do to build his church?

Ponderings

Praise

Petitions

January 27
Exodus 38–40

"So Moses finished the work" (Exodus 40:33b).

The work of building the Tabernacle, God's sanctuary, was finished. No cost was spared in its construction; after all, this was God's house. God had given the instructions for its construction and he had given the people the skills to do the work. The priestly garments had been made, and all the vessels and utensils were complete. They had not given God the leftovers and castoffs, but in his house they had only used the best: the purest gold, the most brilliant of colors, and the finest linens. The craftsmen that had been blessed with the best of skills were employed to do the work. Why is it that we so often give God our leftovers—the used lumber, the old leftover materials, the worn-out clothes. We often use the best for ourselves and let God have whatever might be left over. He deserves and demands the best. His work should be done in excellence. He should get our best.

Ponderings

Praise

Petitions

January 28
Leviticus 1–4

"And the Lord called unto Moses, and spake unto him out of the tabernacle of the congregation" (Leviticus 1:1).

God had called out a people unto himself. They were to be his people and he was to be their God. With the construction of the Tabernacle complete, God gave Moses and the people of Israel specific instructions in how he wanted to be worshiped. It was a way that was completely different than the other nations around them. We do not have the option of worshiping God in a way that pleases ourselves. Our worship should be to glorify and please the Lord. The sacrifices and offerings made to God were to be a picture or a "shadow of good things to come" (Hebrews 10:1). All of these ceremonies would point to the perfect sacrifice that the Lord would provide in his Son. God had a plan that would one day be the complete and perfect sacrifice of his Son on an old, rugged cross. Jesus would become our perfect sacrifice for sin. By faith in that perfect sacrifice, we can have the cleansing of our sin and truly worship the Lord "in spirit and in truth" (John 4:24).

Ponderings

Praise

Petitions

January 29
Leviticus 5–7

"And it shall be, when he shall be guilty in one of these things, that he shall confess that he hath sinned in that thing: And he shall bring his trespass offering unto the Lord for his sin which he hath sinned" (Leviticus 5:5–6a).

There were two things required by God for the cleansing of sin: confession and an offering. Each person had to bring each of these to the Lord. One offering could not be made for all sin. Each sin had to be confessed and atoned for by each individual. In God's plan there would one day be a supreme sacrifice for all sin. It would be in the sacrifice of his only Son. It would not only be a universal sacrifice for all sin for everyone but would also be for each individual. That is why we call Jesus our *personal Savior*. He died so that the price of our sin could be paid. We must also bow before him and confess every sin. He promised, "If we confess our sins, he is faithful and just to forgive us our sins, and to cleanse us from all unrighteousness" (1 John 1:9). The offering has been presented and accepted; now it's time for you to confess your own sin before God and receive his forgiveness.

Ponderings

Praise

Petitions

January 30
Leviticus 8–10

"And Moses brought Aaron and his sons, and washed them with water" (Leviticus 8:6).

Moses prepared Aaron and his sons for serving the Lord in the Tabernacle. First, he washed them so they would be symbolically pure to stand before God. Then he dressed them in the garments of the priest as God had instructed him. Finally, Moses anointed them in order to *sanctify* them for God's service.

We have been prepared in a similar way to serve the Lord. We are washed in the blood of Christ so that we may be presented to the Lord as a pure and holy priesthood. We are given special garments and equipment (the armor of God), as described in Ephesians 6:10–17, to stand against the powers of evil and do the work that God has called us to do. And we are anointed by the Holy Spirit to be set apart (sanctified) for serving the Lord with power and authority. God has called you and equipped you to be holy and fully prepared to serve him. Now, present yourself to him to obey him and serve him this day.

Ponderings

Praise

Petitions

January 31
Leviticus 11–13

"For I am the Lord your God: ye shall therefore sanctify yourselves, and ye shall be holy; for I am holy" (Leviticus 11:44).

God is holy. This means that he is perfectly pure. There is nothing unclean or wicked in him. God has given his Law for a reason. The laws that God gave to the children of Israel were given with the intent to make them a holy people, just like he is holy. We do not often think of ourselves as being a holy people. We know that in ourselves we are incapable of being holy like God is holy. It is because of our lack of holiness that we cannot enter into the presence of God. When we receive Christ as our Savior, he gives us his holiness. With our sins washed in his own blood, we now stand before God a holy people—not because we possesss personal holiness, but because Jesus took our sin upon himself and gave us his holiness. "For he hath made him (Jesus) to be sin for us, who knew no sin; that we might be made the righteousness of God in him" (1 Corinthians 5:21). We must now live out the holiness that Christ has given to us. We must live as purely as we possibly can, being careful to give him all the glory for the holiness we possesss in Christ Jesus.

Ponderings
_____
_____
_____

Praise
_____
_____
_____

Petitions
_____
_____
_____

February 1
Leviticus 14–15

"Thus shall ye separate the children of Israel from their uncleanness; that they die not in their uncleanness, when they defile my tabernacle that is among them." (Leviticus 15:31).

The laws that God issued to his people were not just for ceremonial purposes. Science has proven that the washing and cleansing of one's self helps to prevent the spread of diseases. Leprosy was especially feared for there was no known cure. Notice how God required not only cleansing of the disease but also separation. In order to keep the disease from spreading to all the people, quarantine was necessary. God was not only requiring a ceremonial cleansing for the Tabernacle, but he was also protecting his people. God cares for you very much. When he demands separation from the world, it is for a very good reason. God wants you to be clean and free from the sin and degradation of the world, for these will only lead to pain, misery, and destruction. Through the confession of sin, God will cleanse us. Through separation from the world, God will protect us.

Ponderings

Praise

Petitions

February 2
Leviticus 16–18

"And he shall take the two goats, and present them before the Lord at the door of the tabernacle of the congregation" (Leviticus 16:7).

Two goats were necessary for the atonement. One goat was sacrificed for a sin offering and the other was released as a scapegoat. Jesus became both for us in the atonement of our sin. He was offered up as our sin offering. His blood was spilt in order to pay the penalty for our sin. He is also our scapegoat. The High Priest would place his hands on this second goat, confessing all the sin of the people—in effect placing their sin upon the goat. Jesus took our sin upon himself and took our sin away. Our sin was replaced with his righteousness. II Corinthians 5:21 states, "For he hath made him to be sin for us, who knew no sin; that we might me made the righteousness of God in him." In his death on the cross, Jesus became both our sin offering and our scapegoat. "For Christ is not entered into the holy places made with hands, which are the figures of the true; but into heaven itself, now to appear in the presence of God for us" (Hebrews 9:24).

Ponderings
_____
_____
_____

Praise
_____
_____
_____

Petitions
_____
_____
_____

February 3
Leviticus 19–21

"…but thou shalt love thy neighbor as thyself: I am the Lord" (Leviticus 19:18).

This statement is the second part of what Jesus said was the *greatest commandment*. The first is to "love the Lord thy God with all thy heart, and with all thy soul, and with all thy mind" (Matthew 22:37). Leviticus 19:9–18 gives us a practical application of this great commandment. We are instructed in how to help the poor. We are told not to steal, lie, or cheat. We are told not to make fun of the handicapped or be prejudice in our assessments of other people. These principles should be the foundation of everyday relationships and even business dealings. Notice that they all are connected to a proper self-image. If we are to love others as we love ourselves, then we must have a proper love for self. This is not to be a selfish sort of love but an acknowledgement of our value to God and to others. God loves us very much, and we are important to him. Knowing how much God loves us should translate into a love and respect for all people. It is a love that is unconditional.

Ponderings

Praise

Petitions

February 4
Leviticus 22–23

"They shall therefore keep mine ordinance, lest they bear sin for it, and die therefore, if they profane it" (Leviticus 22:9).

From the time that sin entered into the world by Adam, death has always been the penalty for sin. This is absolute. There is no parole, no time off for good behavior, no probation. There is only one sentence handed down by the Judge—death. This sentence also has never changed. Before God we are all guilty and therefore are sentenced to death. Romans 5:8 proclaims, "But God commendeth his love toward us in that while we were yet sinners, Christ died for us." The sentence of death was never removed or revoked. It was paid by God's only Son at Calvary's cross. It was because of God's love for us that he provided his own son to take our sentence of death upon himself. "For the wages of sin is death, but the gift of God is eternal life through Jesus Christ our Lord" (Romans 6:23). Have you received God gift of eternal life? Jesus paid a great price so that you could have it…for free.

Ponderings

Praise

Petitions

February 5
Leviticus 24–25

"And he that blasphemeth the name of the Lord, he shall surely be put to death" (Leviticus 24:16).

Blasphemy has been defined as using God's name in contempt or in an abusive manner. Blasphemy could be committed by using God's name in vain or by cursing him. God is serious about the use of his name. How it must grieve the heart of God to hear his name used as a curse word or expletive! God's name is holy and must be revered as holy. Even believers fall into the habitual misuse of God's holy name. His name is not to be uttered in a flippant and unholy way. God's name is so holy, its abuse in blasphemy was punishable by death. May we commit to love and revere the holy name of God. In the Ten Commandments, it was stated, "Thou shalt not take the name of the Lord thy God in vain; for the Lord will not hold him guiltless that taketh his name in vain" (Exodus 20:7). May we be careful to only use God's name in reverence and fear.

Ponderings

Praise

Petitions

February 6
Leviticus 26–27

"And I will walk among you, and will be your God, and ye shall be my people" (Leviticus 26:12).

From the time of creation, it was God's intention to walk among the people he had made and fellowship with them. We often describe our fellowship with God as a *walk*. In the Old Testament that *walk* was dependent upon keeping the Law. In the era of the New Testament, it is dependent upon our response to Christ. When you confess Jesus as Lord and believe that God raised him from the dead, you enter into a walk or a relationship with God. He comes into your life; his Holy Spirit dwells in you. You now have a relationship with him. In this walk, he wants to hear from you as well as speak to you. He will speak through his Word or even communicate directly to your heart in a still, small voice. Many claim to know the Lord, but few walk with him every day. God did not want to just give us an empty religion. He wants a relationship. He wants to walk with you in holiness just like he did with Adam in the Garden of Eden.

Ponderings

Praise

Petitions

February 7
Numbers 1–2

"And the children of Israel did according to all that the Lord commanded Moses: so they pitched by their standards, and so they set forward, every one after their families, according to the house of their fathers" (Numbers 2:34).

God is a God of order and design. In these first two chapters of Numbers, God has the children of Israel organize themselves into family groups. The people were counted and recorded. Then he arranged them around the Tabernacle in a particular order. Every time they stopped on their way to the Promised Land, they were to arrange themselves around the Tabernacle in this fashion. God's design and order can be found nearly everywhere. There is design and order in creation. There is to be design and order in our families and churches. They are not to be filled with the confusion and disorder that is so commonplace today. There is even an order to our lives. When you allow him, God will show you the design and order he has for your life. Just follow his leading. "The steps of a good man are ordered by the Lord: and he delighteth in his way" (Psalms 37:23).

Ponderings

Praise

Petitions

February 8
Numbers 3–4

"And I, behold, I have taken the Levites from among the children of Israel…: Therefore the Levites shall be mine" (Numbers 3:12).

Of the twelve tribes of Israel, God chose the sons of Levi to serve him in the work of the Tabernacle. They would be his priests. They would offer the sacrifices that were brought before the Lord and have the responsibility of caring for the Tabernacle. Each of the sons of Aaron (except two that were killed) was given specific jobs when it came time to move on to the next location. Some were given the job of packing everything; some were to take care of materials and utensils needed for worship. Others were to carry the Tabernacle to the next place where they would camp. Every family was given a specific task. This was their service or ministry for God. In the church every person is to have a ministry or place of service. What are you doing to serve the Lord in his sanctuary? Look around and find what needs to be done, then go and do it. Develop a ministry of your own and "serve the Lord with gladness" (Psalms 100:2).

Ponderings

Praise

Petitions

February 9
Numbers 5–6

"And they shall put my name upon the children of Israel: and I will bless them" (Numbers 6:27).

There is a special blessing reserved for the people of God. It was to be spoken by Aaron, the High Priest, to bless the children of Israel. The blessing is for you as well. Look at it again:

"The Lord bless thee, and keep thee: The Lord make his face shine upon thee, and be gracious unto thee: The Lord lift up his countenance upon thee, and give thee peace." (Numbers 6:24–26).

May this blessing of God be upon you today.

Ponderings

Praise

Petitions

February 10
Numbers 7

"And they brought their offering before the Lord" (Numbers 7:3).

The princes of the tribes of Israel brought their offerings for the dedication of the Tabernacle. Although each offering was identical to the other, each offering was recorded separately. It was not an inexpensive gift. At today's values, this offering would be worth approximately $50,000 each. It is interesting that each offering and its value was recording in the Word of God for all to see. What if the offerings that we bring to the Lord were posted, in some way available for all to observe. Would our offerings be greater than they are now? Perhaps some would give more out of guilt and embarrassment; others might give out of pride in an effort not to be outdone. Perhaps some would give less, thinking that the offerings were more than enough to cover ministry expenses. Although our offerings are not generally posted for public scrutiny, they are posted in the annals of eternity. God knows. Are you honoring him in your giving? "Bring ye all the tithes into the storehouse, that there may be meat in mine house, and prove me now herewith, saith the Lord of hosts, if I will not open you the windows of heaven, and pour you out a blessing, that there shall not be room enough to receive it" (Malachi 3:10).

Ponderings

Praise

Petitions

February 11
Numbers 8–10

"At the commandment of the Lord they rested in their tents, and at the commandment of the Lord they journeyed" (Numbers 9:23).

God would lead the children of Israel in a very unique way. By day the Tabernacle was covered with a cloud, and at night there was the appearance of fire. When the cloud moved, they moved; when the cloud sat still, so did they. Notice that they were not moving all the time. There were periods when it was time to sit still and wait on the Lord to show them when to move. Although God might not use a cloud and fire, he directs our lives every day. There are times when we should be moving forward for the Lord in his work. There are times when we are to sit still and wait on him. The time spent waiting on the Lord may often seem the most difficult. It may seem that God is not directing or speaking to us at all. It is in these times that we should just fellowship with him and wait on his timing. Then we must be prepared to move when he says to move. Remember the promise of Proverbs 3:6, "In all thy ways acknowledge him, and he shall direct thy paths."

Ponderings

Praise

Petitions

February 12
Numbers 11–13

"And when the people complained, it displeased the Lord" (Numbers 11:1a).

As the people of Israel made their way toward the Promised Land, they began to take the blessings of the Lord for granted and complain about them. Some complained about God's provision of manna. Moses complained about the burden of leadership that God had given him. Aaron and Miriam complained about the Ethiopian woman that Moses had married. The spies complained about the inhabitants of the Promised Land and how they could not go in to possesss it. Notice that every one of these complaints was made in the midst of God's blessing. God was providing food every day; God was using Moses to lead his people. God had promised to give them the land. Oh, that we would not complain in the midst of God's blessings! God has promised not take you through anything that you cannot handle. When you sense the urge to complain, take it to the Lord and thank him for his leading and provision. He cares very much for you and invites you to cast your cares upon him. Be careful to take your cares to the Lord, not your complaints. There is a difference.

Ponderings
___
___
___

Praise
___
___
___

Petitions
___
___
___

February 13
Numbers 14–15

"And all the congregation lifted up their voice, and cried; and the people wept that night" (Numbers 14:1).

God had sent the spies into the Promised Land. Only two of them came back convinced that they could go in and possesss it. Although the remaining ten agreed that it was a good land, they were convinced that the people of that land were too big for them to conquer. They were not willing to depend on the Lord to lead them to victory. Because of their rebellion, there was weeping and sorrow in the camp. The children of Israel were even considering replacing Moses and returning to their old life in Egypt. When God gives us clear direction, we must follow him. Being unwilling to follow the Lord left the people with few options. Because of their rebellion, there was no happiness or joy. God had one option: send them back into the wilderness to wander until they had all passed away and raise another generation of people that would follow him. When we refuse to follow the Lord by faith, we are destined to wander in the wilderness in weeping and sorrow.

Ponderings

Praise

Petitions

February 14
Numbers 16–18

"But the Levites shall do the service of the tabernacle of the congregation" (Numbers 18:23).

From the miraculous budding of Aaron's rod, it was obvious that God had chosen the Levites to serve him as priests in the Tabernacle. This would mean that they would carry a great responsibility of service to the Lord. It would also mean that they would enjoy special rewards for their service. God has ordained that we should serve him as priests. Concerning the believer, Peter said, "But ye are a chosen generation, *a royal priesthood*, an holy nation, a peculiar people; that ye should shew forth the praises of him who hath called you out of darkness into his marvelous light" (1 Peter 2:9). As priests we also carry a great weight of responsibility in doing the work of God. We should never take our service for him lightly. Along with the responsibilities of the priesthood, there will be great rewards for those who serve the Lord completely.

Ponderings

Praise

Petitions

February 15
Numbers 19–22

"And the Lord spake unto Moses and Aaron, Because ye believed me not, to sanctify me in the eyes of the children of Israel, therefore ye shall not bring this congregation into the land which I have given them" (Numbers 20:12).

Moses was specifically told to speak to the rock in the Desert of Zin so the children of Israel would have water. He had faced this situation before at Rephidim, soon after they had left Egypt. At that time he had been instructed to strike the rock with his rod. It had worked before, so he tried it again. Rather than simply speak to the rock, Moses struck the rock twice. This time by striking the rock he was disobeying God. There are always consequences to disobedience. Moses would pay a price for his sin. He would never enter the Promised Land. Notice that the scripture says his sin was one of not trusting the Lord. We must be careful to obey what God tells us to do. Rather than trying our own way because it worked in the past, we should be faithful to obey God's Word and trust him to take care of the rest.

Ponderings

Praise

Petitions

February 16
Numbers 23–24

"God is not a man, that he should lie; neither the son of man, that he should repent: hath he said, and shall he not do it? or hath he spoken, and shall he not make it good?" (Numbers 23:19).

God had promised to bless Israel. Even though Balaam tried to beseech the Lord to curse Israel, God would not break his promise to his people. God has never and will never break one of his promises. Men make many promises and often will not, or cannot, honor them. God is not like men; he will keep all of his promises to us. In Scripture you will find two kinds of promises that the Lord makes. One of them is called *unconditional*, like the promise to never to destroy the earth again with a flood. The other kind of promise is *conditional*. God says, "If you will… then I will." For example, he tells us that if we put our faith in his Son, then he will give us eternal life in heaven with him. Whether the promise is an unconditional or a conditional promise, you can count on one thing: God will never fail in keeping his promises to us.

Ponderings

Praise

Petitions

February 17
Numbers 25–26

"Wherefore say, Behold, I give unto him my covenant of peace" (Numbers 25:12).

A covenant is a contract God makes between himself and man. He has given us his *covenant of peace*. We can have peace with him through faith in Jesus Christ. Romans 5:1 states, "Therefore, being justified by faith, we have peace with God through our Lord Jesus Christ." Through Christ we also have the peace of God through the indwelling of the Holy Spirit. Jesus said, "Peace I leave with you, my peace I give unto you: not as the world giveth, give I unto you. Let not your heart be troubled, neither let it be afraid" (John 14:27). The peace of God comes through trusting the Lord completely. Concerning peace, Paul told us, "Be careful for nothing; but in every thing by prayer and supplication with thanksgiving let your requests be made known unto God. And the peace of God, which passeth all understanding, shall keep your hearts and minds through Christ Jesus" (Philippians 4:6–7). Trust the Lord in everything and let his peace rule in your heart.

Ponderings

Praise

Petitions

February 18
Numbers 27–29

"And Moses brought their cause before the Lord" (Numbers 27:5).

A problem arose that Moses had never had to deal with before. Several women whose father had died were left with no inheritance of land. Since the land was passed down to the sons, they were left with nothing. What were they to do? Moses took the matter to the Lord for the answer. How often do we find ourselves in new situations, situations in which we do not know how to respond or how to make a right decision? Sometimes we are not even aware of all the options that are available to us. The best course of action is to seek the Lord first. He has the answer, and through prayer, he will show us the way. In fact, he even invites us to come to him when we need such wisdom. "If any of you lack wisdom, let him ask of God, that giveth to all men liberally, and upbraideth not; and it shall be given him" (James 1:5). When you need wisdom in knowing what to do next, ask the One who knows. He will show you the way.

Ponderings

Praise

Petitions

February 19
Numbers 30–32

"If a man vow a vow unto the Lord, or swear an oath to bind his soul with a bond; he shall not break his word, he shall do according to all that proceedeth out of his mouth" (Numbers 30:2).

We live in an age when contracts are required for all transactions because vows alone are not sufficient. Even wedding vows are often accompanied with pre-nuptial agreements. Vows alone are often considered a trivial utterance. Not with God—especially when it comes to vows or promises that are made to him. In times of personal crises, vows are often made to invoke special help or obtain some great blessing from the Lord. Then when God does bless and provide for the need, the vows that were made are often quickly forgotten. God does not take the promises he makes to us lightly. He honors every one. He does not take the vows we make to him lightly either. You must not play games with God. When you make vows to him, make them carefully and keep your word.

Ponderings

Praise

Petitions

February 20
Numbers 33–36

"Then ye shall appoint you cities to be cities of refuge for you" (Numbers 35:11).

Through Moses, God had instructed the children of Israel that there were to be six cities of refuge. According to Israelite law, if someone had murdered someone else, the murderer was to lose his own life in judgment. When a person had killed someone accidentally, he could run to one these cities. In the city of refuge, a person was safe and could not be falsely punished for murder. He was allowed to stay in the city of refuge until the High Priest had died, at which time the perpetrator was free to return to his home. These six cities were specifically built for and by the Levites, the family from which all priests would come. Imagine having to live in one of these cities. Those who had fled into its walls of protection were now just biding their time until the High Priest was dead. Imagine being the High Priest.

In Christ we have a High Priest who will never die. He is eternal, and through the shedding of his blood we have a permanent city of refuge that we will never have to leave. He has prepared a place for you, an eternal city of refuge.

Ponderings

Praise

Petitions

February 21
Deuteronomy 1–2

"These be the words which Moses spake unto all Israel on this side Jordan in the wilderness, in the plain over against the Red sea, between Paran, and Tophel, and Laban, and Hazeroth, and Dizahab" (Deuteronomy 1:1).

The children of Israel had wandered in the wilderness for forty years. They now stood on the banks of the river Jordan, anxious to enter the land that God had promised them. Moses stood before them, knowing that he could not enter. Only Caleb and Joshua remained of the people who had refused to enter at Kadesh-barnea. All the others had died in the wilderness. A new generation was now prepared to go in and possesss the land; but before they did, Moses had a few things to tell them. The book of Deuteronomy is his last instructions before God took him up to Mount Pisgah and ended his life there. Deuteronomy means *second law*. This new generation of people had to understand the Law of God and how they were to obey him before entering this land promised to them. Moses told them everything God had instructed them to do. Would this generation be able to obey God and remain faithful? If you had been in their sandals, what would you have done?

Ponderings

Praise

Petitions

February 22
Deuteronomy 3–4

"And I commanded Joshua at that time, saying, Thine eyes have seen all that the Lord your God hath done unto these two kings: so shall the Lord do unto all the kingdoms whither thou passest" (Deuteronomy 3:21).

We often forget what God has done in the past when we are confronted with new trials in our lives. The mantle of leadership passed from Moses to Joshua shortly after the defeat of the kings of Bashon Heshbon. Moses gave this message of encouragement to Joshua for the new trials he would face. What God had done to these kings he would do to all the kings the children of Israel encountered in the Promised Land. We, too, can be encouraged by what God has done for us in our past. God saw you through the trials in the past and he can do it again. Just trust him.

Ponderings

Praise

Petitions

February 23
Deuteronomy 5–8

"Hear, O Israel: The Lord our God is one Lord: And thou shalt love the Lord thy God with all thine heart, and with all thy soul, and with all thy might" (Deuteronomy 6:4–5).

Jesus said that this was the greatest of all the commandments. If we would just love the Lord with all our hearts, all our souls, and with all our might, then all of the other commandments would fall into place. Notice that in this commandment God does not require any thing of us except to love him supremely. When our love for God is right, he will have the priority in our lives that rightly belongs to him. When we love him supremely, our sin and disobedience to him will break our hearts in such a way that we will not desire to offend him by our foolish ways. Our walk with God is not based on keeping a set of rules and regulations but on a love that takes precedent over every thing and everyone. He loved us first and gave his Son to purchase our salvation. How great is your love for him?

Ponderings

Praise

Petitions

February 24
Deuteronomy 9–11

"And now, Israel, what doth the Lord thy God require of thee, but to fear the Lord thy God, to walk in all his ways, and to love him, and to serve the Lord thy God with all thy heart and with all thy soul, To keep the commandments of the Lord, and his statutes, which I command thee this day for thy good?" (Deuteronomy 10:12–13).

When we love the Lord with all our hearts, all our souls, and all our might, it is shown in how we live. Our love is shown in our fear (reverence) of the Lord, in our walk, through our service, and by our obedience to his Word. The Lord's requirements are all based on a relationship of love. We fear him because we love him. We walk in his ways because we love him. "We love him because he first loved us" (1 John 4:19). We serve him because we love him. And we obey his Word because we love him. His commandments are for our good. They are not designed to take away our enjoyment of life, as the world often claims they are. The fulfillment of God's requirements are not difficult when we love him most of all.

Ponderings

Praise

Petitions

February 25
Deuteronomy 12–15

"For thou art a holy people unto the Lord thy God, and the Lord hath chosen thee to be a peculiar people unto himself, above all the nations that are upon the earth" (Deuteronomy 14:2).

God wanted a people that would be set apart from all other nations to serve him. To be *holy* means to be set apart for a special purpose in purity. God did not want his people to be like everyone else. He wanted them to be a people that would belong to him. The word *peculiar* means that they would be his possesssion. Because he wanted them to be separated unto himself and did not want to be confused with the idols worshipped by many of the other nations in that day, God gave his people special laws and commandments as a demonstration of their holiness. The Lord gave his people specific instructions in how he wanted to be worshiped. He gave his people special dietary laws, which have been proven to have health benefits even today. To be holy does not mean that we are better than anyone else; it simply means that we are set apart by God for his special service.

Ponderings

Praise

Petitions

February 26
Deuteronomy 16–19

"I will raise them up a Prophet from among their brethren, like unto thee, and will put my words in his mouth; and he shall speak unto them all that I shall command him" (Deuteronomy 18:18).

Throughout the centuries, the people of Israel were always on the lookout for this prophet of whom Moses spoke. This prophet to come would have to be like Moses, a prophet *in whose mouth* God would communicate his words. When John the Baptist was preaching on the banks of the Jordan River, the Jews sent priests and Levites to ask him, "Art thou that prophet?" (John 1:21). Of course, John answered, "no." That prophet would be Jesus, who would soon come after him. One of the identifying marks of this prophet was that he would speak all that the Lord commanded him. Jesus said, "And I know that his commandment is life everlasting: whatsoever I speak therefore, even as the Father said unto me, so I speak" (John 12:50). Jesus was the prophet that God promised to the children of Israel. When he came, the Jews rejected him. For those who would receive him, God welcomes into his eternal family. Have you received him? See John 1:11–12.

Ponderings

Praise

Petitions

February 27
Deuteronomy 20–22

"For the Lord your God is he that goeth with you, to fight for you against your enemies, to save you" (Deuteronomy 20:4).

We are in a spiritual battle. This ongoing battle is often called *spiritual warfare*. The enemy is Satan. He is out to destroy the life and work of every person. Our weapon is the Word of God. Though this enemy tries to destroy us and our effectiveness for God, he is already defeated. The devil's end is certain. Our battle strategy is not defensive, for God has already gone on the offensive for us. We are to take our stand and resist the devil. Since he knows he cannot win against an all-powerful God, he flees. In this battle, our part is to watch, stand, and pray. Watch for him to surface with his wicked devices. Take your stand against the wicked one and resist him always. Fully dressed in the armor of God, we are instructed to pray for others who are in this battle with us (see Ephesians 6:10–18). The battle is the Lord's and he has already won. Take your stand, for you are on the winning side.

Ponderings

Praise

Petitions

February 28
Deuteronomy 23–25

"The Lord thy God turned the curse into a blessing unto thee, because the Lord thy God loved thee" (Deuteronomy 23:5b).

God desires the best for us. Even when we had fallen under the curse of Adam's sin and the penalty of that sin, it was God's desire to reconcile us to himself. His everlasting love never diminished for man whom he created. He still wanted to walk and talk with man as he did with Adam in the garden. However, the curse of sin had to be dealt with. Its price had to be paid. Just as God turned the curse of those wicked kings against Israel into blessings, he has turned the curse of sin into blessing. He loves us so much that he did not want that curse to remain on us. It was turned to blessing in the gift of his Son on Calvary's cross. The blessing comes when we place our faith in him and receive his Son into our lives. The curse of sin has been paid for, and we now have the blessing of eternal life. The curse was turned to blessing because he loves us so much.

Ponderings

Praise

Petitions

February 29
Ecclesiastes 3:1-11

"He hath made every thing beautiful in his time: also he hath set the world in their heart, so that no man can find out the work that God maketh from the beginning to the end" (Ecclesiastes 3:11).

When an event starts late, we often speak of it being on *Indian Time*, *Latin Time*, or a time attributed to the late habits of some region or culture. I have even heard of *Baptist Time*—but what about God's time? God is never early or late; he is always right on time. Often we get impatient waiting on God to answer a prayer or move in some way. While we think that God might be late, the truth is that God is always right on time. God has designated a time for everything; from the time that we would be born to when we would die and all of the events of life in between. It's difficult to know God's timing, so we must trust that God knows what is best and that his time is right. He will not be late nor will he be early; he will be right on time. And... *God makes everything beautiful in his time.*

Ponderings

Praise

Petitions

March 1
Deuteronomy 26–27

"And thou shalt rejoice in every good thing which the Lord thy God hath given unto thee" (Deuteronomy 26:11).

Every now and then, it is good to set aside some time to rejoice in everything God has done. God certainly gives cause to rejoice. Even if things are hard and you are going through trials, you can find things over which to rejoice. Make a list of everything that God has done and count your blessings. Look around you and thank him for all he has given you. He has not only blessed us with material things but with spiritual blessings as well. The scripture says to "rejoice in every good thing." There is something about rejoicing that will cause us to burst out in praise. We should never take the good things that God gives us for granted. Thank him for what he has done and rejoice in the Lord. "Rejoice in the Lord always, and again I say, rejoice" (Philippians 4:4).

Ponderings

Praise

Petitions

March 2
Deuteronomy 28–29

"The secret things belong unto the Lord our God: but those things which are revealed belong unto us and to our children for ever, that we may do all the words of this law" (Deuteronomy 29:29).

God has chosen to reveal many things to us in his Word, the Bible. There also remain many *secret things* that he has not revealed to us. He reveals himself to us in creation, in his Son, and in his Word. In the Bible, he has revealed his will and how we can be reconciled with him. We should not be so much concerned with the things he has not revealed but place our attention and efforts in the things he has made known to us. God revealed himself to us for a purpose. His ultimate purpose was to unfold his plan to reconcile man unto himself. His written record is all we need. It is complete, it is true, and it is perfect. God is not playing some kind of game with us. He wants us to come to him, and in his Word he has told us of the great lengths he has gone to in order to do just that. It's all in the Book; we need not look elsewhere for his message.

Ponderings

Praise

Petitions

March 3
Deuteronomy 30–32

"I have set before you life and death, blessing and cursing: therefore choose life" (Deuteronomy 30:19).

God gives us the choice: life or death, blessing or curse. We can find life by making him our first love, by walking in his way, and obeying him in everything. We also have the choice to deny him by turning away from him, ignoring his Word, and worshiping the gods of this world. One would think that the choice is clear and the decision to serve the Lord is an easy one. Yet it seems that many have made the second choice. Rather than loving God supremely, their love is turned away from God and toward self. The consequences of our choices are also clear. Choose to love and obey the Lord and you will have life and blessing. Choose self and this world and the result is death and cursing. John stated it very simply when he said, "He that hath the Son hath life; and he that hath not the Son of God hath not life" (1 John 5:12). Make the right choice.... choose life.

Ponderings

Praise

Petitions

March 4
Deuteronomy 33–34

> "And Moses went up from the plains of Moab unto the mountain of Nebo, to the top of Pisgah, that is over against Jericho" (Deuteronomy 34:1).

When Moses stood on Mount Pisgah and looked out over the Promised Land, it must have been a moment of mixed emotions. From his youth he had heard about the land of Canaan that had been promised to his people. At one time he had nearly entered in at Kadesh-barnea, where the people of Israel were sent into the wilderness because of their unfaithfulness. Now all that Moses could do was view the Promised Land from this lofty height because of his own unfaithfulness. God would keep his promise to his people; they would go in and possesss the land. He would raise up a new leader in Joshua. Moses would not go in, but from Mount Pisgah he was able to see the land of promise. What a sight if must have been! God has promised us a "city not made with hands." Don't miss it because of your own unfaithfulness. Put your faith in the Lord Jesus Christ and prepare to enter into a promised land called Heaven.

Ponderings

Praise

Petitions

March 5
Joshua 1–4

"This book of the law shall not depart out of thy mouth; but thou shalt meditate therein day and night, that thou mayest observe to do according to all that is written therein: for then thou shalt make thy way prosperous, and then thou shalt have good success" (Joshua 1:8).

In all of the Word of God, this is the only verse that provides a promise for success. Notice that to have this success, there are three things that you must do. First, the Word of God must be a constant and consistent part of your life. You should read it and study it until it actually becomes a part of you. Second, you must meditate on the Word of God. This means to think on it. Don't just give it a casual glance, but look at it and carefully consider his Word. Third, our purpose in making the Word of God a part of our lives and carefully considering its message is to do what it says. We must obey the Word of God. In order to do what God says, we must know what God says. Notice that along with the promise of success also comes a promise that you will prosper. Read it, consider it, do it!

Ponderings

Praise

Petitions

March 6
Joshua 5–7

"So the Lord was with Joshua; and his fame was noised throughout all the country" (Joshua 6:27).

When one becomes a follower of Christ, the news cannot be kept a secret. The Lord does not have secret agents. After the fall of Jericho and the means by which it was taken, the people of the surrounding countries knew that Joshua was different. The difference came because he was wholly following the Lord, and it was the Lord who was now giving him the victory. When a person receives Christ and begins to completely follow him, there is going to be a difference in their lives that cannot be hidden. Jesus will shine through. It is amazing how fast the news of a person's salvation gets around, even among the unsaved. They may not fully understand what is happening, but they know that there is a difference and that it was because of the Lord. Of this one thing you can be assured, a believer wholly following the Lord will not go unnoticed.

Ponderings

Praise

Petitions

March 7
Joshua 8–10

"And the men took of their victuals, and asked not the counsel at the mouth of the Lord" (Joshua 9:14).

Joshua made a pact with the Gibeonites not to destroy them. He had been given the impression that they had come from a far city. He had been duped! Joshua's mistake was not in making the pact with the Gibeonites but in failing to take it to the Lord first to determine his will and direction. We often make our plans first and then hope that God will bless them. When our plans fail, we wonder why God did not bless our efforts. It is often because in our arrogance, we try to fit our plans into God's will rather than try to determine God's will first and simply obey him. The Gibeonites would prove to be a problem for Israel for generations to come because Joshua did not seek the counsel of the Lord concerning them. It is vitally important that we take everything to the Lord first, not to ask his blessing on our will but to determine his will and follow his leading. Call upon the Lord first and seek his counsel… he will show you the way.

Ponderings

Praise

Petitions

March 8
Joshua 11–13

"There was none of the Anakims left in the land of the children of Israel: only in Gaza, in Gath, and in Ashdod, there remained" (Joshua 11:22).

In this verse there is the sound of a quiet victory. Did you hear it? It was because of the Anakims that the children feared to enter the Promised Land in the first place. Now there were none left. God had kept his promise. He drove the Anakims out from before them. When they were first told to go and spy out the land, the spies came back with the report that it was a good land, but they saw the children of Anak there. The children of Israel were turned back to wander in the wilderness because of their fear. They did not believe God. It was a matter of choosing fear over faith. Under the leadership of Joshua, a new generation went into the land, defeated the Anakims, and possesssed the land God had promised. Do you have any giants that need to be defeated in your life? They will not be defeated by fear but by trusting the Lord. He will give you the victory over all the Anakims (giants) that stand in your way.

Ponderings

Praise

Petitions

March 9
Joshua 14–17

"Hebron therefore became the inheritance of Caleb the son of Jephunneh the Kenezite unto this day, because that he wholly followed the Lord God of Israel" (Joshua 14:14).

Caleb was one of the spies who went into the Promised Land back at Kadesh-barnea. He voted along with Joshua to follow the Lord and go in and possesss the land. The other ten, who did not believe God and said that they could not go in, voted them down. Now, after over forty years of wandering in the wilderness and helping to take the land that God had given them, Caleb received his portion. Notice that in verse fifteen we are told that this used to be the city of one of the great men among the Anakims. This demonstrates what a great victory it was for Caleb to be able to possesss such a city. God is true to his Word. Caleb wholly followed the Lord from the very beginning when God first told them to go in. He was still faithful in his last days as he continued to follow the Lord and possess his new home in Hebron.

Ponderings

Praise

Petitions

March 10
Joshua 18–20

"So they made and end of dividing the country" (Joshua 19:51).

The fighting was over. The land had been divided. God had kept his promise to the children of Israel. It had been a long, hard road since they had left Egypt to possess the land God had given them. There had been major setbacks because of their lack of faith. There had been disappointments because of disillusionment. There were battles that had to be fought, enemies that had to be driven out. They had been deceived by the enemy and betrayed by their own. But in the end, God was faithful and brought them to their promised homeland. Sometimes life is tough. God has also promised us a land, a land where there are many mansions. A land that is at this very moment being prepared for those who have put their complete trust in the Savior. The road may not be easy. There will be battles, trials, and struggles. But God will keep his promise, and one day we will go in to possess that Promised Land.

Ponderings

Praise

Petitions

March 11
Joshua 21–22

"There failed not aught of any good thing which the Lord had spoken unto the house of Israel; all came to pass" (Joshua 21:45).

From the time that God made the promise to Abraham to make him a great nation and to give him a good land to call his own, God did not fail in keeping his promise. He gave the children of Israel the land he had promised them. He gave them victory over all their enemies and gave them rest. God did not fail to keep all his promises to his people. Even though they failed God often by turning to other gods and doubting his faithfulness to them, he never failed them. God brought them out of Egyptian slavery and safely brought them across the Sinai desert. Even when the people rebelled against God by not going in the first time at Kadesh-barnea, he saw them through the wilderness until a new generation had been raised up that would trust him, go in, and possess the land. God always keeps his promises; he can be trusted to keep his Word. His Word is true and sure. Everything that he told the children of Israel *came to pass*. Don't you think he will keep all the promises he has made to you?

Ponderings

_____
_____
_____

Praise

_____
_____
_____

Petitions

_____
_____
_____

March 12
Joshua 23–24

"Now therefore fear the Lord, and serve him in sincerity and in truth: put away the gods which your fathers served on the other side of the flood, and in Egypt; and serve ye the Lord" (Joshua 24:14).

As Joshua came to the end of his life, he called all of Israel together one last time. He recounted the experiences they had shared together in leaving Egypt and entering into the Promised Land. He reminded them how God had been faithful all along the way and had kept all his promises to them. Joshua encouraged the people to obey the law and love the Lord who had so blessed them. His challenge rings out today as it did back then, to make your choice and serve the Lord. He declared his choice at the end of verse fifteen, "As for me and my house, we will serve the Lord." A few verses later, the people of Israel also declared their stand, "Therefore will we also serve the Lord; for he is our God." Today you are faced with the same challenge. Will you choose to serve the gods of this world or will you choose to serve the Lord? Make your choice.

Ponderings

Praise

Petitions

March 13
Judges 1–3

"I also will not henceforth drive out any from before them of the nations which Joshua left when he died: That through them I may prove Israel, whether they will keep the way of the Lord to walk therein, as their fathers did keep it, or not" (Judges 2:21–22).

The children of Israel did not drive out all of the inhabitants of Canaan, thus disobeying the Lord. Since they did not obey him, God decided to just leave the enemy there as a test determining whether or not the Israelites would completely follow him. Becoming a Christian does not mean that our lives will be free of trouble. There will always be people and distractions in our lives, a constant trial and test of our faith. James tells us that we should "count it all joy when ye fall into diverse temptations" (James 1:2). In the end, the trial will lead us to maturity in Christ. The trials that God leaves in our lives are not necessarily there to make us miserable or to punish us; they are there to help us develop a closer walk with God knowing that he can and will see us through any trial.

Ponderings

Praise

Petitions

March 14
Judges 4–5

"Praise ye the Lord for the avenging of Israel, when the people willingly offered themselves" (Judges 5:2).

Great armies do not always win the battle of the Lord. Sometimes God, using just one individual who is wholly committed to him, wins the victory. Jabel's wife could not have taken on the whole army of Sisera, but she could do her part in winning the battle. She did not wait for someone else to do what needed to be done. She just went ahead and did it herself. *The greatest ability is availability.* Are you available for God to use you? It is easy to see a task that needs to be done and say, "Somebody needs to do that." Perhaps you are that somebody. Take the initiative; go ahead and do what needs to be done. It may be someone else's responsibility to do it, but that does not mean that you can't pitch in and help. Make yourself available to the Lord by surrendering to his will. You may be surprised at the things God can use you to do.

Ponderings

Praise

Petitions

March 15
Judges 6–8

"And the Lord looked upon him, and said, Go in this thy might, and thou shalt save Israel from the hand of the Midianites: have not I sent thee?" (Judges 6:14).

Gideon was just a common laborer threshing wheat and trying to hide from the Midianites when the Lord came to him with a special task. God did not seek out the mighty men of the region nor the noble. He wanted to use Gideon. Gideon was not running for any office nor looking for some great thing to do for the Lord; he just wanted to do his job and stay out of the way of the Midianites. Yet God used him to deliver Israel from the Midianite's oppression. God often uses the ordinary to do the extraordinary. God used Gideon to accomplish his purpose. He had a plan for Gideon's life. He has a plan for your life also and can use you to do the extraordinary. God loves you and the best you will ever find in life is God's plan for you. He can and will use you beyond your ability. Just trust him; follow his leading, and you may be amazed at what God can use you to do for him.

Ponderings

Praise

Petitions

March 16
Judges 9–10

"And the children of Israel said unto the Lord, We have sinned: do thou unto us whatsoever seemeth good unto thee; deliver us only, we pray thee, this day" (Judges 10:15).

The children of Israel had turned away from God to serve other gods. When they came to God for his help, it was necessary that they first confess their sins and turn back to him. As the people confessed their sins before God, they also completely surrendered their lives to him. After they had repented and confessed their sin of idolatry, God began to deliver them out of the hand of the enemy once again. Sin separates us from God. When we rebel against his will for us and turn to our own way, we are engaging in a form of idolatry. It is necessary that we look at our own sin, confess it to him, and then surrender ourselves over to his mercy. He promised that when we confess our sin, he would be faithful to forgive us. "If we confess our sins, he is faithful and just to forgive us our sins, and to cleanse us from all unrighteousness" (1 John 1:9).

Ponderings

Praise

Petitions

March 17
Judges 11–13

"And Manoah said, Now let thy words come to pass. How shall we order the child, and how shall we do unto him?" (Judges 13:12).

Raising a child for the Lord is not an easy task. Manoah's wife had received special instruction concerning the child she was to bear. He was to be a Nazarite, meaning that his life would be given completely to the Lord's service. With such a directive coming from the Lord, Manoah wanted to see that they knew everything they were to do to raise this child to serve God. We are also to bring up our children in the "nurture and admonition of the Lord" (Ephesians 6:4). Every child with which we are blessed should be raised to serve the living God. This responsibility should not be left up to the Sunday school teacher or pastor; it is the parent's responsibility. Deuteronomy 6:4–9 tells us that we should first teach our children to love the Lord. The passage goes on to say that it should be a daily and continual task. Like Manoah, ask for God's wisdom. He will certainly give you all that you need to raise your children for his glory.

Ponderings

Praise

Petitions

March 18
Judges 14–16

"That he told her all his heart, and said unto her, There hath not come a razor upon mine head; for I have been a Nazarite unto God from my mother's womb" (Judges 16:17).

What a paradox we find in the life of Sampson. He was raised to serve the Lord as a Nazarite, yet he spent most of his life serving himself. He took what God had given him and often used it for his own revengeful purposes. However, we find that God used him in spite of himself. Sampson's selfish desire for satisfying his own flesh finally led to his own demise; even so, God used him to destroy the Philistine's stronghold over Israel. We do not hear from the Philistines again for years to come in Israel's history. From his birth, Sampson was set apart to serve the Lord, and even though it seems that everything that Sampson did was to please himself, God still used him to accomplish his purpose. Sometimes God will use us in spite of ourselves. Imagine how much greater he could have been if he had only surrendered to the Lord's will and served him faithfully.

Ponderings

Praise

Petitions

March 19
Judges 17–19

"And they said unto him, Ask counsel, we pray thee, of God, that we may know whether our way which we go shall be prosperous" (Judges 18:5).

There is an important lesson we can learn from these spies of Dan: always seek God's direction before taking on a new endeavor. The Lord promised that when we acknowledge him, he will "direct our paths" (Proverbs 3:6). James warns us that before we even conduct our business plans, we should be careful to see that we are in God's will. "For that ye ought to say, 'If the Lord will, we shall live, and do this, or that'" (James 4:15). When we seek and follow God's direction, we can always be assured that we are in his will. And it is in his will that we find God's best. How often we are arrogant enough to determine what we are going to do and then ask God to place his blessing on our plans. We *should* be seeking God's will first and then continue on with the assurance that God's blessing is already on our human endeavors. When you ask him, God will reveal his way and his will. The problem is that we often don't even ask.

Ponderings

Praise

Petitions

March 20
Judges 20–21

"In those days there was no king in Israel: every man did that which was right in his own eyes" (Judges 21:25).

How sad these words must be to the God of Israel! After he had given the Promised Land to the people, he was supposed to be their King. He had given them his Law, commandments that would separate them from the surrounding nations and give *instruction in righteous*. However, the children of Israel turned away from God and his Law and sought to go either their own way or the way of the false gods of the people they had defeated. When God was supposed to be their King, the record shows that there was "no king in Israel." When the law had been ignored and the sovereignty of God had been denied, the Bible says that "every man did that which was right in his own eyes." How sad that so many today are still rejecting him, resulting in a lawlessness that will one day lead to our own destruction. It is not too late; you can still turn to the King of Kings and Lord of Lords. Is he the Lord of your life? Is he your King?

Ponderings

Praise

Petitions

March 21
Ruth 1–4

"So Boaz took Ruth, and she was his wife" (Ruth 4:13a).

"And he shall be unto thee a restorer of thy life" (Ruth 4:15a).

Boaz became the kinsman-redeemer for Ruth and Naomi. As a near relative, he had the responsibility and right to claim Ruth as his wife. When Naomi and Ruth returned from Moab, they had nothing and were in a word *nobodies*. By marrying Ruth, Boaz would restore the name of her family in Israel and give her a home and hope for the future. He paid the price for their restoration. When we were without hope and separated from God because of our own sin, God gave us a redeemer. He would pay the price for our sin, restoring us to full fellowship with the Father. He would restore our place before him and give us a home and a hope. That redeemer was Jesus Christ, who died in our place paying the price of *our* sin. We now belong to him and are to glorify him in our lives. "For ye are bought with a price: therefore glorify God in your body, and in your spirit, which are God's..." (1 Corinthians 6:20).

Ponderings

Praise

Petitions

March 22
1 Samuel 1–3

> "Wherefore it came to pass, when the time was come about after Hannah had conceived, that she bare a son, and called his name Samuel, saying, Because I have asked him of the Lord" (1 Samuel 1:20).

Hannah, being barren, had prayed for a son. She promised that if the Lord would hear her cry, she would give that son back to God to serve him. After the child was born, she called him Samuel, which means *asked of the Lord* or *the Lord has heard*. As Hannah prayed, it seemed that she was asking for something that was impossible by natural human standards. However, she was praying and trusting in a supernatural God. When your needs seem to be beyond human comprehension, remember that we serve a God who is beyond human comprehension, a God who can do anything he desires to do. We serve a supernatural God who can perform supernatural feats. Go ahead and ask him those things that seem to be impossible. He can make it possible. "For with God, nothing shall be impossible" (Luke 1:37). Just ask Hannah about what God can do.

Ponderings

Praise

Petitions

March 23
1 Samuel 4–7

"And Samuel spake unto all the house of Israel, saying, If ye do return unto the Lord with all your hearts, then put away the strange gods and Ashtaroth from among you, and prepare your hearts unto the Lord, and serve him only: and he will deliver you out of the hand of the Philistines" (1 Samuel 7:3).

For years the children of Israel were at war with the Philistines. In these wars many men had been killed and much of their land taken. They had tried to bring mighty armies against the Philistines to gain victory over them. They even tried to bring the Ark of the Covenant along to see if it would make them victorious; it didn't. The only thing that would bring them victory over their enemy was complete surrender and service to the Lord. All other gods would have to go. Their hearts had to be completely committed to the Lord. They could not defeat the enemy with their own strength and human endeavor. It would take the power of God. When we surrender to the Lord with all of our hearts to serve him only, he takes over and he gives us the victory over the enemies of our lives.

Ponderings

Praise

Petitions

March 24
1 Samuel 8–12

> "And the Lord said unto Samuel, Hearken unto the voice of the people in all that they say unto thee: for they have not rejected thee, but they have rejected me, that I should not reign over them" (1 Samuel 8:7).

The people of Israel looked around them and saw that all the other nations had a king. They wanted a king too. The tragedy of their desire for a king was the fact that God was supposed to be their King. They were to serve him and him only. Their desire for a king brought great distress to Samuel, who knew that God was supposed to be the king. God explained to him that the people had not rejected the leadership of Samuel, but the authority of God as their king. We must be careful that when we receive Christ into our lives as Lord, that he really is in control. How often we have claimed Christ as our Lord and then decided that, rather then obey him, we just do things our own way? As Lord, Jesus becomes our Master and King. Our position in life is to obey his every command. If he is truly the king of your life, then obey him. Don't rebel against his leading and Lordship in your life.

Ponderings

Praise

Petitions

March 25
1 Samuel 13–14

"…the Lord hath sought him a man after his own heart" (1 Samuel 13:14).

God is looking for someone who will be *after his own heart*. What does it mean to be after the heart of God? God is looking for those who would have a heart that is just like his. A heart that hears him when he speaks and obeys his perfect will. It is a heart that is surrendered and open to God's leading. To have a heart like God's requires a heart that is purified by the shed blood of Jesus Christ. When we have the heart of God, we will begin to be like him. We will love as he loves. We will give as he gives. We will forgive as he forgives. God is still searching for those who would be *after his own heart*. Will you be that one? Has your heart been washed in the blood? Are you seeking and obeying God's will? In order for us to have a heart that is after God's heart, we first give him our heart to cleanse, to keep, and to use as he sees fit. Give him your heart today and do everything you can to be a person *after God's own heart*.

Ponderings

Praise

Petitions

March 26
1 Samuel 15–16

"And Samuel said, Hath the Lord as great delight in burnt offerings and sacrifices, as in obeying the voice of the Lord? Behold, to obey is better than sacrifice, and to hearken than the fat of rams" (1 Samuel 15:22).

Saul had disobeyed the Lord in failing to carrying out his orders concerning King Agag and the Amalekites. He made up the excuse that the best of the livestock was kept for sacrifice to the Lord. He also tried to blame his disobedience on the people. This disobedience was the beginning of Saul's downfall. When we receive Jesus Christ into our lives as Lord and Savior, it becomes our purpose in life to obey the Word of the Master. It is not enough to just hear the voice of God in reading his Word; we must also be careful to obey everything he tells us. Saul knew what God wanted him to do and rather than do it, he did what he wanted to do and then made up excuses as to why he was disobedient. God is not interested in our petty excuses; he requires complete obedience to his Word. James said it this way, "But be ye doers of the word, and not hearers only" (James 1:22).

Ponderings

Praise

Petitions

March 27
1 Samuel 17–18

"And the men of Israel said, Have ye seen this man that is come up?" (1 Samuel 17:25).

"And all this assembly shall know that the Lord saveth not with sword and spear: for the battle is the Lord's, and he will give you into our hands" (1 Samuel 17:47).

What a contrast! While the men of Israel looked at Goliath, saying, "Have you seen this man?" David said, "The battle is the Lord's." It is a difference of perspective. One looked at the enemy and said, "I can't." The other looked to the Lord and said, "He can." There will be many Goliaths in our lives and how we deal with them will depend on our perspective. Rather than looking at the problem in comparison to our own inadequacies, may we look to God and see that he is able to help us deal with these giants. Remember, *the battle is the Lord's*. Let him fight it....

Ponderings

Praise

Petitions

March 28
1 Samuel 19–21

> "And Jonathan said to David, Go in peace, forasmuch as we have sworn both of us in the name of the Lord, saying, The Lord be between me and thee, and between my seed and thy seed forever" (1 Samuel 20:42).

There was no closer friendship in Scripture than that of Jonathan and David. They had fought side-by-side in Saul's army. They had become closer than brothers. Jonathan had gone to great lengths to protect David from Saul's wrath. Every person needs a close friend, one in whom they can confide and fully trust. In a recent survey of 1500 people, nearly a quarter of the people surveyed said they had "zero" close friends with whom to discuss personal matters. More than fifty percent named two or fewer confidants [http://www.gopala.org/_evo/index.php/2006/06/27/statistics_americans_circle_of_close_fri]. The friendship of Jonathan and David should be an example to us of the kind of friendship that we should endeavor to develop in our own lives. Proverbs 18:24 says, "A man that hath friends must shew himself friendly: and there is a friend that sticketh closer than a brother." To have a friend we must be a friend. Make it a priority to find someone you can make your close friend. Don't wait for someone to come to you. Go and be that friend first.

Ponderings

Praise

Petitions

March 29
1 Samuel 22–24

"And every one that was in distress, and every one that was in debt, and every one that was discontented, gathered themselves unto him; and he became a captain over them: and there were with him about four hundred men" (1 Samuel 22:2).

As David began to gather his army, he found quite a rag-tag group of men. They would not be the elite fighting men or the rich and adventurous that joined up with him. David accepted those who were *in distress, in debt*, and *discontented*. David did not look at what they were but at what they could be. This is how God sees us when we come to him. He takes us as we are and makes us what he wants us to be. He doesn't wait until our lives are all cleaned up and polished. He takes us with all our sin and he does the cleansing. Jesus said, "All that the Father giveth me shall come to me; and him that cometh to me I will in no wise cast out" (John 6:37). You can come to Jesus just like you are, with all your sin, unrighteousness, and imperfection. Come to him, trust him, and he will do the rest.

Ponderings

Praise

Petitions

March 30
1 Samuel 25–27

> "And David said in his heart, I shall now perish one day by the hand of Saul: there is nothing better for me than that I should speedily escape into the land of the Philistines; and Saul shall despair of me, to seek me any more in any coast of Israel: so shall I escape out of his hand" (1 Samuel 27:1).

It seemed to David that with Saul hot on his heels, his best course of action was to run. Notice that in this verse there is no mention of the Lord's leading in his going to the Philistines. He was simply looking for a place to hide. How often we try to run from our troubles and trials! Many of the trials that come into our lives are placed there by the Lord for a reason (read James 1:1–5). The answer is not to run but to ask for God's wisdom and then follow his leading. He will show you what the proper course of action should be. Running from our difficulties will often just lead to… well, look what happened to Jonah when he tried to run away from God.

Ponderings

Praise

Petitions

March 31
1 Samuel 28–31

"So Saul died, and his three sons, and his armor-bearer, and all his men, that same day together" (1 Samuel 31:6).

Saul's death would not seem so tragic except that his demise was a result of his own disobedience to God. In his last days when he tried to find God's direction, he only found silence. In the silence he turned to witchcraft to inquire of the old prophet Samuel. There he received the news of his own death and the reason that God had turned a deaf ear to him. Saul was told in specific words that his kingdom was taken from him because he had not obeyed God completely. It was because of the disobedience of Adam that sin was thrust upon all mankind and the end result was the same—death. The only difference is that the price of death was paid for us when Jesus died on Calvary's cross. Because he died in our place we can have eternal life. "For as by one man's disobedience many were made sinners, so by the obedience of one shall many be made righteous" (Romans 5:19).

Ponderings

Praise

Petitions

April 1
2 Samuel 1–3

"The beauty of Israel is slain upon thy high places: how are the mighty fallen!" (2 Samuel 1:19).

David had just received word that King Saul had been slain. As he laments Saul's demise, he cries out the question, "How are the mighty fallen?" He often referred to Saul as God's anointed and had great respect for him and his position as king. It was hard for him to accept that God's anointed had fallen in battle. It is always hard for us to understand how people that God has used in a leadership position often fall because of some sin. The fall often comes because of pride and self will. The scripture admonishes us, "Wherefore let him that thinketh he standeth take heed lest he fall" (1 Corinthians 10:12). When Saul thought that he could take things into his own hands without the help and direction of the Lord, he began to fall. The admonition is still true today. When we think we can stand on our own, we will fall flat on our faces. Learn to lean on the One who will uphold you with his mighty hand.

Ponderings
___
___
___

Praise
___
___
___

Petitions
___
___
___

April 2
2 Samuel 4–7

"And David went on, and grew great, and the Lord God of hosts was with him" (2 Samuel 5:10).

Without question, David was the greatest king of Israel. He was known as the *champion of Israel*, defeating her enemies under God's direction and power. This is not to say that David was perfect. He was human and often failed his people and his God. Still, he was a man "after God's own heart." From the time of David, all the kings who followed David would be compared to him. When a king was doing right and serving the Lord, Scripture records that "he did that which was right in the sight of the Lord, according to all that David his father did" (2 Kings 18:3). When a king was not doing right, David again became the standard for what a good king should be. "And he walked in all the sins of his father, which he had done before him: and his heart was not perfect with the Lord his God, as the heart of David his father" (1 Kings 15:3). What kind of legacy do you want to leave behind—one that speaks of righteousness and obedience or one that speaks of sin and destruction?

Ponderings

Praise

Petitions

April 3
2 Samuel 8–11

"And David said unto him, Fear not: for I will surely shew thee kindness for Jonathan thy father's sake, and will restore thee all the land of Saul thy father; and thou shalt eat bread at my table continually" (2 Samuel 9:7).

Here we see a picture of grace. It was common practice in David's time that when a new king ascended the throne, he saw to it that all of the kindred of the previous king were killed in order to prevent them from taking over the throne. In this case, David sought out those who were still alive in Saul's family; and instead of death, those he found received life. Mephibosheth was given all of his father's land and servants. Besides all that, he was given a place at the king's table every day. David would see that Mephibosheth was treated like royalty. This is such an example of God's grace to us. When we should have been condemned to a sinner's death, he gave us life. He made us one of the King's children. There was nothing we did on our part to deserve such treatment, yet God loved us so much that he provided a way giving us the honor to feast at his table for eternity. Perhaps that is why we consider God's grace so amazing.

Ponderings

Praise

Petitions

April 4
2 Samuel 12–13

"And David said unto Nathan, I have sinned against the Lord. And Nathan said unto David, The Lord also hath put away thy sin; thou shalt not die" (2 Samuel 12:13).

David had committed a great sin against the Lord in committing adultery with his neighbor Bathsheba and in the murder of her husband, Uriah. The prophet Nathan confronted David with his sin. David had thought that his sin was hidden and that somehow he could get away with it. We can never get away with sin before an all-seeing God. David immediately confessed his sin, and although he finds God's forgiveness, David would live with the consequences of his sin the rest of his life. First, there would be the blasphemy of his enemies and then the death of the child wrought in his sin. When we confess our sin before God, he promises to forgive us. How much pain and sorrow we suffer because of our own wickedness! Forgiveness of sin does not mean that God will remove all consequences of our sin. They serve as a constant reminder of our own foolishness.

Ponderings

Praise

Petitions

April 5
2 Samuel 14–16

"For thy servant vowed a vow while I abode at Geshur in Syria, saying, If the Lord shall bring me again indeed to Jerusalem, then I will serve the Lord" (2 Samuel 15:8).

Have you ever made that kind of promise to the Lord? Something like, "Lord, if you will just do so and so, then I will serve you for the rest of my life." Did God answer that prayer? Did you mean it when you promised to serve him? Why is it that we think that God must do something for us before we can commit to serve him? After all, he did the greatest thing for us that he could do. He sent us his only Son to die a death that we could not die and to pay a price for our sin that we could not pay. In Romans 12:1–2, Paul said that it was our *reasonable service* to present ourselves to the Lord as a *living sacrifice*. Our service to the Lord should be out of a heart of love and a desire to do his will, not out of a sense of duty because he bailed us out of some kind of trouble. Serve the Lord because you love him, not just for what he might do for you.

Ponderings

_____
_____
_____

Praise

_____
_____
_____

Petitions

_____
_____
_____

April 6
2 Samuel 17–19

"And the king was much moved, and went up to the chamber over the gate, and wept: and as he went, thus he said, O my son Absalom, my son, my son Absalom! Would God I had died for thee, O Absalom, my son, my son!" (2 Samuel 18:33).

The cries of David could be heard all through the night as he mourned the loss of his son, Absalom. Even though his son had tried to overthrow David as king and assume his throne, David had requested that they *deal gently* with Absalom in battle. Now he was dead. David's mourning was somewhat confusing to Joab because Absalom had become his enemy. And even so, David still greatly loved his son. There is nothing like the love of a father for his son. Imagine what love it must have taken for the heavenly Father to give up his Son so that we could be reconciled to him. It was a love that transcends all human knowledge and understanding. The scripture plainly states, "But God commendeth his love toward us, in that, while we were yet sinners, Christ died for us" (Romans 5:8). What kind of love did it take for God to give up his only Son so that we could have everlasting life in him?

Ponderings

Praise

Petitions

April 7
2 Samuel 20–22

"And David spake unto the Lord the words of this song, in the day that the Lord had delivered him out of the hand of all his enemies, and out of the hand of Saul" (2 Samuel 22:1).

David began to praise the Lord because he knew that throughout all his life, God had been with him and had blessed him. God had taken David from being a shepherd boy to being the King of Israel. David recognized that all the victories that he had ever won were because God was with him. He praised the Lord because he knew that God was worthy of his praise. Without the Lord, perhaps David would now be a crusty old shepherd still watching the sheep. God had made all the difference in his life. Has God made a difference in your life? Where would you be today if you had never met the Lord? By saving us, God took us from a destiny of hell and destruction to the abundant life and a home in heaven. He is worthy of our praise! Take time today to praise the Lord for the help and blessings he has given to you. Like David, look over your life and praise the Lord for he is worthy to be praised.

Ponderings

Praise

Petitions

April 8
2 Samuel 23–24

"Now these be the last words of David. David the son of Jesse said, and the man who was raised up on high, the anointed of the God of Jacob, and the sweet psalmist of Israel" (2 Samuel 23:1).

What a great description of David as we come to the closing days of his life! He was the son of Jesse, making him an Israelite and one of God's chosen people. He was *the man raised up on high*. God had taken David from the sheepfold to the king's palace. He was *the anointed of the God of Jacob*. As a young lad Samuel had anointed him to be king. God chose him for this position. When the sons of Jesse lined up before Samuel, David was not even considered to be worthy of such a position. Then finally the scripture describes him as *the sweet psalmist of Israel.* How often we have been comforted and encouraged by the Psalms of David! Psalms that came from a heart that would seek to please God and reflect a total dependence on him. David loved the Lord and was the man who truly was after his own heart.

Ponderings

Praise

Petitions

April 9
1 Kings 1–2

"And keep the charge of the Lord thy God, to walk in his ways, to keep his statutes, and his commandments, and his judgments, and his testimonies, as it is written in the law of Moses, that thou mayest prosper in all that thou doest, and whithersoever thou turnest thyself" (1 Kings 2:3).

On his deathbed, David advised his son, Solomon, as to how he could prosper as the new king of Israel. He was told, "Keep the charge of the Lord," meaning to obey all of God's Word. He was told that if he expects to prosper, he is to follow the Lord and his laws in everything he does. This was the secret of David's success as king. Why is it that we look everywhere else for prosperity except where it is promised? We look to finances and accept the world's standard for prosperity. To find true joy and happiness, one need look no further than the Word of God. True prosperity is always found in obedience to the Lord and his Word. Solomon became one of the richest men the world has ever known. His prosperity came by listening to his father's advice.

Ponderings

Praise

Petitions

April 10
1 Kings 3–5

"Behold, I have done according to thy words: lo, I have given thee a wise and an understanding heart; so that there was none like thee before thee, neither after thee shall any arise like unto thee" (1 Kings 3:12).

God came to Solomon and said to him, "Ask what I shall give thee?" Solomon could have asked for anything and everything. However, he simply asked that God would give him an understanding heart so that he could wisely rule over God's people. God gave him that and more. Since Solomon had asked for wisdom instead of riches or long life, God gave him these as well. And just like God had promised, Solomon rose to be a great king. Concerning Solomon, 2 Chronicles 1:1 states, "And Solomon the son of David was strengthened in his kingdom, and the Lord his God was with him, and magnified him exceedingly." God has also promised wisdom to every believer. "If any of you lack wisdom, let him ask of God, that giveth to all men liberally, and upbraideth not; and it shall be given him" (James 1:5). Imagine—the wisdom that was available to Solomon is also available to you. All you have to do is ask.

Ponderings

Praise

Petitions

April 11
1 Kings 6–7

"And I will dwell among the children of Israel, and will not forsake my people Israel. So Solomon built the house, and finished it" (1 Kings 6:13–14).

It was David's hope to build a house for the Lord, but God did not allow him to build it because of all the blood he had shed in battle. The task of building the Temple was passed on to Solomon. The materials were gathered and prepared, and the workmen were assembled. It would be a great undertaking, and no detail would be spared. God had promised David that there would be a place where God could dwell among the children of Israel. God's dwelling place would now be among his people. After Jesus died on Calvary, God established a new dwelling place, the heart of the believer. If you have received Christ, you are now the Temple of God. "What? know ye not that your body is the temple of the Holy Ghost which is in you, which ye have of God, and ye are not your own? For ye are bought with a price: therefore glorify God in your body, and in your spirit, which are God's" (1 Corinthians 6:19–20). Are you taking good care of God's temple?

Ponderings

Praise

Petitions

April 12
1 Kings 8–9

"Blessed be the Lord, that hath given rest unto his people Israel, according to all that he promised: there hath not failed one word of all his good promise, which he promised by the hand of Moses his servant" (1 Kings 8:56).

God had promised Abraham that he would make of him a nation and a people and that he would dwell among them. He had promised Moses that he would build a dwelling place among the people and gave Moses the design of the Tabernacle. He had promised David that he would establish his throne forever and that he would have a permanent dwelling place among his people. God had kept all of his promises. After Solomon had completed the Temple, there was one task left, moving the Ark of the Covenant into its permanent place. Once that was done, Solomon gave God the glory and praise for keeping all the promises that he had made to the patriarchs of Israel. God has never broken one of his promises to his people. He will not break his promises to you.

Ponderings

Praise

Petitions

April 13
1 Kings 10–12

"For it came to pass, when Solomon was old, that his wives turned away his heart after other gods: and his heart was not perfect with the Lord his god, as was the heart of David, his father" (1 Kings 11:4).

Solomon's great downfall was marrying the women of many different nations. God had warned him that by him marrying them, they would bring their gods made of stone and wood with them to his cities. To appease his many wives, Solomon built them temples and *high places* so that they could worship these foreign gods. This was no small offense, for the scripture records that Solomon had *seven hundred wives and three hundred concubines*. He not only built them temples to accommodate their gods, he eventually turned to worshiping some of them himself. We must be so careful to give God our whole heart. Compromise is one of Satan's most dangerous tools. When we decide to allow sin in our life, it is not long until that sin consumes us. Ephesians 4:27 advises, "Neither give place to the devil." We may consider a little sin harmless at first, only to lose everything in the end. Solomon lost a kingdom. What do you have to lose?

Ponderings

_____
_____
_____

Praise

_____
_____
_____

Petitions

_____
_____

April 14
1 Kings 13–15

"And this thing became sin unto the house of Jeroboam, even to cut it off, and to destroy it from off the face of the earth" (1 Kings 13:34).

You cannot continue in sin and get away with it. Both the *man of God* and Jeroboam came to a destructive end because they refused to obey God and his Word. God is serious when it comes to sin. God hates sin. It seems that in our culture today there is small regard for sin against God. Sin has one result, death. Jeroboam turned to other gods even to the point of becoming a priest to them. Growing up in David's home, he knew that it was a violation of God's law to worship these false gods, yet he chose to do so anyway. Because of his sin, God's judgment came down upon him. The wages of sin have never changed. It is still death. God must deal thusly with sin, yet he loves us so much that he provided a way that we could escape the punishment of our sin. He sent his Son to die in our place. "But God commendeth his love toward us, in that, while we were yet sinners, Christ died for us" (Romans 5:8). Have you received the gift of God's love?

Ponderings

Praise

Petitions

April 15
1 Kings 16–18

"And Elijah came unto all the people, and said, How long halt ye between two opinions? if the Lord be God, follow him: but if Baal, then follow him. And the people answered him not a word" (1 Kings 18:21).

God's people had turned to other gods. They had turned to Baal and the other gods of wood and stone. Except for a few people who still feared the Lord, like Obadiah, God had been all but forgotten. Elijah lays down the challenge to test these false gods to determine their power and existence. It would be a test of faith and fire. The prophets of the false gods took their turn and failed. Now it was Elijah's turn to make God known among the people. He repaired the altar at the evening sacrifice and offered a simple prayer to his God. To Elijah, it was no surprise that God answered his prayer by consuming the altar with fire. The people fell on their faces and cried out, "The Lord he is the God, the Lord, he is the God" (1 Kings 18:39). Elijah's prayer was answered. The important thing was not that the altar was consumed with fire, but that it resulted in the people recognizing who their God really was.

Ponderings

Praise

Petitions

April 16
1 Kings 19–20

"Yet I have left me seven thousand in Israel, all the knees, which have not bowed unto Baal, and every mouth, which hath not kissed him" (1 Kings 19:18).

Elijah felt as though he was all alone. He felt as though he was the only one who was trying to truly serve the Lord. God told him that in Israel there were seven thousand who had not *bowed the knee* to Baal. Have you been there, feeling like you were the only one that was serving the Lord, that somehow you were left to do all the work? Well, you are not alone. There are many around you who love the Lord and want to serve him also. Others may be feeling the way you do. To them you must reach out. Seek out their fellowship. Someone is noticing your work for the Lord. Perhaps, it will be a testimony to them when they see your faithfulness. You should remember this also: we are told to "run with patience the race that is set before us, Looking unto Jesus the author and finisher of our faith" (Hebrews 12:1–2). Keep your eyes on Jesus and remember your "labour is not in vain in the Lord" (1 Corinthians 15:58).

Ponderings

Praise

Petitions

April 17
1 Kings 21–22

"Seest thou how Ahab humbleth himself before me? Because he humbleth himself before me, I will not bring the evil in his days" (1 Kings 21:29).

Because of his wickedness, God had already pronounced judgment on Ahab. When Ahab knew that he would come to an expected end under the judgment of God, "he rent his clothes and put sackcloth upon his flesh and fasted and lay in sackcloth, and went softly" (1 Kings 21:27). He humbled himself before God. Now, due to his humility, God is gracious to him. James reminds us, "But he giveth more grace. Wherefore he saith, God resisteth the proud, but giveth grace unto the humble" (James 4:6). Is your pride keeping you away from the Lord? When we try to puff ourselves up and think of ourselves more highly than we ought to think, God will resist that pride and often cause us to fail in our endeavors. However, the promise of Scripture is that God will exalt those who humble themselves before him. Jesus said, "And whosoever shall exalt himself shall be abased; and he that shall humble himself shall be exalted" (Matthew 23:12). Humble yourself today before Almighty God.

Ponderings

Praise

Petitions

April 18
2 Kings 1–3

"He took up also the mantle of Elijah that fell from him, and went back, and stood by the bank of Jordan" (2 Kings 2:13).

When Elijah was caught up to glory on a chariot of fire in the midst of a whirlwind, his mantle fell to Elisha. The mantle represented authority and power. The authority of Elijah the Tishbite as a man of God would now fall to Elisha. Elisha would speak for God just as Elijah had done. It is so important in our Christian walk that we maintain a ministry of mentoring younger believers. This is especially important for pastors and Christian leaders. As older believers move off the scene, younger believers must be trained to win and disciple new believers. Paul told young Timothy, "And the things that thou hast heard of me among many witnesses, the same commit thou to faithful men, who shall be able to teach others also" (2 Timothy 2:2). Whom have you won to the Lord? Whom are you training to walk with him? God had prepared Elisha to take Elijah's place. Someday someone will need to fill your shoes. Train them well.

Ponderings

Praise

Petitions

April 19
2 Kings 4–5

"Are not Abana and Pharpar, rivers of Damascus, better than all the waters of Israel? May I not wash in them and be clean?" (2 Kings 5:12).

The scripture says, "The things which are impossible with men are possible with God" (Luke 18:27). Why is it that when we are faced with trials and difficulties, we seek for solutions in the world? And when all sources that the world has to offer have been exhausted, we then turn to God? Naaman with his leprosy thought that perhaps there was a better river back home in which he could dip himself. Yet the instructions of the prophet were clear, "Go and wash in the Jordan." God's way and God's plan are the best. Solutions offered by the world are often inadequate. Problems that seem insurmountable by the world's standards are solved under the hand of an Almighty God. Rather than chasing after the solutions that the world offers, seek out God and the answers he has already given in his Word. Naaman could have gone back to Damascus, but there he would have only gotten wet in the rivers of Abana and Pharpar. When he followed God's plan, he was healed.

Ponderings

Praise

Petitions

April 20
2 Kings 6–8

"And he prepared great provision for them: and when they had eaten and drunk, he sent them away, and they went to their master. So the bands of Syria came no more into the land of Israel" (2 Kings 6:23).

The Syrian army was marching toward Israel to overthrow it. Elisha had miraculously led the King of Israel and his army to meet them. When their eyes were open and they found themselves face-to-face with the enemy, the first reaction of the king was to attack. But Elisha had another plan. He instructed the king to "set bread and water before them that they may eat and drink, and go to their master" (2 Kings 6:22b). The plan was to offer them blessing instead of cursing. Jesus said, "But I say unto you, Love your enemies, bless them that curse you, do good to them that hate you, and pray for them which despitefully use you, and persecute you" (Matthew 5:44). When the army of Israel blessed their enemies by giving them food and drink, they simply went away without a fight. Next time your enemy comes to fight… give him a blessing. You'll be amazed at the results.

Ponderings

Praise

Petitions

April 21
2 Kings 9–10

"Know now that there shall fall unto the earth nothing of the word of the Lord, which the Lord spake concerning the house of Ahab: for the Lord hath done that which he spake by his servant Elijah" (2 Kings 10:10).

Because of their sin, God had pronounced judgment on both Ahab and Jezebel. Not only did Jezebel and Ahab fall under the judgment of God, but their demise came about in the exact way that God said it would happen. God always keeps his word. He will always do what he says he will do. There are many promises and prophecies in Scripture that are yet unfulfilled. As certainly as God was true to his word in the past, he will fulfill his word in what is yet to come. One day every person will stand before the judgment of God. There is but one sentence for sin—death. God sent his Son to die that death for us. Have you received the gift of God? Jesus said, "He that believeth on the Son hath everlasting life; and he that believeth not the Son shall not see life; but the wrath of God abideth on him" (John 3:36). You can escape the judgment of God by trusting in the Son of God. Have you fully trusted him?

Ponderings

Praise

Petitions

April 22
2 Kings 11–13

"And the Lord gave Israel a savior" (2 Kings 13:5).

The Israelites were under the oppression of the Syrians. When King Jehoahaz called out to God for help, God sent a savior. This savior would deliver them from the oppression of the Syrians. One cannot read this phrase without realizing that God sent another Savior, one who would save Israel from the oppression of sin. This Savior was promised to the people of Israel first. For generations they would wait and watch for him, for they knew from the time of the Patriarchs that he would one day come. And when he finally came, they rejected him. "He came unto his own, and his own received him not" (John 1:11). The promise of this Savior was not only given to Israel but to all who believe. "But as many as received him, to them gave he power to become the sons of God, even to them that believe on his name" (John 1:12). God so loved the world that he sent his own Son to be the Savior of the world. One question remains: Have you rejected him or will you believe on his name and receive him?

Ponderings

Praise

Petitions

April 23
2 Kings 14–16

> "And he did that which was right in the sight of the Lord, yet not like David his father: he did according to all things as Joash his father did" (2 Kings 14:3).

King Joash only served the Lord halfway. Although the scripture records that "Joash did that which was right in the sight of the Lord, yet not like David, his father," this phrase indicates that it was only halfway. There were areas in his life where he did not allow the Lord to reign. He compromised with some of the foreign gods in his kingdom. How often we see the same kind of surrender in many believers of our day! Many are willing to serve the Lord but reserve certain areas of their life to continue in their sin. Don't be a halfway servant. Serve the Lord with all of your heart. Search your heart today and see if there is any area that you have not completely surrendered to the Lord. Confess that sin that you want to hang on to and repent of it. God needs people who are completely surrendered to him. Don't be like Joash and other kings of Israel who would only follow the Lord halfway. Surrender your all today.

Ponderings

Praise

Petitions

April 24
2 Kings 17–18

"Now it came to pass in the third year of Hoshea son of Elah king of Israel, that Hezekiah the son of Ahaz king of Judah began to reign" (2 Kings 18:1).

Under the leadership of evil kings, Israel had left the Lord and his Word. Hezekiah was a good king who tried to set things right. The Bible has only good things to say about him. When he began to reign, he first removed all the idols and their temples of worship. Hezekiah began to turn the people back to the Lord. Of him the Bible says, "He trusted the Lord," and "He clave to the Lord." He was careful to do all that the Lord commanded in his Word. Because of his desire to obey the God of Israel, the Lord greatly blessed him and caused him to prosper. He did not give in to his heathen enemies, he simply trusted the Lord. Under Hezekiah there was a great revival in the land of Israel. Most of other kings had given in to the world and had given in to those who wanted to serve other gods. Hezekiah turned the people to God and his Word. He "did that which was right in the sight of the Lord" (2 Kings 18:3).

Ponderings

Praise

Petitions

April 25
2 Kings 19–21

"Now therefore, O Lord our God, I beseech thee, save thou us out of his hand, that all the kingdoms of the earth may know that thou art the Lord God, even thou only" (2 Kings 19:19).

When Sennacherib came with his armies and his threats against the people of Israel, King Hezekiah went to the Lord in prayer. Rather than threaten back or try to scheme some sort of response, he went to the Lord first and committed his dilemma to him. When Jesus was threatened and beaten, he did the same thing. Concerning the Savior, 1 Peter 2:23 states, "Who, when he was reviled, reviled not again; when he suffered, he threatened not; but committed himself to him that judgeth righteously." It is our human response to return threats or to find some means of revenge when we are mistreated. It is best to seek the Lord first and commit the wrongs done against us to him. He knows what to do and has the power to intervene on our behalf. When you are mistreated, follow Hezekiah's example and take it to the Lord. He's listening.

Ponderings

Praise

Petitions

April 26
2 Kings 22–23

"And the king stood by a pillar, and made a covenant before the Lord, to walk after the Lord, and to keep his commandments and his testimonies and his statutes with all their heart and all their soul, to perform the words of this covenant that were written in this book. And all the people stood to the covenant" (2 Kings 23:3).

Hilkiah the high priest had found a book. It was the Word of God. It had been forgotten as the people had turned to serving other gods over the years. When the book was found, King Josiah was greatly troubled, for he and his people had disobeyed God. As soon as they knew what needed to be done, Josiah began to clean house. The old gods of wood and stone were destroyed and the people returned to the Lord. Before his people the king made a commitment "to walk after the Lord and to obey his Word." Later it was said of Josiah, "And like unto him was there no king before him, that turned to the Lord with all his heart, and with all his soul, and with all his might, according to all the law of Moses, neither after him arose there any like him" (2 Kings 23:25). Is it time to clean house and make a new commitment to "walk after the Lord"?

Ponderings

Praise

Petitions

April 27
2 Kings 24–25

"And he burnt the house of the Lord, and the king's house, and all the houses of Jerusalem, and every great man's house burnt he with fire" (2 Kings 25:9).

For years God had pleaded with his people to return to him. In their rebellion they had turned to other gods—gods of wood and stone. Through his prophets, God had warned his people over and over again that judgment would come; and come it did. Using the armies of the great king Nebuchadnezzar of Babylon, God destroyed Jerusalem. The Temple was also demolished and its treasures carried away. Thousands of people were killed. Only the young people who were strong and suitable for the king's use were kept alive and carried away to Babylon. God's judgment had finally come. There is another judgment to come. The Bible says, "We shall all stand before the judgment seat of Christ" (Romans 14:10). God's judgment is sure and swift. When we stand before the final judgment at God's throne, the only thing that will matter is what you have done with Christ. Receive the payment for your sin that Christ paid on Calvary's cross or face the Judgment of God.

Ponderings

Praise

Petitions

April 28
1 Chronicles 1–2

"These are the sons of Israel; Reuben, Simeon, Levi, and Judah, Issachar, and Zebulun, Dan, Joseph, and Benjamin, Naphtali, Gad, and Asher" (1 Chronicles 2:1–2).

It is sometimes a difficult and laborious task reading through the genealogies of the Bible. Families are important. It was important to establish your lineage in order to occupy the throne as a king. Matthew and Luke both included genealogies showing the place of Jesus as a King and son of Abraham. To be found in the family of God requires more that a listing in a genealogical chart. It requires faith. To be in the family of God requires that one be born again. We are not children of God because he created us. That simply makes us his creation. John 1:11–12 states, "He came unto his own, and his own received him not. But as many as received him, to them gave he power to become the sons of God, even to them that believe on his name." To be in the family of God as one of his children requires that you receive Christ as your personal Savior. If you have never trusted him, do it now and come into the family of God.

Ponderings

Praise

Petitions

April 29
1 Chronicles 3–4

"And Jabez called on the God of Israel, saying, Oh that thou wouldest bless me indeed, and enlarge my coast, and that thine hand might be with me, and that thou wouldest keep me from evil, that it may not grieve me! And God granted him that which he requested" (1 Chronicles 4:10).

The Bible does not tell us much about Jabez. We do know that he was of Caleb's family and that his mother bore him in sorrow. The meaning of his name is literally *sorrow*. The Bible also tells us that he was more honorable than all his brethren. Jabez wanted God's blessing on his life, so he called out to the God of Israel and requested of him four things: that God would bless him, that God would increase his territories, that God's hand would be with him, and that the Lord would keep him from the presence and suffering of evil. We don't know exactly how God did it; all that we are told in Scripture is that "God granted him that which he requested." Perhaps sometimes we are missing the blessings of God simply because we are not asking. James reminds us, "Ye have not, because ye ask not" (James 4:2). Go ahead…ask.

Ponderings

Praise

Petitions

April 30
1 Chronicles 5–6

"And they transgressed against the God of their fathers, and went a whoring after the gods of the people of the land, whom God destroyed before them" (1 Chronicles 5:25).

In the first of the Ten Commandments, God says, "Thou shalt have no other gods before me" (Exodus 20:3). The people of Israel had a choice. They could choose to serve the God of their fathers or the gods of the people of the land. Their choice was to worship the gods of the people of the land in which they were living. The devil is always quick to see that there are other gods around to worship. They are all around us still today. It is vital that you keep your eyes and heart on the Lord. Be careful not to fall into the trap of worshiping the gods of this world. The people of Israel did and they paid dearly for it. God is a jealous God and will not take a backseat to any of the gods of human making. See that you put him first in everything. Do not let the gods of materialism, greed, and self stand in the place of the God who created you and loves you most.

Ponderings

Praise

Petitions

May 1
1 Chronicles 7–9

"Ishmerai also, and Jezliah, and Jobab, the sons of Elpaal" (1 Chronicles 8:18).

Consider Jezliah. Who was he? Why is he mentioned in the scripture? His name is only mentioned once in the entire Bible. All that we really know about him is that he was the son of Elpaal and that his name means *whom God will preserve*. Although he seems to be an insignificant individual, God thought that it was necessary to include him in his inspired Word. Wouldn't it be something to read your own name in the Word of God? There is no record that Jezliah ever did anything that would cause him to be worthy to be included in the pages of the Bible. Though it may seem that you have never accomplished anything of great significance, if you have put your faith in Jesus Christ for the cleansing of your sin, you are also in a book that is very important to the Lord. It is called The Book of Life. Revelation 20:15 states, "And whosoever was not found written in the book of life was cast into the lake of fire." Those who are in the book will be saved to life everlasting. Is your name in his book?

Ponderings

Praise

Petitions

May 2
1 Chronicles 10–12

"for there was joy in Israel" (1 Chronicles 12:40b).

There was joy in Israel, and with that joy came much celebration. Israel had a new king, a king who was after God's own heart, a king who had led them to victory over their enemies and had given them peace. There was joy because of the abundant blessing that God had poured out upon them. The vineyards were filled and the harvests were abundant. It would seem, at least for now, that things were looking up. David had become their champion in war and was ready to lead them as God had designed. The secret of their joy can be found in 1 Chronicles 11:9, "So David waxed greater and greater; for the Lord of hosts was with him." Where their former king, Saul, had been disobedient and full of pride, David was obedient and humble before the Lord. Joy is not found in circumstance, but in the presence of the Lord and in the obedience of his Word. When David became king, there was joy in Israel.

Ponderings

Praise

Petitions

May 3
1 Chronicles 13–16

"And the anger of the Lord was kindled against Uzza, and he smote him, because he put his hand to the ark: and there he died before God" (1 Chronicles 13:10).

Is it possible to do the right thing the wrong way? It was right for David to bring the Ark of the Covenant up to Jerusalem. It was even determined that it was God's will to bring the ark to its proper home. So what went wrong? Why did the simple touch of the ark by Uzza result in his death. The fact is they were doing it all wrong. God had given specific instructions in the Law as to how and by whom the ark was to be moved. It seems they had failed to obey God's Word. After a period of about three months, David had found in the Scripture that there was a right and proper way to move the Ark of the Covenant. When the Levites were summoned, sanctified, and prepared to move the ark in the way that God had instructed, David told them, "For because ye did it not at the first the Lord our God made a breach upon us, for that we sought him not after the due order" (1 Chronicles 15:13). It is always best to do God's work, God's way.

Ponderings

Praise

Petitions

May 4
1 Chronicles 17–19

"Then Nathan said unto David, Do all that is in thine heart; for God is with thee" (1 Chronicles 17:2).

God had put it in David's heart to build a temple for him. David had a burden and a vision that had come from God. Nathan encouraged him to do what God was leading him to do. What has God placed in your heart to accomplish for him? When God gives you the burden and the vision to do his work, do not hesitate to do it. Don't be concerned with the method or the means. If God has placed a ministry in your heart, he will show you how to accomplish it. Take on the task, one step at a time, and just do it. It has been said that "God's work, done God's way, will not lack God's supply." God will not only show you how to accomplish what he is leading you to do, he will also supply the means. Just be faithful to take the matter to him and ask for his direction and help. God will not lead you to do something that is impossible to complete. If you are certain that God has put a task or ministry into your heart, trust him, follow him, and do it!

Ponderings

Praise

Petitions

May 5
1 Chronicles 20–23

"At that time when David saw that the Lord had answered him in the threshingfloor of Ornan the Jebusite, then he sacrificed there" (1 Chronicles 21:28).

The threshing floor of Ornan has now become the holiest site on all the earth. Little did Ornan know that when he gave David his threshing floor that it would become the site of the Temple, the very place where countless sacrifices and offerings would be made to the Lord. It would be the site of many battles. It would also be the site where God would meet with his people. The site where the Messiah would one day walk, teach, and heal the sick. It would be the site where some of the world's greatest sermons would be preached by the apostles. Many would come just to see the place where God had established his house, a place where even today many go to pray and seek the Lord's favor. The site that had been a common threshing floor would become the focal point of Bible prophecy. It is doubtful that Ornan even knew how significant his old threshing floor would become to the world throughout eternity. Do you suppose he knows now?

Ponderings

Praise

Petitions

May 6
1 Chronicles 24–26

> "All these were under the hands of their father for song in the house of the Lord, with cymbals, psalteries, and harps, for the service of the house of God, according to the king's order to Asaph, Jeduthun, and Heman" (1 Chronicles 25:6).

There were 288 men appointed to the task of writing and performing the music for the house of God. They were not just appointed but also given great skill and talent in all kinds of music. Scripture says they were *instructed in the songs of the Lord*. From these musicians came many of the psalms we read today. In reading the introductory notes in the Psalms, you will often find the name Asaph. He along with his family would play their instruments and sing praises to the God of Israel. What joy they must have experienced as they wrote and sang beautiful songs of praise to the Lord! It is sad that we do not have the musical composition for their songs. We do have the words to many of them in the Psalms but the musical score has been lost. God still gives to his servants the ability to compose and sing songs and psalms to his glory. If you have such a gift, you should feel honored to be in the company of Asaph and his singers.

Ponderings

Praise

Petitions

May 7
1 Chronicles 27–29

"And thou, Solomon my son, know thou the God of thy father, and serve him with a perfect heart and with a willing mind: for the Lord searcheth all hearts, and understandeth all the imaginations of the thoughts: if thou seek him, he will be found of thee; but if thou forsake him, he will cast thee off for ever" (1 Chronicles 28:9).

The reign of King David was coming to a close. He had gathered together all the military and spiritual leaders for one final address. He told how God had put it in his heart to build the Temple and how God had then denied him that privilege because of all the blood he had shed in battle. David then turned to his son Solomon with some special advice as he passed the throne of Israel to him. He told him first to know God and then to serve him with a perfect heart and a willing mind. He also told him that if he would seek the Lord he would be certain to find him. David could give Solomon this instruction because it is what David had attempted to do all his life. Certainly there were times when he had failed the Lord, but nonetheless it is advice that is good for us even in these modern times.

Ponderings

Praise

Petitions

May 8
2 Chronicles 1–4

"And Solomon sent to Huram the king of Tyre, saying, As thou didst deal with David my father, and didst send him cedars to build him a house to dwell therein, even so deal with me" (2 Chronicles 2:3).

Solomon was determined, under the leadership of God, to build the Temple. He knew he did not have the skill or ability to do it alone, so he wrote to Huram, King of Tyre. He asked him for help, not only in materials but in labor as well, both skilled and unskilled. God has a plan and a purpose for everyone. When God is leading you to accomplish a task for him, don't assume that he expects you to do it alone. God has equipped different people with different talents and abilities. Solomon knew he needed the skill of the craftsmen to do the fine art work that would be required in the Temple. He knew he would need the materials that could only be found in Lebanon. In writing to Huram, Solomon was using all the resources at his disposal. When God has a plan, he will provide the personnel as well at the materials to finish his work. He may send them from places you do not expect.

Ponderings

Praise

Petitions

May 9
2 Chronicles 5–7

> "If my people, which are called by my name, shall humble themselves, and pray, and seek my face, and turn from their wicked ways; then will I hear from heaven, and will forgive their sin, and will heal their land" (2 Chronicles 7:14).

What a great day it was when Solomon and the people of Israel dedicated the Temple to the Lord. The Ark of the Covenant was put into place, there was much music, and many sacrifices offered up to the Lord. Solomon prayed, committing himself and all of Israel to the Lord. God responded by filling the Temple with all of his glory. It was later that night when the Lord appeared to Solomon and told him that his prayer had been heard. It was at this time that God made the above promise to the King of Israel. God promised that when Israel found themselves under his judgment as a result of their own sin, their recourse was to humble themselves before God, seek his face, and turn away from their sin. God then promised that when they did so, he would hear their cry, forgive their sin, and would heal their land from whatever judgment had been poured out on them. Perhaps the time has come when our nation should call out to God in such a manner.

Ponderings

Praise

Petitions

May 10
2 Chronicles 8–11

"And Solomon reigned in Jerusalem over all Israel forty years" (2 Chronicles 9:30).

In the forty years that Solomon reigned over Israel, he became the greatest king the world has ever known. Solomon was known for his wisdom, his wealth, and for building the Temple in Jerusalem. When visited by the Queen of Sheba, she came with all manner of questions for him—all of which wise Solomon was able to answer with great skill. When Solomon gave her a tour of his kingdom, she told him, "One half of the greatness of thy wisdom was not told me, for thou exceedest the fame that I heard" (2 Chronicles 9:6). She also saw how happy his people were. Though Solomon was such a great king, his reputation is tarnished by the way he lived. He began to surround himself with wives from all over the world. When they came to Jerusalem, they also brought with them their idols and false gods. Solomon allowed them to flourish in his kingdom. Compromise is so easy and yet so detrimental to our walk with God. Of Solomon, the Bible goes on to tell how Solomon did not completely follow the Lord. Don't make the same mistake as Solomon. Don't allow the things of this world to keep you from fully following the Lord.

Ponderings

Praise

Petitions

May 11
2 Chronicles 12–16

"And when Judah looked back, behold, the battle was before and behind: and they cried unto the Lord, and the priests sounded with the trumpets" (2 Chronicles 13:14).

Have you ever found yourself between a rock and a hard place? This was the position in which Judah found itself when it fought against Israel. When they found that they were surrounded and it seemed there was nowhere to go, they cried out to the Lord. When they called upon the Lord, he stepped in and gave them the victory. The outcome of this predicament is found in 2 Chronicles 13:18. "Thus the children of Israel were brought under at that time, and the children of Judah prevailed, because they relied upon the Lord God of their fathers." Notice the reason for their victory was because they relied upon the Lord. This is the place where you will also find victory when you are in a position of uncertainty. When is seems that there is nowhere to turn, there is always the Lord. He will hear your cry and he will come to your aid. The Psalmist said, "God is our refuge and strength, a very present help in trouble" (Psalms 46:1).

Ponderings

Praise

Petitions

May 12
2 Chronicles 17–20

"…thus saith the Lord unto you, Be not afraid nor dismayed by reason of this great multitude; for the battle is not yours, but God's" (2 Chronicles 20:15b).

The armies of Moab, Ammon, and others had conspired to attack Judah. Jehoshaphat, the king, went to enquire of the Lord about what they should do. His prayer is recorded in 2 Chronicles 20:3–13. The Lord reassured them that the battle was not theirs to fight, but his. Without so much as shooting an arrow, the invading armies were defeated by the Lord. In our spiritual lives, there are often battles that we fight; battles with Satan, sin, and self. Many times we fight battles that really belong to the Lord. When we fight these battles ourselves, we are certain to fail. When we take them to the Lord and allow him to fight the battles for us, then victory is certain. Whatever battles you face today, do as Jehoshaphat did: first take it to the Lord. 2 Chronicles 20:3 notes that Jehoshaphat "set himself to seek the Lord." Rather then trying to fight an apparent losing battle, take it to the one who can bring certain victory to your life.

Ponderings

Praise

Petitions

May 13
2 Chronicles 21–24

"Joash was seven years old when he began to reign…And Joash did that which was right in the sight of the Lord all the days of Jehoiada the priest" (2 Chronicles 24:1–2).

Imagine a seven-year-old king. Most seven-year-olds today are just learning to read a book or ride a bicycle; yet, when Joash became king, the scripture records that he set out to please the Lord. When he discovered that the Temple was in ruins, he gathered the priests and assigned them to special tasks and to restore the offerings and sacrifices. A special offering was collected, and so much money was given that there was more than enough to repair and furnish the house of the Lord. Finally, Temple worship was restored, and as much as he could, Joash attempted to turn the people's hearts back to the Lord. Perhaps there is some repair work that needs to be done in your life so you can come and worship the Lord again. The weight and ravages of sin have left you in ruins. It's not too late to seek the Lord, make the necessary repairs, and worship him again.

Ponderings

Praise

Petitions

May 14
2 Chronicles 25–28

"The Lord is able to give thee much more than this" (2 Chronicles 25:9c).

Amaziah was building a war machine. He gathered together some 300,000 fighting men from Judah and another 100,000 from Israel. The fighting men from Israel were to be paid for their services. When the man of God came and told Amaziah that he would not prevail with the men of Israel fighting for him, his first concern was the money he had put out to hire them. How often we look for human solutions, which often prove to be inadequate! Amaziah was trusting in his own abilities when he should have trusted the Lord all along. Sound familiar? The man of God then told Amaziah that the Lord could provide much more than he had paid out in money. The Lord is able. Why is it that when God is able and willing to help us that we turn to human efforts to solve our problems? Under the mighty hand of God Amaziah would be successful in his battles. Under the mighty hand of God his need would be met. Look unto the Lord and seek him, for God has the power to help.

Ponderings

Praise

Petitions

May 15
2 Chronicles 29–31

"And in every work that he began in the service of the house of God, and in the law, and in the commandments, to seek his God, he did it with all his heart, and prospered" (2 Chronicles 31:21).

When Hezekiah determined that he would serve the Lord, he did it all the way. When he became King, he began leading his people back to the Lord. He cleaned out the Temple and restored the service of the priests. He saw that they were prepared and sanctified for service. He destroyed all of the altars and high places of all the false gods that previous kings had set up. He began celebrating the Passover Seder again. Hezekiah wanted to serve God fully without reservation. Not everyone followed him, but many did. At his invitation, the people came from all over the country to celebrate the restoration of the Law and the Temple sacrifices. Everything that Hezekiah did to turn himself and his people back to God, he did with all of his heart. Is there any other way to serve the Lord? God is not interested in our half-hearted efforts to serve him. He blesses those who seek and serve him completely.

Ponderings

Praise

Petitions

May 16
2 Chronicles 32–34

"Be strong and courageous, be not afraid nor dismayed for the king of Assyria…With him is an arm of flesh; but with us is the Lord our God to help us, and to fight our battles" (2 Chronicles 32:7–8).

The king of Assyria had come to attack Jerusalem. His army stood outside the wall and cast forth their threats. They tried to intimidate the people into surrendering. They would soon be coming to accomplish all they had threatened to do against the people. The king and his army would attempt by all earthly means to destroy Jerusalem and take her people captive: "With him is an arm of flesh." Paul said in 2 Corinthians 10:4, "For the weapons of our warfare are not carnal, but mighty through God to the pulling down of strongholds." Hezekiah encouraged his people to be strong and courageous. There was one weapon that Sennacherib did not have: the power and presence of God. "What shall we then say to these things? 'If God be for us, who can be against us'" (Romans 8:31)? When you have the Lord, you can be certain of victory.

Ponderings

Praise

Petitions

May 17
2 Chronicles 35–36

"And the Lord God of their fathers sent to them by his messengers, rising up betimes, and sending; because he had compassion on his people, and on his dwelling place" (2 Chronicles 36:15).

Time and time again, God had sent his messengers to his people trying to tell them how much he loved them. He told them to obey him and he would be their God and they would be his people. Yet, often the people refused to listen to him and rebelled against him. Sure, there were some, like Hezekiah, who tried to obey and honor the Lord; but for the most part, there was rebellion in the leadership as well as in the populace. God had warned them that if they would not abandon their idols and worship him and him alone that judgment was going to come. Finally, that judgment did come in the form of a Babylonian king named Nebuchadnezzar. The people were taken captive, many were killed, and Jerusalem was destroyed. God is still sending his message today; you will find it in his Word. And like the people of old, many refuse to listen in their rebellion. What about you, are you listening?

Ponderings

Praise

Petitions

May 18
Ezra 1–4

"And they sang together by course in praising and giving thanks unto the Lord; because he is good, for his mercy endureth forever toward Israel" (Ezra 3:11).

The Babylonian exile was coming to an end. Many of the children of Israel who had been taken captive were allowed to return to Jerusalem to rebuild its wall and the Temple. The rebuilding had begun. There was much cause to praise the Lord. There had been a day when among the people of Israel there was great sadness and despair because of their captivity. God had completed his work of chastisement and was ready to fully restore his people. The children of Israel had once turned their back on God. Now they were ready and willing to come home and worship him again. Though the days may seem dark and you see no light at the end of the tunnel, do not despair. God has not forgotten you. He loves you very much. His desire is to restore you to full fellowship with him through the shed blood of his only Son. Perhaps the time has come to rebuild your life and restore your fellowship with the Lord. His mercy endures forever and he will give you cause to worship and praise him because *he is good*.

Ponderings

Praise

Petitions

May 19
Ezra 5–7

"And thus they returned us an answer, saying, We are the servants of the God of heaven and earth, and build the house that was builded these many years ago, which a great king of Israel builded and set up" (Ezra 5:11).

When a letter was sent to Darius attempting to stop the restoration of the Temple it was recorded that the workers were asked to identify who they were. The only answer they would give was that they were the "servants of the God of heaven and earth." The only way they wanted to be identified was as *servants of God*. They were not interested in making a name for themselves. It is true that they may have feared retribution for their part in building the new Temple. Nonetheless, they saw themselves as doing God's work and for God's glory. Too often Christian workers attempt to take the glory that belongs to God for themselves. Rather than trying to exalt the name of God, they are trying to establish a name for their own glory. In all your labor for the Lord, be careful that all the glory is given unto him. "Give unto the Lord the glory that is due unto his name" (Psalms 29:2).

Ponderings

Praise

Petitions

May 20
Ezra 8–10

"Then I proclaimed a fast there, at the river of Ahava, that we might afflict ourselves before our God, to seek of him a right way for us, and for our little ones, and for all our substance" (Ezra 8:21).

On their way back to Jerusalem, Ezra and his companions stopped at the river of Ahava to consider their situation. They had not asked their former king for soldiers to protect them on their journey and it came to them that they were now completely dependent on the Lord for protection. As they stopped by the river, Ezra calls for a fast in which they would humble (afflict) themselves and seek God's direction for their journey. It is so important for us in our hectic lives to take occasional opportunities to assess where we are in God's will for our lives. He has a plan that is perfect for us. It is a plan for good and represents God's best. Often we attempt to plot out our own lives without even considering what God's plan for us might be. It is then when we find ourselves in a mess of our own making that we cry out to God to somehow straighten out the mess we have created. Perhaps it is time to stop for a while and seek out God's plan and direction for your life. Humble yourself before him, and seek of him a *right way*.

Ponderings

Praise

Petitions

May 21
Nehemiah 1–3

"Then answered I them, and said unto them, The God of heaven, he will prosper us; therefore we his servants will arise and build" (Nehemiah 2:20).

When Nehemiah had revealed his intentions concerning the rebuilding of Jerusalem, his enemies began to mock him. They laughed at him and accused him of rebellion. Nehemiah was quick to point out that this was God's work. It was not an everyday construction project; it had been bathed in prayer. God had sent Nehemiah on a mission. It was God's work and God was going to bless it. Nehemiah had seen God's hand on this project ever since he told King Artaxerxes about it. God had directed his every step. The fact that it was God's work would be their motivation to carry them on to complete it. Never lose sight of the fact that when you are working for the Lord that it is his work. Its success will depend not on us but on God's blessing. We are to be concerned with simply obeying and following his direction. What is God leading you to do? Don't be concerned with the critics and naysayers. If you are convinced that God is in it, and that he is leading you, then allow God to use you to do the work and leave the rest to him.

Ponderings

Praise

Petitions

May 22
Nehemiah 4–7

"Nevertheless we made our prayer unto our God, and set a watch against them day and night, because of them" (Nehemiah 4:9).

Nehemiah was doing the work that God had sent him to do. When God's work is progressing, it is not long until the enemy shows up to try to stop it. For Nehemiah the enemy appeared in form of Sanballat and Tobiah. However, their threatening and mocking did not stop the work. There came a point when it seemed that the whole world was against Nehemiah and the rebuilding of the wall around Jerusalem. Nehemiah went to the one place where he knew he could find help. We do not find Nehemiah plotting a scheme against his enemies. Nor do we find him casting threats or reprisals. Nehemiah simply called upon God. Why is it that we so often think that our own solutions are better than God's? That we somehow have a greater wisdom than he has? When the enemy strikes (and he will), take it to the Lord first. Allow him to fight the battle. Not only did Nehemiah pray, but he also set a watch. Watch and pray. Isn't that what our Lord Jesus Christ taught us to do? "Take ye heed, watch and pray" (Mark 13:33). It worked for Nehemiah.

Ponderings

Praise

Petitions

May 23
Nehemiah 8–9

"Also day by day, from the first day unto the last day, he read in the book of the law of God" (Nehemiah 8:18).

As the children of Israel were once again discovering the Law of God, they also began to obey what God had told them to do. There were public readings of the Law and the people would stand for hours just to hear what God had said. How their hearts were overcome with conviction, as they understood their own neglect of the Word of God! The Feast of Tabernacles was restored as well as a newfound obedience to the Word of God. Notice that their obedience came from the reading and preaching of God's Word. Day by day, the Scriptures were read aloud and explained to the people. The fact that you are reading this book shows that you too are listening to the voice of God in his Word. May you be encouraged to continue in the Word of God every day. It will be food for your soul, bring you strength, and cause you to grow in the Lord. His Word will not fail you. As you read his Word, seek the Lord and how you can be obedient to his Word. Do this and revival will come to your own life.

Ponderings

Praise

Petitions

May 24
Nehemiah 10–11

"They clave to their brethren, their nobles, and entered into a curse, and into an oath, to walk in God's law, which was given by Moses the servant of God, and to observe and do all the commandments of the Lord our Lord, and his judgments and his statutes" (Nehemiah 10:29).

Once the Temple and the walls of Jerusalem had been rebuilt, the people entered into a covenant among themselves. There was an agreement among them that they would now do all they could to walk in God's law. They had seen the judgment of God in their captivity in Babylon and knew that it had come about because their fathers had forsaken the Lord and his Law. Now that they were back in Jerusalem and able to worship the Lord as he had directed, they were ready to commit themselves together to serve him. There was still much to be done, but they knew that if they were to have the blessing of God upon them that they must obey the Lord completely. Their commitment to the Lord and to each other was sealed with an oath. They did not want to go back to their old life. They wanted to build a new life that was centered on the Lord and on serving him. Are you ready to make such a commitment? Are you ready for new life?

Ponderings

Praise

Petitions

May 25
Nehemiah 12–13

"…howbeit our God turned the curse into a blessing." Nehemiah 13:2).

The mercy of God is great toward us as he turns the curses that have come upon us into blessings. He turned the curse of Adam's sin into to blessing of eternal salvation. He took the curse of death and turned it into the blessing of eternal life through the death, burial, and resurrection of his only begotten Son. The death of Christ on the cross turned the curse of our sin into the blessing of sanctification. Where we were once separated from God in our sin, we are now made clean and acceptable to him. The cross turned the curse of a sinner's hell into the blessing of promised heaven. God's desire is to bless you. He has given you every opportunity for blessing. He has turned the curse into a blessing. Now he gives you a choice. In Deuteronomy 30:19, he says to you, "I call heaven and earth to record this day against you, that I have set before you life and death, blessing and cursing: therefore choose life, that both thou and thy seed may live." God gives you the choice of blessing and cursing, life and death. The choice is yours to make. What will you choose?

Ponderings

Praise

Petitions

May 26
Esther 1–3

"And the letters were sent by posts into all the king's provinces, to destroy, to kill, and to cause to perish, all Jews, both young and old, little children and women, in one day, even upon the thirteenth day of the twelfth month, which is the month Adar, and to take the spoil of them for a prey" (Esther 3:13).

Hate is a great destroyer. Because Mordecai had not shown Haman the respect that he thought he deserved, a great plot was devised to destroy all of the Jews that were under Ahasuerus' reign. Haman was a man of great pride and demanded that everyone bow down to him as he passed though the streets of Shushan. Mordecai would not do it. Scripture records in Esther 3:5, "And when Haman saw that Mordecai bowed not, nor did him reverence, then was Haman full of wrath." That wrath was now passed on to all Jews through the scheming of Haman. Hate destroys everything in its path. Hate has no place in the family of God. Jesus taught, "Love your enemies, do good to them which hate you. Bless them that curse you, and pray for them which despitefully use you" (Luke 6: 27–28). Love and prayer is the best response to hate.

Ponderings

Praise

Petitions

May 27
Esther 4–7

"And Mordecai came again to the king's gate. But Haman hasted to his house mourning, and having his head covered" (Esther 6:12).

Having thought that the king wanted to honor him, Haman instead had to give the honor to Mordecai. Haman thought that when the King wanted to give honor to someone, it would surely be him. He was so full of pride that in his mind no one else was worthy of the King's honor. When Haman gave the King the means by which he could honor someone, he was thinking that this would be the way *I* want to be honored. When he found out that the honor would go to Mordecai, Haman was greatly humiliated. Jesus said, "And whosoever shall exalt himself shall be abased; and he that shall humble himself shall be exalted" (Matthew 23:12). When Haman tried to exalt himself, he ended up being abased (humiliated) and embarrassed. How often we have tried to toot our own horn only to find out that it played a sour note. Self-exaltation will only lead to humility and embarrassment. The next time you think you want to exalt yourself, think of Haman, you could end up like him.

Ponderings

Praise

Petitions

May 28
Esther 8–10

"And that these days should be remembered and kept throughout every generation, every family, every province, and every city; and that these days of Purim should not fail from among the Jews, nor the memorial of them perish from their seed" (Esther 9:28).

From the time of Esther, the Jews have celebrated Purim every year. It is a day of rejoicing, games, plays, and feasts. A special pastry called Hamantashan (Haman's ears) are prepared and eaten. The freedom that was gained under Queen Esther is remembered and celebrated. The story of Queen Esther, Mordecai, and Haman is retold and often reenacted in plays performed by the children. The fact that they were rescued from certain death and given life is the cause for much celebration. Purim is usually celebrated in the spring around Easter. There is another time when we celebrate the deliverance from death to life. Only this time it is a celebration of eternal life. Jesus said, "Verily, verily, I say unto you, he that heareth my word, and believeth on him that sent me, hath everlasting life, and shall not come into condemnation; but is passed from death unto life" (John 5:24). Trust the Lord and celebrate life!

Ponderings

Praise

Petitions

May 29
Job 1–4

"There was a man in the Land of Uz, whose name was Job; and that man was perfect and upright, and one that feared God, and eschewed evil" (Job 1:1).

Job has become our standard for suffering. When a loved one is suffering, we often try to offer comfort by reminding them of the suffering of Job. We look at all that he lost and how he suffered pain and attempt to compare his suffering to their situation. Job certainly went through more than any of us care to even consider. Notice Job's first reaction to his loss and suffering. In Job 1:20 we read, "Then Job arose, and rent his mantle and shaved his head and fell down upon the ground, and worshiped." His immediate reaction was that of humility and worship. In our suffering, we often pose the question. Why me? Job asked, *Why Lord?* His first thoughts were not about how bad it was, but what the Lord wanted to accomplish in his life. The first place that he went was to the Lord and there, rather than complaining and whining, the Bible says he *worshiped*. The scripture goes on to point out that, "In all this, Job sinned not, nor charged God foolishly." Job simply turned all his attention to the Lord proclaiming, "Blessed be the name of the Lord." How difficult it seems for us to worship the Lord in our most difficult hour! Job did it. Why can't we?

Ponderings

Praise

Petitions

May 30
Job 5–8

"I would seek unto my God, and unto God would I commit my cause; Which doeth great things and unsearchable; marvelous things without number" (Job 5:8–9).

Jesus said, "But seek ye first the kingdom of God, and his righteousness; and all these things shall be added unto you" (Matthew 6:33). Our first priority every day should be to seek the Lord. We should seek him in prayer as well as in reading his Word. We should seek his presence and search out the direction in which he would have us walk. This kind of daily seeking of the Lord requires that we are totally committed to him and his will for us. As we seek the Lord, we must also commit everything to him. We give him our lives, our love, and our loyalty. When you commit to following the Lord, he will give you direction, wisdom, and the strength to do what he has planned for you. He will not lead you or give you some task that you cannot accomplish. He will never give you more than you can handle. We often seek the Lord only when we feel we need him. Our need for the Lord is daily and so we should seek him and commit ourselves to him every day.

Ponderings

Praise

Petitions

May 31
Job 9–12

"Then Job answered and said, I know it is so of a truth: but how should man be just with God?" (Job 9:1–2)

When Scripture speaks of being *just*, it is speaking of being made *right* with God. In our natural state, we stand before God condemned in our sin. We could not be made just through the law. Galatians 3:11 states, "But that no man is justified by the law in the sight of God." It is evident we cannot be made righteous before God by keeping the Law. However that same verse goes on to say, "For the just shall live by faith." There is the answer. We are made right with God by faith—but faith in what or in whom? The answer lies in what it took for our sin to be forgiven so that we could be *made right* before God. That price is death and was paid by the blood of Jesus Christ. "Much more then, being now justified by his blood, we shall be saved from wrath through him" (Romans 5:9). So, how should man be just with God? Man can be made just (right) with God by placing his faith in the shed blood of Jesus Christ. "For Christ also hath once suffered for sins, the just for the unjust, that he might bring us to God, being put to death in the flesh, but quickened by the Spirit" (1 Peter 3:18).

Ponderings

Praise

Petitions

June 1
Job 13–16

"If a man die, shall he live again? all the days of my appointed time will I wait, till my change come" (Job 14:14).

The scripture tells us that because of our sin every man will come to an expected end. "The wages of sin is death" (Romans 3:23). Yet the question that remains is *what then?* When death comes, can man expect to find life again? Jesus answered this question standing outside the tomb of his friend Lazarus. Lazarus had died and Jesus had just told Martha, "Thy brother shall rise again." She assumed that Jesus was talking about the last resurrection when she offered her affirmation of what Jesus had said to her. Then Jesus went on to say, "I am the resurrection and the life: he that believeth in me, though he were dead, yet shall he live" (John 11:25). The answer to Job's question is a resounding yes! However, don't miss the fact that there is one qualification. You must have placed your faith in the Son of God. John put it very simply in his epistle. "He that hath the Son hath life; and he that hath not the Son of God hath not life" (1 John 5:12). The answer to Job's questions is yes, as long as you have put your faith in the Son of God, you will "live again."

Ponderings

Praise

Petitions

June 2
Job 17–20

"For I know that my redeemer liveth, and that he shall stand at the latter day upon the earth" (Job 19:25).

With all the pain and suffering that Job was going through, there was one thing that Job could declare that he knew. With all the advice that his friends were trying to give him, and in all the questions Job would be asked, the one thing the Job would hang on to was the fact that his *redeemer liveth*. We do not serve a dead and uncaring God. The tomb in which Jesus was buried is empty. It is not empty because someone stole his body; it is empty because he lives. A living person has no need for a grave. Many religions will speak of their dead leaders. Their gravesites are places of worship and adoration, their bones are revered in their graves. At the tomb of Jesus, however, there is rejoicing because he is not there. As the women who came to the grave of Jesus after he had been crucified peered into the open tomb, an angel told them, "He is not here: for he is risen, as he said. Come, see the place where the Lord lay" (Matthew 28:6). We can rejoice that we serve a living God.

Ponderings

Praise

Petitions

June 3
Job 21–24

"He draweth also the mighty with his power: he riseth up, and no man is sure of life" (Job 24:22).

Life is a fragile thing. We would like to think that we are invincible, but this is just not true. No man is sure of his life. Do you know the day and hour when your life will come to an end? Many set out on a journey thinking that they would eventually arrive home safe and sound. Yet the sound of crushing metal and breaking glass came, and a life was suddenly ended. We can never be sure when our time will come, when *life's fleeting days will be o'er*. The scripture says, "It is appointed unto men once to die" (Hebrews 9:27). You have an appointment with death, and only God knows when that time will come. This is an appointment for which you will not be late; it is not an appointment that you can postpone to another time. No one can say that they will for a surety live through another day. God made a way so that when that day does arrive we can be with him for eternity. Are you trusting in Jesus to save you? Are you prepared should your appointment with death come today? Are you sure?

Ponderings

Praise

Petitions

June 4
Job 25–30

"But where shall wisdom be found? And where is the place of understanding?" (Job 28:12).

Often comes the time in a person's life when they are faced with a situation and have not the wisdom to know what to do. In the midst of Job's suffering and with the misguided advice of his friends, no doubt Job had come to a point in his life when he needed wisdom. As his friends explore the possible reasons for Job's affliction and suffering and try to find a solution to his dilemma, there is the question of what to do now. So where will the wisdom be found to deal with this situation? Where do you find the wisdom to deal with the situations that come into your life when you just don't know what to do? In the book of James the Bible tells us that when we need wisdom, all we have to do is ask the Lord and he will give it to us. You will also find Job answers his own question when you reach the last verse of Job 28. "Behold the fear of the Lord, that is wisdom, and to depart from evil is understanding" (Job 28:28). The kind of wisdom that we need for daily living will only be found in recognizing God and the part that he plays in our life. In the fear of God you will find wisdom. Just ask him.

Ponderings

Praise

Petitions

June 5
Job 31–34

> "He looketh upon men, and if any say, I have sinned, and perverted that which was right, and it profited me not; He will deliver his soul from going into the pit, and his life shall see the light" (Job 33:27–28).

When most people come face to face with their own sin, they will usually do one of two things. They will either try to deny it or they will confess their sin. It is often hard to admit our own sin. Yet it is the confession of our sin before God that brings his forgiveness. Every day we should examine ourselves to determine if we have sinned against God. The Holy Spirit will reveal our sin to our hearts when we are openly seeking to please the Lord by a pure life. It is when we try to deny or excuse our sin that we find ourselves getting deeper and deeper into the trouble of our own making. John said in his little epistle, "If we say that we have no sin, we deceive ourselves, and the truth is not in us. If we confess our sins, he is faithful and just to forgive us our sins, and to cleanse us from all unrighteousness" (1 John 1:8–9). When we bow before God and confess our sin rather than try to excuse or deny it, we will find the forgiveness of God who judges all men righteously.

Ponderings

Praise

Petitions

June 6
Job 35–38

"Hearken unto this, O Job: stand still, and consider the wondrous works of God."(Job 37:14).

Have you ever stood on a mountaintop viewing the landscape below or on a sandy beach looking out over an ocean? Have you ever been overwhelmed by the vastness of a clear winter sky? There you will see the wondrous works of God. When we stand still for a few moments and soak in the creation of God, it gives us a sense of how small and weak we really are. At the same time, it also gives us a confidence in the wisdom and strength of an Almighty God. In our hurried lives, perhaps it would be good for us to occasionally take a drive to a place where we can just stand still and consider the wondrous works of God. His creation is filled with beauty and wonder. To see how he perfectly blended colors and textures in such a magnificent work of creation is almost beyond description. The artist's brush is hard pressed to replicate what God has already done. How mighty and awesome he really is! When we gaze at the wonder of God's creation, it shows us his splendor, his magnificence, and his power. When you are feeling down and discouraged, give yourself some time to stand still and consider the wondrous works of God. It will help you put things in perspective.

Ponderings

Praise

Petitions

June 7
Job 39–42

"So the Lord blessed the latter end of Job more than his beginning: for he had fourteen thousand sheep, and six thousand camels, and a thousand yoke of oxen, and a thousand she asses. He had also seven sons and three daughters" (Job 42:12–13).

There is much that we can learn from Job concerning patience, prayer, the sovereignty of God, and suffering. However, the greatest lesson seen in a sort of undercurrent in Job's story is a lesson of faithfulness. In all of his suffering and loss, Job did not loose faith in the God he served. Often when tragedy strikes we are quick to blame God or someone else. Job never gave up on God or blamed him as though God had forsaken him. Job was faithful. When Job's friends came to comfort and console him, they wondered why he did didn't just turn his back on God. Job told them, "Though he slay me, yet will I trust in him: but I will maintain mine own ways before him" (Job 13:15). Job simply trusted the Lord. He believed that God had a great plan and would bring him through this crisis. May God give you an unshakable faith in the Lord like Job had.

Ponderings

Praise

Petitions

June 8
Psalms 1–8

"What is man that thou are mindful of him? and the son of man that thou visitest him?" (Psalms 8:4).

When one considers the whole of creation, when one stands under a clear sky and gazes at the vastness of space, it causes one to wonder, *What is man?* When we try to see our place in such a big universe, man seems to become so insignificant. Yet, we are very important to God. God's plan through the ages was to bring us salvation. God loves us with an unconditional love. We matter to God. He created us and he knows us individually. Jesus said that even the *very hairs of your head are all numbered*. God knows your voice and cares very much about what happens to you. He even has a plan for your life that is filled with good things. Yes, he cares about you. He wants to hear from you and he wants you to trust him. The scripture promises, "Humble yourselves therefore under the mighty hand of God, that he may exalt you in due time: Casting all your care upon him; for he careth for you" (1 Peter 5:6–7). You may feel insignificant in such a big universe, but you are not insignificant to God.

Ponderings

Praise

Petitions

June 9
Psalms 9–17

"But the Lord shall endure for ever: he hath prepared his throne for judgment. And he shall judge the world in righteousness, he shall minister judgment to the people in uprightness" (Psalms 9:7–8).

There is no doubt that one day we will all stand before the judgment seat of God. His judgment will not be according to man's law nor according to the mood God might happen to be in on that fateful day. God's judgment will be according to his righteousness. We will not be judged according to other people's character or behavior. Each individual will be judged by the righteousness of God. When we have received Christ, we also receive his righteousness and will be spared the punishment of our sin. "For he hath made him to be sin for us, who knew no sin; that we might be made the righteousness of God in him" (2 Corinthians 5:21). For those who have never received Christ there will be but one sentence—death. There will be no parole, no time off for good behavior, no second chance. God's judgment will be final and eternal. How will you stand before his judgment? Will you have the righteousness of Christ or will you be condemned to eternal punishment because of your sin? It's your choice.

Ponderings

Praise

Petitions

June 10
Psalms 18–21

"The heavens declare the glory of God; and the firmament sheweth his handiwork." (Psalms 19:1).

The creation itself speaks of God's power and majesty, but more than these it also speaks of his glory. The stars in all their beauty and brilliance in a summer night's sky bring glory to the One who placed them there. How can one not consider the vastness of space and wonder at the Creator who gave it order and beauty? Scientists can only guess at the size of the universe and the number of stars that it contains. Yet God knows its size and the place of each star. The Universe is no mystery to the One who created it. We also see order and complexity in the earth clearly demonstrating God's handiwork. To see the array of colors in a mountain ridge or the ever-changing beauty of a sunset is to see the very handiwork of God. Artists can try to copy the beauty of the earth on canvas, but they cannot replicate the real thing. Only God can display his handiwork in the universe that he created. God even gave us the capacity to see his handiwork and to marvel at its unique beauty. *To God be the glory, great things he hath done!*

Ponderings

Praise

Petitions

June 11
Psalms 22–27

"The Lord is my shepherd; I shall not want." (Psalm 23)

The twenty-third Psalm has been a comfort and encouragement time and time again. It is a psalm that is bursting with meaning and significance. It always seems to fit the need whenever and wherever it is repeated. It is a psalm of comfort. Knowing that the Lord is our Shepherd brings to us a confidence that he is looking out for our best interests. It reminds us that he is sufficient to meet all of our needs every day. It assures us of his protective hand over us. It is a psalm of encouragement. Just to know that the Lord is with us wherever we are and wherever we go encourages us to face life with all of its difficulties and sorrows. Even when we come to the *valley of the shadow of death*, God does not leave us alone. It is a psalm of blessing. Surely the Lord gives us more than we deserve. So great is his blessing on us that our cup is full and *runneth over*. It is a psalm of hope, a hope that we will one day be in the *house of the Lord forever*. For sheep that have gone astray, God has provided himself as the perfect Shepherd who provides, protects, and guides us all the way into his fold.

Ponderings

Praise

Petitions

June 12
Psalms 28–33

"Give unto the Lord the glory due unto his name; worship the Lord in the beauty of holiness" (Psalms 29:2).

Everything that we are, everything that we have, everything that we have the capacity to do is because of the Lord. All of the praise and credit that we receive should be redirected to him. Why is it that when a singer sings a beautiful song or a preacher delivers a great sermon, that we are inclined to give them the glory instead of giving the glory to the Lord? It is the Lord that gives the song, and it is the Lord that gives the singer the talent to sing the song so beautifully. It is the Lord's message delivered through his servant. Therefore, it is the Lord who should receive the glory. Servants who are truly serving the Lord will give the glory unto the Lord and not receive it unto themselves. It is said that we ought to give credit where credit is due. Certainly the credit and glory is due to the Lord. When God gives you his strength, his wisdom, his grace, a special talent to do his work, or a special blessing, give credit where credit is due. Give the Lord the glory that he so greatly deserves.

Ponderings

Praise

Petitions

June 13
Psalms 34–37

"The steps of a good man are ordered by the Lord: and he delighteth in his way. Though he fall, he shall not be utterly cast down: for the Lord upholdeth him with his hand" (Psalms 37:23–24).

It is true that a Christian will occasionally fall. There will be some stumbling block or temptation that will cause him to stumble and fail the Lord. However, this does not mean that the believer has to stay down. No, the Lord is always there to pick us up, dust us off, forgive our sin, and guide us with his hand. God's purpose for us is forgiveness and reconciliation. His desire for us is that we continue to walk with him in a manner that will glorify him. When we fall and cry out to him, he will lift us up. Often we think it is the Christian's duty to hold onto the Lord. But we will find that when the going gets rough and the trials come, it is actually the Lord that is holding on to us. When we fall, the Lord is always there. He does not want us to stay down in the folly of our sin. No matter how far we may stray, the Father is always faithful to forgive and restore us. When you fall, don't give up; God has not given up on you. He still loves you very much.

Ponderings

Praise

Petitions

June 14
Psalms 38–42

"As the hart panteth after the water brooks, so panteth my soul after thee, O God. My soul thirsteth for God, for the living God: when shall I come and appear before God?" (Psalms 42:1–2).

Are you thirsty for God? When man is thirsty, it is an indication that he has a great need. When he is thirsty, he will do whatever it takes to satisfy that thirst. Thirst is more than simply wanting for something; it represents a real need. It is a need that causes one to search until that need is met. Do you have a longing for God, a desire to be closer to him? Do you have a deep felt need for him? The psalmist illustrated his thirst for God by comparing it to the thirst of a deer (hart) for water. The deer is in such a need and has such a heart for seeking out the water brook that he is literally panting with thirst. Do you have that kind of desire to seek the Lord? He is able and stands ready to meet your every need, no matter how big it may seem nor how insignificant. He is sufficient to meet all of your needs. Knowing that he is our sufficiency causes us to thirst for him, to search him out and bring to him our deepest need. Are you thirsty? Only he can satisfy your thirst.

Ponderings

Praise

Petitions

June 15
Psalms 43–49

"Why art thou cast down, O my soul? and why art thou disquieted within me? hope in God; for I shall yet praise him, who is the health of my countenance, and my God." (Psalms 43:5).

Have you ever caught yourself worrying about nothing? Have you ever found yourself depressed and down for some unknown reason? It seems here that the psalmist had found himself in a depressed and sorrowful state. When those times come, it is helpful to remind ourselves of the promises of God. We are not hopeless. God cares about us very much and has promised to provide our every need. Our hope is in the Lord. Our hope is not in the things that we possesss or in our schemes to solve our own problems. You trusted Christ to save you; can you trust him to sustain you? Look at this promise. "Be careful for nothing; but in every thing by prayer and supplication with thanksgiving let your requests be made known unto God. And the peace of God, which passeth all understanding, shall keep your hearts and minds through Christ Jesus" (Philippians 4:6–7). When you find yourself filled with worry and fear, just take it to the Lord and put your hope and trust in him. He will take care of you.

Ponderings

Praise

Petitions

June 16
Psalms 50–55

"Cast thy burden upon the Lord, and he shall sustain thee."(Psalms 55:22a).

The Lord invites you to bundle up all the burdens that you carry and bring them to him. Jesus restated the invitation this way, "Come unto me, all ye that labour and are heavy laden, and I will give you rest" (Matthew 11:28). The burdens that we carry demand our attention. Their weight causes us to focus on them rather than on the Lord. The burdens cause worry, fear, and a self-dependency. By casting our burdens upon the Lord, he gives us a freedom to enjoy the abundant life. It is unnecessary for the believer to be burdened down with the cares of this life when there is a greater purpose, to serve and glorify the Lord. When we give the Lord our burdens, we are free to worship and glorify him. Of course, placing our burdens on the Lord requires that we trust him to take those burdens from us. We must trust that he is able to care for them. With our burden removed, we can run the race and do the work that he calls us to do. It is the Lord that will give you freedom and sustain you through anything. Are you tired of the load? Do you need a rest? It's time to unload.

Ponderings

Praise

Petitions

June 17
Psalms 56–61

"What time I am afraid, I will trust in thee" (Psalms 56:3).

It sounds simple, doesn't it? When those times come, when for some reason, our heart is filled we fear, Scripture teaches us to just trust the Lord. Worry is grounded on fear. Worry is usually a fear of what might happen or perhaps of what won't happen the way we expect it to. Daniel is a good example of trusting the Lord in the face of fear. Imagine facing a lair of hungry lions just waiting to make you their next meal. Daniel trusted the Lord and was delivered out of the mouth of the lions. David, who penned this Psalm, faced fear on many occasions. He was often in life threatening situations from the time he faced Goliath to the rebellion of his own son, Absalom. David had learned to trust the Lord in the face of fear the hard way. When you trust the Lord, he has a way of calming your fears and giving you peace. No matter what causes you to fear, God already knows about it and has the power to help you though anything. You are never alone, the Lord is always at your side to help you and guide you. Learn to trust the Lord; he will calm your fears.

Ponderings

Praise

Petitions

June 18
Psalms 62–68

"If I regard iniquity in my heart, the Lord will not hear me" (Psalms 66:18).

Our greatest barrier to prayer is sin that we are not willing to confront and confess to the Lord. The word *regard* in this verse refers to sin that we are willing to just look at and ignore. God hates sin. Oh, that we would hate the sin in our own lives as much as God does. He says that if we are willing to just look at our sin and do nothing to confess and repent of it that he will not hear our prayer. How many times have we held onto some sin and tried to petition something from the Lord. What foolishness! When we are comfortable with our own sin, we cannot expect anything from the Lord. The human race has become masters at excusing and attempting to ignore sin. When we know we have sinned against a holy God, we must confess that sin to him and repent of it immediately. He promises, "If we confess our sins, he is faithful and just to forgive us our sins, and to cleanse us from all unrighteousness" (1 John 1:9). When it seems that your prayers are not being heard, perhaps the first step should be to search your heart and confess every sin before the Lord.

Ponderings

Praise

Petitions

June 19
Psalms 69–72

"O God, thou knowest my foolishness; and my sins are not hid from thee" (Psalms 69:5).

The hiding of sin has become a time consuming project for many. People may try to hide their sin in darkness. In an effort to hide past deeds, some have even gone so far as to have their name as well as their whole identity changed. Lies and elaborate schemes are devised to cover up sinful deeds. One might be somewhat successful at hiding their sin from others. But they will never be successful at hiding their sin from God. He knows! Before God, we are totally without a hiding place. You can try to run; but no matter where you go, God will already be there. He knows our very thoughts as well as the intents of our heart. We cannot hide from God. When we stand before him in the judgment, there is no scheme of the human mind that can hide sin from an all-knowing God. We may try to ignore sin, hide sin, or excuse sin; but God will ultimately be the judge of sin. No sin can be hidden from him. It's time to quit trying to excuse and cover up your sin. Bring it all to the Lord in repentance and confession and you will find the forgiveness of a merciful, gracious, and loving Lord. After all, it was for your sin that Jesus died.

Ponderings

Praise

Petitions

June 20
Psalms 73–77

"But it is good for me to draw near to God: I have put my trust in the Lord God, that I may declare all thy works." (Psalms 73:28).

It is a good thing to draw near to God. You can draw near to him through prayer and through meditating on his Word. In this busy world, it is so important to give time to drawing near to our heavenly Father. The Lord said in Psalms 46:10, "Be still, and know that I am God." Find a quiet place and give yourself time to draw near to the Lord. As you draw near to him, you will find that he is waiting for you and desires to draw near to you as well. James said, "Draw nigh to God, and he will draw nigh to you" (James 4:8). God loves you very much and wants to be close to you in much the same way he was close to Adam in the Garden of Eden. In the quietness, listen for his voice and sense his presence. In his presence, you will find comfort, peace, and a sense of joy. Drawing near him requires that you are seeking and trusting him. Are you so far away from God that you have forgotten what it is like to be near him? It is not too late to draw close to him again. He is as near as your next prayer. Determine in your heart that every day you will draw near to the Lord. It is good, you know.

Ponderings

Praise

Petitions

June 21
Psalms 78–80

"So will not we go back from thee; quicken us, and we will call upon thy name. Turn us again, O Lord God of hosts, cause they face to shine; and we shall be saved." (Psalms 80:18–19).

It is when God's people realize their own sinfulness and how far from God they really are that they understand their need for revival. Revival comes from God. It begins with a renewed commitment to seek the blessings and power of God by calling out to him in repentance and confession. It is the plea of a desperate people. In David's time the people had turned their backs on God and served idols. Notice that revival involves commitment. "So will not we go back from thee." Revival also requires prayer where we call upon God's name in repentance and confession of our sin. Do you desire revival in your church, community, or in your own life? Commit now to the Lord to serve him fully, turn away from the false gods that have taken your attention and devotion away from him, confess all your sin before him with repentance, and call unto him. God is waiting to hear from you. It's time to come home.

Ponderings

Praise

Petitions

June 22
Psalms 81–88

"For thou, Lord, art good, and ready to forgive; and plenteous in mercy unto all them that call upon thee" (Psalms 86:5).

God is often seen as seeking vengeance and condemnation. He is thought to be fierce and revengeful looking to destroy those who will not trust in him. Certainly, God will ultimately judge those who forsake and blaspheme his name. However, God is good and rather than looking for condemnation, he is looking to forgive and bless. Condemnation is the result of our sin and not the final desire of God upon man. God's desire is forgiveness and restoration. He sent Jesus to keep us from condemnation. Jesus said, "For God sent not his Son into the world to condemn the world; but that the world through him might be saved" (John 3:17). God loves you very much and his desire is to restore you to a loving relationship with him. He does not want to condemn you, but must in order to be perfectly just. Call upon him today, and find the complete forgiveness of sin that the Lord gives.

Ponderings

Praise

Petitions

June 23
Psalms 89–94

"Thou hast set our iniquities before thee, our secret sins in the light of thy countenance" (Psalms 90:8).

We seem to live in a time when the rule of life is to do whatever you think you can get away with. One speeds down the highway without regard to the speed limit hoping that there is no law enforcement officer in sight. People cheat on expense reports and try to get away with all manner of sin. Jesus said, "And this is the condemnation, that light is come into the world, and men loved darkness rather than light, because their deeds were evil" (John 3:19). Men will try to hide their sin in darkness and secrecy. However, there is no sin that can be hidden from the eyes of the Lord. He sees all and knows all. You may hide your sin from other people and may even seem to get away with some evil deed, but you cannot hide from the all-seeing eye of God. He knows. This should motivate us to always do what is right and good. Knowing that our sin cannot be hidden from the eyes of the Lord we should always live in such a way that pleases him. The sin that is done is darkness will be made known in the light of his countenance.

Ponderings

Praise

Petitions

June 24
Psalms 95–103

"Make a joyful noise unto the Lord, all ye lands. Serve the Lord with gladness: come before his presence with singing" (Psalms 100:1–2).

How often have you heard this verse quoted as an excuse to sing badly? Some have often said, "I can't sing very well, but I can make a joyful noise." The phrase *joyful noise* is in fact one Hebrew word that means *to shout*, as in a shout of victory or a shout for joy. When an army would win a battle, they would raise their voice in a victory shout. Today, this shout is often heard as a football is carried over a goal line or a baseball is hit out of a stadium. How often is it heard in the congregation of the saints? Does this say something about our priorities? When you consider that Jesus died to pay the price for your sin and that he has prepared a place for you in heaven, when you consider that he gave us victory over death, hell and the grave, when you consider that he gives you the ability to live a victorious life overcoming the world, shouldn't that be enough to lift your voice in a shout of victory. Go ahead, make a joyful noise.

Ponderings

Praise

Petitions

June 25
Psalms 104–106

"O give thanks unto the Lord; call upon his name: make known his deeds among the people. Sing unto him, sing psalms unto him: talk ye of all his wondrous works. Glory ye in his holy name: let the heart of them rejoice that seek the Lord" (Psalms 105:1–3).

Here is a great prescription for praise and worship. In praise we should offer our thanks to the Lord for all that he has done. Call upon his name in prayer. Through personal testimonies, we should also make known what God had done among his people. We also express our worship and adoration in song, singing unto him. We should glory in the name of the Lord. This means that we should give him all the glory for what he has done. No one should take the glory or the credit for anything. All glory should be given to the Lord. "Give unto the Lord the glory due unto his name; worship the Lord in the beauty of holiness" (Psalms 29:2). Our worship should include rejoicing, both in song and testimony. Finally, we must talk of his wondrous works as found in his Word. This plan can be used in both public and private worship.

Ponderings

Praise

Petitions

June 26
Psalms 107–111

"Let the redeemed of the Lord say so, whom he hath redeemed from the hand of the enemy" (Psalms 107:2).

It is time for believers to speak up. How often a word is said about religion or God and the believer remains silent in embarrassment or fear. We who have been redeemed from the hand of the enemy ought to have enough courage to speak up when it is appropriate to do so. When the subject of God comes up in a conversation, don't be afraid to speak up for your faith. God does not have secret agents. We are to declare ourselves to be his and do it without fear. We who know what it is to be washed in the blood, to have our sins forgiven, to be saved from the hand of the enemy should speak up and declare that it is the Lord that saved us. Do your coworkers know that you are a believer in Jesus Christ? Do they know that you have found the plan of eternal redemption? Are you ready to take a stand for the one who saved you? It's time to stand up and say so. After all, when Jesus told us to go and tell the world about the Good News, he promised, "I am with you always" (Mathew 29:20). Go ahead, speak up!

Ponderings

Praise

Petitions

June 27
Psalms 112–118

"Precious in the sight of the Lord is the death of his saints" (Psalms 116:15).

How often we have stood grieving at the graveside of a dear saint. Yet, the grieving is not for the departed but for our own sakes. When a child of God closes their eyes in death, they are opened in glory. The death of a saint is a precious thing to the Lord. It is precious because the plan for salvation that was put in place before the foundation of the world is finally completed. A child of creation, born into sin, is now redeemed, born into the family of God. It is also precious because the fellowship with God that was destroyed in the Garden of Eden is now fully restored. Yes, we can have fellowship now, but there is something precious about being in heaven for all eternity, without worldly woes. When we grieve for a departed saint, don't weep for them, they are in the presence of God. Weep for those who do not know the Lord and have no hope of eternal salvation without Christ. The funeral for a departed saint should be a victory party, knowing that the victory has been won over death and the grave. The departed saint has only gone ahead before us.

Ponderings

Praise

Petitions

June 28
Psalms 119

"O how love I thy law! it is my meditation all the day" (Psalms 119:97).

Psalms 119 is the longest chapter in the Bible. Its primary focus is the Word of God and our relationship with the Lord. The psalmist speaks of the permanency of God's Word. "Forever, O Lord, thy word is settled in heaven" (verse 89). He also speaks of the truth of the Word of God. "Thy word is true from the beginning: and every one of thy righteous judgments endureth for ever" (verse 160). This psalm is just bursting with declarations concerning God's Word. One could spend many hours searching its treasure. Notice all the ways that the Word of God is presented. It is called his commandments, testimonies, statutes, and precepts. The psalmist speaks of how our relationship with the Word of God determines our relationship with God himself. "Wherewithal shall a young man cleanse his way? By taking heed thereto according to thy word" (verse 9). And "Thy word have I hid in mine heart, that I might not sin against thee" (verse 11). With obedience to the Word of God comes the blessing of God. "Blessed are the undefiled in the way, who walk in the law of the Lord" (verse 1). Don't you just love it?

Ponderings

Praise

Petitions

June 29
Psalms 120–133

"My help cometh from the Lord, which made heaven and earth" (Psalms 121:2).

Why is it that we often look everywhere but to the Lord when we are in trouble and need help? People will run to the psychologists, the psychics, and other worldly places, seeking advice and guidance when all they need is the instruction found in the Word of God. It is the Lord that can help us. Just think. He is omniscient (all knowing) and omnipotent (all-powerful). He is willing and waiting to help us. Is there any problem or difficulty that is too hard for the Lord? He has promised to give us wisdom. James 1:5 states, "If any of you lack wisdom, let him ask of God, that giveth to all men liberally, and upbraideth not; and it shall be given him." All we have to do is ask. God has also promised to guide us when we trust him and completely lean on him. "Trust in the Lord with all thine heart; and lean not unto thine own understanding. In all thy ways acknowledge him, and he shall direct thy paths" (Proverbs 3:5–6). The help that we really need comes from the Lord. We must go to him with everything, knowing that the help he gives us is the best that we can receive.

Ponderings

Praise

Petitions

June 30
Psalms 134–140

"Whither shall I go from thy spirit? or whither shall I flee from thy presence?" (Psalms 139:7).

The word *omnipresence* is used to describe the universal presence of God. There is no place that you can go where you can escape the Lord's presence. The psalmist attempted to provide a list of such places. Yet, at every place that he mentions, God is there. Even in the darkness, God is there. Why is it that man thinks that somehow sin can be hidden from God in darkness? Jesus said that, "men loved darkness rather than light, because their deeds were evil" (John 3:19). It may be possible to hide from people, even hide sin from those close to us. But there is no place you can go to hide from God. Even Adam and Eve tried to hide from God in the Garden of Eden after their disobedience, but they could not do it. It seems that the only reason man has to hide from God is because of his sin. It is almost beyond our comprehension how that God can be every place at once. We cannot put God in a box or define his existence. Knowing that there is no place we can be that his helping hand cannot reach out to help us should bring comfort rather than fear.

Ponderings

Praise

Petitions

July 1
Psalms 141–150

"The Lord is nigh unto all them that call upon him, to all that call upon him in truth" (Psalms 145:18).

God is only a prayer away. God is longing to be near us. He created us to fellowship with him. When we call upon the Lord, he will come to our side to aid us in every way. It does not matter where we are or what time of day it is. Would you say that you are close to the Lord? There was once a bumper sticker that read, *If you feel far from God, guess who moved.* All you need to do to draw closer to the Lord is to call upon him. In repentance, confess your sin to him. He is anxious to forgive you. His desire is to be near you and to walk with you. Talk to him about everything. Talk to him like you would talk to your best friend. Tell him of your fears and your deepest burdens. Perhaps it seems God is so far away because you have ignored his presence. Today, draw near to him by calling on his name. "The Lord is nigh unto all them that call upon him, to all that call upon him in truth" (Psalms 145:18). He is waiting.

Ponderings

Praise

Petitions

July 2
Proverbs 1–3

"Trust in the Lord with all thine heart; and lean not unto thine own understanding. In all thy ways acknowledge him, and he shall direct thy paths" (Proverbs 3:5–6).

God has a plan for your life. God's plan can only be found by trusting the Lord to lead you every day. God may not reveal his entire plan to you all at once. He asks you first to trust him and then follow him each step of the way. How often we have tried our own way only to stumble and fail? God has your best interest at heart. He will not lead you where he does not intend for you to be. Sometimes his direction may not make much sense, which is why he says, "Lean not unto thine own understanding." In every decision that you make it is important that you take it first to God in prayer. Seek his direction and guidance in everything. God will reveal his plan for you a little at a time. What he requires of you is just to trust him and acknowledge his working in your life. God will not lead you to the wrong place. He may take you through some times of testing. Just be faithful to follow him as he leads you each day. You will find his way is always best.

Ponderings

Praise

Petitions

July 3
Proverbs 4–7

"Wisdom is the principal thing; therefore get wisdom: and with all thy getting get understanding" (Proverbs 4:7).

Of all the things we need to live for the Lord in this world, wisdom is the most important. For if we have wisdom, we will know how to live righteous and godly lives. When given an opportunity to ask for anything he wanted, Solomon asked the Lord for wisdom. God granted him his request and along with that wisdom, Solomon was also given great riches. The wisdom we should seek is not the wisdom that the world has to offer. Rather, our quest should be for Godly wisdom. Do not equate wisdom with knowledge. Many who had great scholastic credentials had very little wisdom. Wisdom, as used here in Proverbs, is defined as having a skill in how to live. Life is filled with choices. Godly wisdom gives us the ability to make the right choices. In our pursuit for happiness, peace, and surviving in this world, wisdom is our most valued possesssion. So, how do we get this wisdom? Scripture says all we have to do is ask in faith. "If any of you lack wisdom, let him ask of God, that giveth to all men liberally, and upbraideth not; and it shall be given him" (James 1:5).

Ponderings

Praise

Petitions

July 4
Proverbs 8–11

"Give instruction to a wise man, and he will be yet wiser: teach a just man, and he will increase in learning" (Proverbs 9:9).

We should never come to a point in our lives where we stop learning. There is so much to know about the world around us. There is so much to know about the Word of God. Often some would come to the conclusion that they have learned all that they need to get along in the world. How enriched their lives would be if they would just keep on learning. In our Christian growth we never get to the place were we can stop learning about the Lord and his Word. We could never exhaust the truth or the depth of God's Holy Word. You may have read a passage of Scripture many times, and yet, the Lord can show you something you have never seen before. Let the Holy Spirit be your guide. When one comes to the place where they think they know it all, they are on a pathway to self-destruction. We must keep learning about how to live for the Lord and how we can bring him glory in our lives. Every time you read the scripture, pray and ask the Lord to show you what he wants you to learn. Ask him to show you something new. You may be surprised by what the Lord gives you. Never stop learning and never stop asking!

Ponderings

Praise

Petitions

July 5
Proverbs 12–14

"The backslider in heart shall be filled with his own ways" (Proverbs 14:14a).

A person does not backslide from the Lord accidentally. The backslider chooses to backslide. His choices change from doing what is pleasing to the Lord to what is pleasing to himself. The backslider says in his heart, "I know what God says, but I'll do what I want to do." Backsliding is not usually the result of making one wrong choice, but from making many wrong choices. The backslider decides in his heart that there are some sins that he can live with, knowing well that such sin causes him to be separated from the Lord. It is only when the backslider finds himself suffering from the consequences of his sin that he realizes that obedience to the Lord was the best choice. The problem with backsliding is its subtlety. The choice may begin with choosing to participate in some sin that is excused as being harmless. There is no such thing as *harmless* sin. Sin comes from choosing to obey our own lusts rather than the Word of God. We can choose to obey the Lord and walk close to him. We can also choose to backslide by trying our own way. How will you choose?

Ponderings

Praise

Petitions

July 6
Proverbs 15–17

"A soft answer turneth away wrath: but grievous words stir up anger." (Proverbs 15:1).

Our natural response to someone who is angry with us is to get angry in return. We somehow feel that someone who is angry with us must not get the advantage of us. Anger begets anger. However, Scripture teaches that the best way to deal with anger is not by getting angry in return, but by responding with a soft answer. Jesus is our best example of how to handle the wrath of people. 1 Peter 2:23 records how Jesus responded to those who wanted to hurt him. "Who, when he was reviled, reviled not again; when he suffered, he threatened not; but committed himself to him that judgeth righteously." When we are attacked in anger, our response should be to answer with a soft voice in a humble manner. Then, like Jesus, commit it to *him who judges righteously*. With such a response, the sting is taken out of the attacker. When we answer with soft words and a humble spirit, it is not the response the attacker is expecting. However, it is the godly response and is honoring to the Lord. James said that we should be "swift to hear, slow to speak, slow to wrath" (James 1:19b).

Ponderings

Praise

Petitions

July 7
Proverbs 18–20

"There are many devices in a man's heart; nevertheless the counsel of the Lord, that shall stand" (Proverbs 19:21).

It seems that men are often making plans for the future. Many have dreams of what they want to accomplish in life. Some set their sights on making huge amounts of money, others on finding some way to be famous. Man is filled with all kinds of ambition. His heart is filled with many schemes and designs that he hopes will bring him some kind of happiness and security. But the best plans are those that come from knowing and obeying the will of God. God has a plan for the life of every person. When we are in the will of God, we will have the best that God has for us. There is nothing wrong with dreams and ambitions as long as they are within the perfect will of God. There is nothing we can attain or accomplish that will bring the satisfaction and joy of knowing that we have done as God has led us. James spoke of how man should plan out his life. "For that ye ought to say, If the Lord will, we shall live, and do this, or that" (James 4:15). Seek the Lord first in all things; don't depend only on the devices of your heart "for the counsel of the Lord, that shall stand."

Ponderings

Praise

Petitions

July 8
Proverbs 21–23

"Have not I written to thee excellent things in counsels and knowledge, that I might make thee know the certainty of the words of truth; that thou mightest answer the words of truth to them that send unto thee?" (Proverbs 22:20–21).

As you read through the Proverbs, it is important that you read them carefully and thoroughly. The Proverbs are *wise sayings* that God gave to Solomon. Each proverb should be read and considered one at time. In reading the Proverbs, you will find many comparisons and contrasts. Often the foolish is contrasted with the wise or the righteous is compared to the wicked. Each time you read through each chapter select one or two of the proverbs to muse over. It would do you good to commit many of them to memory. Just reading the Proverbs is not enough, it is also important to make them a part of your life. They are of little use unless the truths that they teach become a part of you. The Proverbs give the wisdom of God, which is high above the wisdom of man. Putting into practice the wisdom of God can keep you close to him and help you live a life that is pleasing to the Lord.

Ponderings

Praise

Petitions

July 9
Proverbs 24–26

"Be not thou envious against evil men, neither desire to be with them" (Proverbs 24:1).

There is something alluring about evildoers. Why is it that we are so drawn to be like evil men? The heroes of many in our generation are not those who seek after righteousness and justice, but those who rebel and seem to get away with sin. Our young people are drawn to be like the *bad guys* rather than emulate the *good guys*. The Bible tells us that we are not to envy evil men nor desire to *hang out* with them. The end of the evil man is stated clearly in Psalms 37:1–2, "Fret not thyself because of evildoers, neither be thou envious against the workers of iniquity. For they shall soon be cut down like the grass, and wither as the green herb." Our desire should be to emulate the life of Christ. Rather than seeking to do evil, we should always be seeking what God says is right. To be sure, this is not the way of the world, but it is the way of Christ. Jesus calls us to holiness and righteousness. By the shedding of his blood, we are cleansed from sin and told to go and sin no more. Let your light shine by doing what is right.

Ponderings

Praise

Petitions

July 10
Proverbs 27–29

"The rod and reproof give wisdom: but a child left to himself bringeth his mother to shame" (Proverbs 29:15).

Many a mother with an errant child will attest to the truth of this verse. Thinking that a child should not be punished or corrected for his misbehavior is not showing him love; a child grows up to have no respect for the law or any authority. We must not forget that a child is born with the burden of Adam's sin that is played out in sinful behavior. When a child is young, that sin must be dealt with severely and quickly or it will grow to be the controlling factor in that child's life. Another proverb states, "Foolishness is bound in the heart of a child; but the rod of correction shall drive it far from him" (Proverbs 22:15). The rod should never be used in an abusive manner. It is to be used for correction by a loving and caring parent. When a child is left to himself without correction, he will ultimately begin to make foolish decisions that lead to self-destruction bringing shame to his mother. A child that is taught righteousness through the teachings of Scripture will grow to be a mature responsible adult.

Ponderings

Praise

Petitions

July 11
Proverbs 30–31

"Favour is deceitful, and beauty is vain: but a woman that feareth the Lord, she shall be praised" (Proverbs 31:30).

Much can be said for the virtuous woman of Proverbs 31. She is a rare woman indeed. Of all her character qualities, the greatest is her fear of the Lord. Certainly this is the foundation of all the other qualities that surround her. Because of her fear of the Lord, she is trustworthy, industrious, and caring. The virtuous woman possessses a wisdom that only comes from knowing God and his Word. Remember at the beginning of Proverbs, we found the words "The fear of the Lord is the beginning of wisdom: and the knowledge of the holy is understanding" (Proverbs 9:10). A woman becomes virtuous by putting God first in her life. Her character qualities come not of a desire to be praised by others, but by having a deep desire to please the Lord. When the Lord is feared in a holy and reverent manner, the qualities of the virtuous woman will fall into place. Her purpose is not to satisfy herself or her family, but to honor the Lord with all of her life. When a woman genuinely fears the Lord, the results will be evident in her life.

Ponderings

Praise

Petitions

July 12

Ecclesiastes 1–4

"To every thing there is a season, and a time to every purpose under the heaven" (Ecclesiastes 3:1).

How often we have said, "I just don't have the time." We actually have the time to do everything we ought to do. We often don't have the time to do what *we want* to do. God gives us 1,440 minutes every day to accomplish his will. When our life is given completely over to the Lord, we have ample time to do all that he wants us to do. Our difficulty with time is when we try to crowd in the activities that are for our own amusement and entertainment. Each day, time should be given to searching out God's will and then going on to accomplish what he leads us to do. It's interesting that we never read of Jesus running out of time and yet he accomplished all that God had given him to do. In our modern day of fast cars, microwave ovens, and computers, it would seem that we should have ample time to do it all. The problem is we are so caught up in trivial and temporary things that we forget the eternal matters. God has a work for you to do. He will give you the time you need to do it. He "hath made everything beautiful in his time" (Ecclesiastes 3:11).

Ponderings

Praise

Petitions

July 13
Ecclesiastes 5–8

"Be not rash with thy mouth, and let not thine heart be hasty to utter any thing before God: for God is in heaven, and thou upon earth: therefore let thy words be few. For a dream cometh through the multitude of business; and a fool's voice is known by multitude of words" (Ecclesiastes 5:2–3).

It is better to remain silent and be thought a fool than to speak out and remove all doubt. How often have we blurted something out and as quickly as it came out of our mouth we wished we could retract it? It is better to withhold your tongue until you have had time to consider what you are saying. Words are powerful, they have the ability to encourage and bless as well as the ability to hurt and damage. The preacher of Ecclesiastes gives us this warning concerning the flow of words from our mind to our tongue. "Be not rash with thy mouth, and let not thine heart be hasty to utter anything before God." It is better to be a person of few words and speak them wisely than to let every thought be uttered revealing our own foolishness. Say what you mean, mean what you say, and let your words be few.

Ponderings

Praise

Petitions

July 14
Ecclesiastes 9–12

"Let us hear the conclusion of the whole matter: Fear God, and keep his commandments: for this is the whole duty of man" (Ecclesiastes 12:13).

God had given Solomon great wisdom to rule his people. He had also blessed Solomon with great riches. In his lifetime, Solomon had tried it all. He had given himself to folly and frivolity. He had tried hard work and acquiring great knowledge. Solomon built great houses and magnificent stables for his mass of livestock. When the Queen of Sheba came to visit Solomon and saw all of his great wealth and the wisdom with which he ruled, she exclaimed, "Howbeit I believed not the words, until I came, and mine eyes had seen it: and, behold, the half was not told me: thy wisdom and prosperity exceedeth the fame which I heard" (1 Kings 10:7). When Solomon had considered all that he had and all that God had given him, after exploring the meaning of his life and what it had amounted to on this earth, he concludes it all by saying that the whole duty of man is but *to fear God, and keep his commandments*. Perhaps we should heed the advice of one of the wisest men that ever lived.

Ponderings

Praise

Petitions

July 15
Song of Solomon 1–4

"The song of songs, which is Solomon's. Let him kiss me with the kisses of his mouth: for thy love is better than wine" (Song of Solomon 1:1–2).

The Song of Solomon, also known at the Canticles, is probably one of the most misunderstood and misinterpreted books of the entire Bible. Many theologians and Bible teachers have suggested that Song of Solomon is to be taken as a letter from Christ to his bride, the church. We should not attempt to turn this beautiful work of poetry into something that was not intended to be. Read the book carefully, and you will find that it is a love story between Solomon and his bride. The book shows an expression of pure love between a husband and his wife. Read it with delight as you see how deep their love was for each other and how that love was expressed through the beautiful dialogue of a couple deeply in love. Ascribe other interpretations to it if you will, but don't miss its original intention of the expression of deep affection and commitment. It would do married couples good to revive such romance and the expression of Song of Solomon in their own marriage relationship. Perhaps they could borrow some expressions of love from this very book.

Ponderings

Praise

Petitions

July 16
Song of Solomon 5–8

"Many waters cannot quench love, neither can the floods drown it: if a man would give all the substance of his house for love, it would utterly be contemned." (Song of Solomon 8:7).

There is no greater entity on the earth than love. It is stronger and mightier than anything known to man. Many have given their lives or sometimes even killed in the name of love. Love drives one to attempt and accomplish feats beyond his dreams. Love causes a man to act foolishly as well as wisely. Many a life has been changed in the giving and receiving of love. It was love that caused the Creator and Judge of this world to give his only Son to die for us. Because of love, the One who did no sin died a sinner's death. Love allows us to look beyond what a person is to see what he can become. Love has been the subject of many stories, songs, and poems. As Solomon so eloquently stated, love cannot be quenched and it cannot be drowned. Its worth is greater than anything that a man could own. Love is the very essence of God, for Scripture proclaims that, *God is love* (1 John 4:16). It is no wonder that the Apostle Paul said, "And now abide faith, hope, love, these three; but the greatest of these is love" (1 Corinthians 13:13).

Ponderings

Praise

Petitions

July 17
Isaiah 1–3

"Hear, O heavens, and give ear, O earth: for the Lord hath spoken, I have nourished and brought up children, and they have rebelled against me" (Isaiah 1:2).

Isaiah is the first book of the Major Prophets. God spoke through them to his people. You would think that when God speaks people would sit up and take notice, that they would turn their ears toward him to hear every word. Yet we find that for years Israel had turned a deaf ear to the Word of the Lord. Even after God had brought them out of the slavery of Egypt and had brought them into a land flowing with milk and honey, they refused to listen to him. The people of Israel had rebelled against the Lord and refuse to follow him. God had some things to say to them now. They would be words of judgment and a call to repentance. God spoke words of warning to his people and yet they continued in their rebellious way. At the same time, God was giving them an opportunity to turn from their wicked way, repent of their sin, and worship him again. God is still speaking today and yet millions refused to hear him. He sent his Son to redeem mankind, and while some have received him, millions reject him. God has spoken through his Word. Are you listening?

Ponderings

Praise

Petitions

July 18
Isaiah 4–8

"Woe unto them that call evil good, and good evil; that put darkness for light, and light for darkness; that put bitter for sweet, and sweet for bitter!" (Isaiah 5:20).

Sometimes it seems we live in an upside down world. The things that are evil and wrong have become the appropriate things to do. Movies and television programs present evildoers as the heroes and the righteous as some kind of weird creature. This twisting of values is a scheme of Satan to tempt us away from God and into a life of acceptable sin. The individual who loves God, reads his Word, and lives a righteous life is cast as a person who is dangerous or to be avoided. While the person who kills randomly, beats up people, drinks alcoholic beverages to excess, and has no regard for anyone but himself is cast as the person to emulate. Often the thief is presented as the person who we are too support and cheer. It's time we listen to God's warning and honor the honorable and stand against such twisted thinking. We must begin to do the right thing because it is the right thing to do. Rather then following worldly heroes and allowing our children to emulate them, we should be honoring what is right and good.

Ponderings

Praise

Petitions

July 19
Isaiah 9–11

"For unto us a child is born, unto us a son is given: and the government shall be upon his shoulder: and his name shall be called Wonderful, Counselor, The mighty God, The everlasting Father, The Prince of Peace" (Isaiah 9:6).

Even in the time of Isaiah God revealed that he would send his own Son to the earth. So that there would be no mistaking him, the Lord gave us his identity. He would sit on the throne of David, the son of Jesse. He could be identified by five different titles: *Wonderful, Counselor, The Mighty God, The Everlasting Father, The Prince of Peace.* These were more than just titles, they also identified his character and his nature. From the beginning of time, God had planned on providing a Savior. At the writing of Isaiah, Israel was in one of the darkest periods in her history. In the midst of that darkness, God revealed that he had not forgotten his people, but that he had a plan. And that plan would involve the coming of a child, his own Son. That Child would be the Lamb of God sent to bear the burden of the judgment of sin and death. He was sent for you. Have you received him or will you reject him too?

Ponderings

Praise

Petitions

July 20
Isaiah 12–14

"How art Thou fallen from heaven, O Lucifer, son of the morning! how art thou cut down to the ground, which didst weaken the nations!" (Isaiah 14:12).

There was a time in the history of eternity past that Lucifer was a beautiful angel. He served in the presence of the Lord perhaps in some musical manner. Then one day he began to grow proud of his own beauty and strength and rose up in pride against the Lord. The one thing that caused Lucifer, the beautiful angel, to turn into Satan, the enemy of God, was his pride. Pride has been the downfall of many people as well. Pride causes us to turn our eyes from to Lord to ourselves. It causes us to have a self-dependency rather than a dependency on the Lord. There are many warnings in Scripture concerning pride. In fact it is one of the seven things that God hates (Proverbs 6:17). When man begins to get so full of himself that he does not feel that he needs the Lord any longer, he is walking on dangerous ground. Perhaps the fall of Lucifer is our greatest example of the consequences of pride. James said it this way, "But he giveth more grace. Wherefore he saith, God resisteth the proud, but giveth grace unto the humble" (James 4:6).

Ponderings

Praise

Petitions

July 21
Isaiah 15–19

"At that day shall a man look to his Maker, and his eyes shall have respect to the Holy One of Israel" (Isaiah 17:7).

Oh, that every person would somehow get a glimpse of his Maker. All around us are visible manifestations of the power and glory of the Lord. Yet, somehow, man refuses to pay attention. "For God speaketh once, yea twice, yet man perceiveth it not" (Job 33:14). If man would only look up to his maker and recognize the *Holy One of Israel,* he would find One who loves him more than anyone on this earth. He would have a reverence and holy awe of the greatness and glory of God. Paul said, "As it is written, there is none righteous, no, not one: There is none that understandeth, there is none that seeketh after God" (Romans 3:10–11). However, there will be a day when every eye will be turned to the throne of heaven and there declare that Jesus Christ is Lord to the glory of God the Father. The question is, are you willing to lift up your eyes and fear him now or will you wait until your soul is condemned for eternity and proclaim him as Lord then. Do it now!

Ponderings

Praise

Petitions

July 22
Isaiah 20–24

> "They shall lift up their voice, they shall sing for the majesty of the Lord, they shall cry aloud from the sea" (Isaiah 24:14).

As you read through these chapters of Isaiah, you read much of God's judgment upon the nations that had forsaken and rejected him. Yet God in his judgment is also full of mercy and grace. All of these heathen nations are without excuse. They had the opportunity to serve and worship the Lord. His judgment is swift and final. Among those who had rejected the Lord and gone on the serve other gods is a remnant that will truly acknowledge the Lord and serve him. It is refreshing to read Isaiah 24:13–15 and discover that there were some who lifted up their voices to sing for the majesty of the Lord. It is that way today also. Sometimes it seems that we live in such an ungodly generation. The media, entertainment outlets, and even the government are bent on demeaning the Lord and his people. And in the midst of all the attacks, there is a remnant that remains faithful and loyal to the Lord. God always has a people that will worship and honor his name. The question is, are you among them?

Ponderings

Praise

Petitions

July 23
Isaiah 25–28

"Thou wilt keep him in perfect peace, whose mind is stayed on thee: because he trusteth in thee" (Isaiah 26:3).

The person who is at peace in his heart is the person who is trusting in the Lord. His mind and heart are toward the Lord continually. This peace comes from a confidence in the Lord to take care of every situation, every burden, and every need. When we trust in ourselves or in the things of the world, there is an uncertainty. We cannot control circumstances or see into the future like the Lord can. Although it seems man would rather trust in his own wisdom and strength, the life of peace comes from having an abiding faith in the Lord. The peace that God gives is not the same as the world gives, nor can it ever be. Jesus said, "Peace I leave with you, my peace I give unto you: not as the world giveth, give I unto you. Let not your heart be troubled, neither let it be afraid" (John 14:27). True peace comes from knowing and abiding in Christ. It comes from having such a confidence in the Lord that the things of this world cannot shake you. The mind and heart that dwells on the Lord and his Word is exhibited in a life that is filled with peace.

Ponderings

Praise

Petitions

July 24
Isaiah 29–31

"Wherefore the Lord said, Forasmuch as this people draw near me with their mouth, and with their lips do honour me, but have removed their heart far from me, and their fear toward me is taught by the precept of men" (Isaiah 29:13).

It's called *lip service*. I suppose we have all known people who claim to know and love the Lord, yet their heart if far from him. It seems that those who yell, "Praise the Lord," the loudest are often those who are just putting on a show. They honor the Lord with their lips, but do not love him with their hearts. Lip service people are usually easy to identify. They are usually the ones who are bragging on all they have done for the Lord rather than talking about what God has done for them. They are very much like the Pharisees whom Jesus often encountered. On the outside they had all the trappings of being the most holy and righteous people in town. But Jesus knew their hearts and said that inside they were full of *dead men's bones*. God certainly wants us to honor him with our mouth, but unless it comes from the heart, it is not genuine. You may fool the world with lying lips, but you won't fool God with a dishonest heart.

Ponderings

Praise

Petitions

July 25
Isaiah 32–34

"And the work of righteousness shall be peace; and the effect of righteousness quietness and assurance forever" (Isaiah 32:17).

One of the names of Jesus given in Scripture is the *Prince of Peace* (Isaiah 9:6). The peace that he brings will come through righteousness. *Righteousness* means to be right or in a right relationship with the Lord. Jesus was without sin, yet he took our sin upon himself to give us his righteousness. "For he hath made him to be sin for us, who knew no sin; that we might be made the righteousness of God in him" (2 Corinthians 5:21). We are made at peace with God through faith in the work of righteousness of Jesus Christ at Calvary. "Therefore, being justified by faith, we have peace with God through our Lord Jesus Christ" (Romans 5:1). Having placed our faith in the Lord Jesus Christ and having been brought to a peaceful relationship with the Lord, we now have a quiet assurance of eternal life with him. It may be difficult to find peace on earth, but through the shed blood of Jesus Christ and his imputed righteousness, we can find a peace that passes all understanding in our walk with him.

Ponderings

Praise

Petitions

July 26
Isaiah 35–37

"And Hezekiah received the letter from the hand of the messengers, and read it: and Hezekiah went up unto the house of the Lord, and spread it before the Lord. And Hezekiah prayed unto the Lord" (Isaiah 37:14–15).

When threatened, the human response is to threaten back or to seek some kind of vengeance on our attacker. When Hezekiah was threatened by the army of Assyria, his response was quite different. We know from 2 Kings 18:3 that Hezekiah "did that which was right in the sight of the Lord, according to all that David his father did." When Hezekiah was faced with the army of the Assyrians, he did three things. First, he went to the Word of God as it was delivered through the prophet Isaiah. There he received the promise of victory and was encouraged. Next, he went to the House of God. Finally, he went to the throne of God and poured out his heart to the Lord. In answer to his prayer, Hezekiah received the assurance that he and his kingdom would come to no harm. In the end, the Lord destroyed the Assyrians and King Sennacherib who had threatened Hezekiah. The best answer to threats is to take them to the Lord and let him deal with them in a way that only he can.

Ponderings

Praise

Petitions

July 27
Isaiah 38–40

"Then Hezekiah turned his face toward the wall, and prayed unto the Lord" (Isaiah 38:2).

When Hezekiah heard that his life was to come to an end, he "turned his face to the wall, and prayed unto the Lord." God answered his prayer by moving heaven and earth and giving him fifteen more years to live. Why was Hezekiah's prayer so quickly and graciously granted? First, Hezekiah had a right walk with the Lord. He had removed all the idols from the land and had restored Temple worship. The Bible records in 2 Kings 18:6 that "he clave to the Lord, and departed not from following him." Secondly, Hezekiah had a right heart before the Lord (2 Kings 20:3). Hezekiah had no personal agenda in his reign as king. He simply wanted to do what was right in the sight of God. He was not in office for personal gain or glory, only to honor the Lord. His heart was right with God. Thirdly, Hezekiah had a right relationship with the Lord, a relationship of obedience. Hezekiah was obedient in every way. He had done all that he knew to do to obey God's commands. When we pray, we should also come before the Lord with a right walk, a right heart, and a right relationship with him.

Ponderings

Praise

Petitions

July 28
Isaiah 41–43

"Fear thou not; for I am with thee: be not dismayed; for I am thy God: I will strengthen thee; yea, I will help thee; yea, I will uphold thee with the right hand of my righteousness" (Isaiah 41:10).

God is able to supply our every need. He cares about everything that comes into our lives. The Lord has promised that he would never leave us nor forsake us. There is no reason for us to be discouraged or to give up hope. When we trust the Lord, he will give us all we need for today. He promises to strengthen us when we need strength. He promises to give us his help when we need it most. Why is it that when we are in need, we often go to every source that the world has to offer and when we have exhausted all of them, we finally turn to the Lord. The psalmist said, "God is our refuge and strength, a very present help in trouble" (Psalms 46:1). When we fall, the Lord is there to pick us up and sustain us. When we try to find our own solutions in our own strength and wisdom, we often find ourselves in even more trouble than when we started. When the Lord promises to do so much for us, why do we always seem to search him out as a last resort?

Ponderings

Praise

Petitions

July 29
Isaiah 44–46

"Fear ye not, neither be afraid: have not I told thee from that time, and have declared it? ye are even my witnesses. Is there a God beside me? yea, there is no God; I know not any" (Isaiah 44:8).

God says that you are his witness. A witness is described as someone who tells of something they have seen, heard, or experienced. So what are we to be a witness to? Simply that God is and that there is none else. Our witness is not to be only a spoken witness but also we are to show the existence of God and our relationship to him by how we live. Does your life show your faith in the Lord? There are many who claim to believe in God when asked about him. However, their life shows a great contradiction. James said that our faith is shown in our actions or works (James 2:14–26). While it is good to proclaim our faith in the Lord, it is just as important to show our faith by our conduct. Someone once asked the question, *If you were arrested for believing in God, would there be enough evidence to convict you?* The witness of your life must show that there is only one God that you serve. What kind of a witness for the Lord is demonstrated by your life?

Ponderings

Praise

Petitions

July 30
Isaiah 47–49

"Thus saith the Lord, thy Redeemer, the Holy One of Israel; I am the Lord thy God which teacheth thee to profit, which leadeth thee by the way that thou shouldest go." (Isaiah 48:17).

God is declaring his place in the universe to a people that had rejected him in the past. He is reestablishing himself as their God and the one who will redeem them from their slavery in Babylon. He also promises to lead them according to his will in the way that they should go. Certainly, God leads and directs our lives when we put our trust in him; however, there seems to be a greater meaning to this promise. It was God's intention to not only lead them back to their native land, but also give them a way to an eternal home. Jump forward about seven hundred years and you will find the Son of God saying, "I am the way, the truth and the life, no man cometh unto the father but by me" (John 14:6). Through the work of Jesus Christ on the cross, God was leading his people right back to himself. The way would be through the death, burial, and resurrection of his Son. There is no other God but the Lord, the Holy One of Israel, and there is no other way to salvation, but through his Son.

Ponderings

Praise

Petitions

July 31
Isaiah 50–52

"Who is among you that feareth the Lord, that obeyeth the voice of his servant, that walketh in darkness, and hath no light? let him trust in the name of the Lord, and stay upon his God" (Isaiah 50:10).

The question is a rhetorical one. *Who fears the Lord, obeys his prophets, and continues to walk in darkness?* The answer, of course, is no one. John says "If we say that we have fellowship with him, and walk in darkness, we lie, and do not the truth" (1 John 1:6). You cannot have fellowship with the Lord and continue to walk in darkness. The person who continues in sin and claims to fear the Lord and serve him is a liar, plain and simple. The key to walking in darkness is given is the last part of our verse. Trust the Lord and *stay upon* him. We must learn to trust the Lord for everything. It is amazing how we can trust him for our salvation and refuse to trust him in our daily life. We must continually keep our eyes on the Lord. The writer of Hebrews encourages us to "lay aside every weight, and the sin which doth so easily beset us, and let us run with patience the race that is set before us, looking unto Jesus the author and finisher of our faith" (Hebrew 12:1a-2b). Walk in the light keeping your eyes on the Lord!

Ponderings

Praise

Petitions

August 1
Isaiah 53–56

"For my thoughts are not your thoughts, neither are your ways my ways, saith the Lord. For as the heavens are higher than the earth, so are my ways higher than your ways, and my thoughts than your thoughts" (Isaiah 55:8–9).

We do not always understand what God is doing in our lives. Why does tragedy come? Why does disease take away our loved ones? Why do accidents happen? In tragedy, we often lift our eyes to heaven and cry out to the Lord. We must remember that God has a great plan for our lives. As he reveals his plan to us day by day, we do not always understand, or see the road ahead clearly. That is why we "walk by faith and not by sight" (2 Corinthians 5:7). God knows everything about us including what he wants to accomplish through us. Since his thoughts are higher than our thoughts and his ways higher than our ways, we are compelled to just trust him for everything. God loves you very much and wants the best for you. Trust him and obey his will and you will never find a happier life. He knows what he is doing and is working out his plan for you. Trust the Lord; he knows what he is doing.

Ponderings

Praise

Petitions

August 2
Isaiah 57–59

"Behold, the Lord's hand is not shortened, that it cannot save; neither his ear heavy, that it cannot hear: But your iniquities have separated between you and your God, and your sins have hid his face from you, that he will not hear" (Isaiah 59:1–2).

Have you ever prayed and it seemed that the windows of heaven were tightly shut? Did it seem that your prayers were barely reaching the ceiling? The problem is not that the Lord doesn't answer prayer; after all, he promised, "Call unto me, and I will answer thee, and shew thee great and mighty things, which thou knowest not" (Jeremiah 33:3). God is capable of answering any prayer and meeting any need that you bring before him. The problem with unanswered prayer is often our own unconfessed sin. Often there is some sin that we just want to hold on to without ever turning from it. How can we expect anything from God if we are not willing to obey his Word? We must not continue in sin. When we pray, the first thing we should do is confess all our sin and ask the Lord to search our hearts to see if there is any wickedness that we are harboring in our hearts. With confession comes cleansing and an assurance that God will hear our prayer.

Ponderings

Praise

Petitions

August 3
Isaiah 60–63

"I will mention the loving-kindnesses of the Lord, and the praises of the Lord, according to all that the Lord hath bestowed on us…and according to the multitude of his loving-kindnesses" (Isaiah 63:7).

The psalmist said, "…it is good to sing praises unto our God; for it is pleasant; and praise is comely" (Psalms 147:1). Every now and then, it is good to stop and consider the *lovingkindnesses of the Lord* and the *praises of the Lord*. Like the old song says, "Count your many blessings, name them one by one." We often fail to contemplate the depth of God's love for us. His love is eternal and unmerited. He loves us no matter who we are or what we have done. And nothing can separate us from his love. When was the last time you just sat down and counted the ways that God has shown his love to you? His love is in the sunrise and in the rain. His love is in a child's laughter and in an elder's gentle smile. God has given us so much, how can we do any thing else but praise his name. Take time today to make a list of the ways that God has blessed you, and praise him all day long.

Ponderings

Praise

Petitions

August 4
Isaiah 64–66

"For since the beginning of the world men have not heard, or perceived by the ear, neither hath the eye seen, O God, beside thee, what he hath prepared for him that waiteth for him" (Isaiah 64:4).

We try to imagine what heaven might be like. Often we think of the streets of gold and perhaps a flowing crystal river. We try to imagine what our mansion must be like and who might be next door. In our finite mind we create pleasant images that heaven will be a beautiful place. But our minds are limited to the things we have experienced or seen. What God has prepared for us is beyond our wildest imaginations. Paul said it this way, "Eye hath not seen, nor ear heard, neither have entered into the heart of man, the things which God hath prepared for them that love him" (1 Corinthians 2:9). We really don't know what heaven will be like apart from what the Bible tells us. What we do know is that we will be in the presence of God and that we will be there for eternity. To be sure, heaven will be a beautiful place, a place where there will be eternal peace and joy. Put together the best image of heaven you can, and then try to imagine that it will even be better than that. Only God knows what he has in store for us.

Ponderings

Praise

Petitions

August 5
Jeremiah 1–3

"For though thou wash thee with nitre, and take thee much soap, yet thine iniquity is marked before me, saith the Lord God" (Jeremiah 2:22).

We cannot wash away our own sin. As much as we may try to hide, excuse, or rectify our own sin, it still remains before the eyes of the Lord. We can attempt to wash it away with soda water and mounds of soap, but it will not be enough to remove our sin. Man has become a master at excusing and explaining away his wrongdoing. We try to make it sound better than it is, or we think if we have a good reason to sin that it somehow becomes acceptable to the Lord. John said, "If we say that we have no sin, we deceive ourselves, and the truth is not in us. If we confess our sins, he is faithful and just to forgive us our sins and to cleanse us from all unrighteousness" (1 John 1:8–9). When we try to remove our own sin, we are just deceiving ourselves. The only way to receive the cleansing of our sin is confession. When we honestly confess our sin to God, he does the cleaning. The cleaning agent is the very blood of his Son, Jesus Christ, "and the blood of Jesus Christ his Son cleanseth us from all sin" (1 John 1:7). Only confession brings cleansing of sin through the blood of Christ. It's guaranteed.

Ponderings

Praise

Petitions

August 6
Jeremiah 4–5

"Your iniquities have turned away these things, and your sins have withholden good things from you" (Jeremiah 5:25).

Sin is deceiving. While trying to find some pleasure in life, the world will lure you into sinful behavior. But mark it down: sin will never make you happy. Sin is followed by the consequences that it produces. We often expect some good thing will come from sin, such as a good feeling or financial gain, but in the end, those expectations will be unrealized or short lived. Rather than give you what you were hoping for, sin will rob you. Sin does not bring joy; sin robs you of joy. Just as the children of Israel could not expect anything good from chasing after foreign gods, neither should you expect anything good to come from sin. You cannot continue in sin and expect the blessings of God. Instead, you will find the blessing of God will most likely be held back from your life. God expects us to fear and serve him. He did not save us to continue in sin trying to find some kind of joy and happiness. He gave us these as a result of his grace. Why should we look to the world to give us joy and blessing when God has already promised to give them to us? Don't let sin rob you.

Ponderings

Praise

Petitions

August 7
Jeremiah 6–8

"Thus saith the Lord, Stand ye in the ways, and see, and ask for the old paths, where is the good way, and walk therein, and ye shall find rest for your souls" (Jeremiah 6:16).

In our hustle and bustle world, we often seek new ways to live our Christian life. The mantra of the modern Christian era is to find Christ in a new way. While our lives and methods may change, the Lord is always the same. Sometimes the new paths of modernism lead us to greater consumerism and materialism and we find ourselves wondering what happened to our walk with the Lord. Why are we not as close to him as we used to be? Perhaps the need is not to seek new paths, but return to the old paths. The path of just trusting the Lord, reading his Word, and communing with him in prayer. We often make our lives too complicated with daily planners, computers, and other so-called conveniences that are supposed to make our lives simpler. Every now and then, it is good to just stand still for a while and look at where you are going. It may require that we change paths. The Bible says, "Ask for the old paths," and there you will find "rest for your souls."

Ponderings

Praise

Petitions

August 8
Jeremiah 9–11

"O Lord, I know that the way of man is not in himself: it is not in man that walketh to direct his steps" (Jeremiah 10:23).

Without the Lord, man is totally lost. He cannot even find his own way through the journey of his own life. Hear the prophet cry out, "I know that the way of man is not in himself." How often have we heard the advice to follow our instincts or do what our heart tells us to do? The prophet goes on to say, "It is not in man that walketh to direct his steps." The direction that we are to follow cannot be found within ourselves, which is why we need the Lord to direct our lives. He promised that if we would just acknowledge him that he would *direct our paths* (Proverbs 3:6). The Lord knows what is best for us; he also knows what is on the road ahead. Rather than trying to stumble our way through life, God has offered his help and direction. To follow him means that we give up our own will and surrender to his. The Lord has a plan for your life and he will reveal it to you little by little as you seek him and his direction. This requires a day-by-day intimate walk with him. To be on the right path—just follow the Lord. He knows the way.

Ponderings

Praise

Petitions

August 9
Jeremiah 12–14

"Are there any among the vanities of the Gentiles that can cause rain? or can the heavens give showers? art not thou he, O Lord our God? Therefore we will wait upon thee: for thou has made all these things" (Jeremiah 14:22).

The "vanities of the Gentiles" are the gods of wood and silver that the people had made. These gods could not make it rain or "cause the heavens to give showers." Only the Lord, the Creator, can do these things. Even today in times of trouble and distress, people often look to the gods of this world for solutions. It is believed that the god of money can solve humanity's ills and problems. Or perhaps the gods of intellectualism hold all the answers to life's dilemmas. Yet neither money nor worldly education can give us the wisdom that the maker of the rain possessses. If we are to walk with the Lord, we must also learn to wait on the Lord. Waiting on the Lord is not always easy. Waiting on him suggests that we trust him and him alone to carry us through the dilemmas that we face. The One who made you knows you the best. And he knows what the best is for you. It is best to seek him first in everything. Seek his wisdom, seek his will, and you will find the best in life that God has planned for you.

Ponderings

Praise

Petitions

August 10
Jeremiah 15–17

"I the Lord search the heart, I try the reins, even to give every man according to his ways, and according to the fruit of his doings" (Jeremiah 17:10).

While we may hide our hearts from each other, we cannot hide them from the Lord. He searches and knows the heart of every person. He knows our motives. He knows our imaginations. He knows our dreams. The Lord is the perfect judge because he already knows the truth. Every day we must come before the Lord and ask him to purify our hearts and our thoughts. When we come to church, we dress up in fine clothes; we wash our face, comb our hair, and try to put on a good appearance. However, we cannot dress up our hearts for show. No one can see our heart. Only God can. He knows what we are trying to hide from those we greet with a Sunday morning smile. When it is time to give an account of ourselves to God, we won't have to tell him anything as he will already know us and judge us in righteousness and holiness. The secrets of your heart will be known to him. It's best to just come clean before the Lord. Confess your sin and God promises to forgive you and cleanse you. So, how's your heart today?

Ponderings

Praise

Petitions

August 11
Jeremiah 18–21

"And unto this people thou shalt say, Thus saith the Lord; Behold I set before you the way of life, and the way of death" (Jeremiah 21:8).

God is a righteous judge and will judge every man according to his works. He has set before us *the way of life* and *the way of death*. He then gives us the free will to choose life or death. Actually, the choice given to us is to choose life, for in our sin death has passed upon us already. Jesus said, "Most assuredly, I say to you, he who hears my word and believes in him who sent me has everlasting life, and shall not come into judgment, but has passed from death into life" (John 5:24). Jesus came to give us life and in choosing him, we also choose life. In refusing to make a choice, you have chosen the *way of death* by default. By receiving Jesus Christ into your life and making him your Lord, you have chosen life. For "in him was life; and the life was the light of men" (John 1:4). So the question is, will you receive Jesus Christ, who is the *way of life*, or will you continue in your sin and thus choose the *way of death*? The choice is yours to make. God says, *Choose life.*

Ponderings

Praise

Petitions

August 12
Jeremiah 22-24

"And I will give them an heart to know me, that I am the Lord; and they shall be my people, and I will be their God: for they shall return unto me with their whole heart." (Jeremiah 24:7).

People who genuinely know the Lord cannot continue in sin without returning to him eventually. Perhaps it has even happened in your own life, a time when you turned away from God and began to live in the world. The children of Israel had turned away from God and began to serve idols and other gods. God in his chastisement sent them away captive to Babylon. It seemed that all hope was lost for Jerusalem and God's people. Here God promises them that he had not forsaken his people. There would be a day when they would once again have a heart to know the Lord. There would be a time when the people would be fully restored to fellowship with him. A person who continues in sin without ever returning or falling under the chastisement of God was probably never really saved to begin with. If you are praying for a loved one who is away from God right now, there is hope. If they do not return soon, then perhaps you should be praying for their salvation. Either way, pray that God would give them a heart to know him.

Ponderings

Praise

Petitions

August 13
Jeremiah 25–27

"…for of a truth the Lord hath sent me unto you to speak all these words in your ears." (Jeremiah 26:15b).

The people of Israel had turned their backs on the Lord. They had forsaken his laws and commandments and turned to serving other gods and idols. God sent Jeremiah to preach to them. He told them that certain destruction would come if they continued in their ways and not repent of their sin. The people rejected the word of the Lord and his prophet Jeremiah. Now they are set on killing him. They knew that they could not change the message, even though their own false prophets had tried. Since they did not like the message that Jeremiah was bringing to them they decided to reject the truth and kill God's messenger. The truth is not always easy to take. Truth can be rejected, but truth cannot be changed. How many preachers are raked over the coals on Sunday afternoon because the hearers did not like the message? When God speaks through his Word or through his chosen servants, we must be careful to listen and obey what he says. For when we reject truth the only thing left is certain destruction.

Ponderings

Praise

Petitions

August 14
Jeremiah 28–30

"For I know the thoughts that I think toward you, saith the Lord, thoughts of peace, and not of evil, to give you an expected end" (Jeremiah 29:11).

God has a plan for our life. He knows what the best is for us and wants us to have it. Sometimes it may seem that the Lord is playing some cruel game with us when things aren't like we think they should be. You can be confident of this truth—God loves you very much. Although, he may take you through some trials, he is working out his plan for your life. The trials we are given are so that we will learn to endure, mature, and grow in our faith. We must remain faithful to the Lord for his way is the best you will ever find for your life. As you grow in your faith and in your walk with the Lord, you will begin to see his plan for you unfold a little at a time. Don't expect to have God lay out his entire plan before you all at once. Live one day at a time seeking out his will. God already knows about tomorrow and will lead you through it when you get there. For now, just follow his leading every day. God wants you to call upon him and seek his face every day. When you follow him you cannot go wrong, for he knows what is best for you.

Ponderings

Praise

Petitions

August 15
Jeremiah 31–32

"The Lord hath appeared of old unto me saying, Yea, I have loved thee with an everlasting love: therefore with loving kindness have I drawn thee" (Jeremiah 31:3).

God loves you very much. God's love is not like human love. Most of the time, human love is based on how we act, look, or on some other criteria. God loves you because you are you. There are no conditions or criteria; there are no *ifs, ands, or buts*. God loves you just like you are. His love is unconditional. His love is perfect. His love is demonstrated in the gift of his Son for the remission of our sin. Romans 5:8 states, "But God commendeth his love toward us, in that, while we were yet sinners, Christ died for us." God also tells us that his love is *everlasting*. His love has no end. There will never come a day when it will be said that God does not love you. It is also by his love that he draws us unto himself. He does not force us to come. He does not threaten us or entice us, but gently draws us to himself with his matchless love. Only the Lord could love us in such a way. It is God's very nature to love for the scripture also declares, "God is love" (1 John 4:8).

Ponderings

Praise

Petitions

August 16
Jeremiah 33–36

"Call unto me, and I will answer thee, and shew thee great and mighty things, which thou knowest not" (Jeremiah 33:3).

An evangelist was once heard to say that Jeremiah 33:3 is *God's phone number*. The Lord invites us to call upon him. God cares about us very much. We are important to him. When God created man and placed him upon the earth, it was not his intention to abandon him to his own devices. God created us in order to maintain a relationship with us. That relationship was severed by Adam's disobedience in the Garden of Eden and reestablished by the death of Christ on the cross. God wants very much for us to bring all of our burdens and needs to him. God promises that when we call upon him that he will answer us. When we call upon the Lord, we will never hear a *busy signal*. The Lord is able and willing to answer our prayers in ways that we do not expect. Often when we pray we have an expected outcome. Our knowledge is limited, but God is not limited by anything or anyone. "For with God nothing shall be impossible" (Luke 1:37). In answering our prayers, he will often show us *great and mighty* things that we were just not aware of. Call upon the Lord; he is waiting to hear from you. Ask him for the impossible.

Ponderings

Praise

Petitions

August 17
Jeremiah 37–39

"Obey, I beseech thee, the voice of the Lord, which I speak unto thee: so it shall be well unto thee, and thy soul shall live" (Jeremiah 38:20).

Jeremiah's advice to Zedekiah is also good for us today. To put it simply; obey the Lord. As a believer, it should be our desire to do the will of God. His will is that we obey his Word. Yes, we are saved by faith, but we cannot cast out the Word of God in disobedience. God wants us to obey him. Our obedience to him demonstrates our faith. Like the old hymn says, *Trust and Obey*. The problem with many Christians is that they do not know what God says in his Word and thus do not know how to obey him. We must become students of the Word of God, so that we can know what God wants us to do and how he wants us to be. Our obedience to him will result in growth toward Christian maturity. Not only are we to obey the written Word of God, but also the voice of God. He often speaks through the indwelling Holy Spirit. We are also to obey his voice. How many opportunities to witness or minister to someone have been lost because we failed to obey the gentle voice of the Holy Spirit. Whatever God says, simply obey.

Ponderings

Praise

Petitions

August 18
Jeremiah 40–43

"That the Lord thy God may shew us the way wherein we may walk, and the thing that we may do" (Jeremiah 42:3).

The people who remained in Israel had come to Jeremiah to request prayer. They were perplexed about what to do having been attacked by Nebuchadnezzar's army. They came with a good and right petition. "Jeremiah," they said, "ask the Lord what we should do and where we should go." So Jeremiah prayed for ten days and came back with their answer. "Stay put," was what God had said. "Do not flee to Egypt." They had promised Jeremiah that whatever the Lord said, they would do it. So, what did they do? They dismissed the Word of God as being untrue and packed their bags to go to Egypt. How foolish! God had promised them death and destruction if they went to Egypt, yet they were determined to go anyway. May God help us to listen to his voice and then obey what he says. God knows what is best and will lead us in the way that we should go. We must be careful to obey his every word. God cares for us too much to lead us down a wrong path.

Ponderings

Praise

Petitions

August 19
Jeremiah 44–46

"As for the word that thou hast spoken unto us in the name of the Lord, we will not hearken unto thee" (Jeremiah 44:16).

How tragic! God had sent his messengers to his own people. He had sent Jeremiah and other prophets to communicate his word and will to them. Yet, when the people knew what God expected of them they refused to listen. God's message was neither difficult nor burdensome. He simply wanted the people to trust him, obey him, and observe the ordinances that he had given for proper worship. The people, however, turned to other gods and refused even to listen to God's Word. All around us there are people who have reacted to God's commands in the same way. Many claim to know and follow the Lord. They know what God says, they know what he expects of his people, and yet they refuse to listen and obey the Word of God. Many think that they have found a better way to live. But their way leads to destruction and disappointment. They are trusting in themselves or some form of a false god. Then they wonder why God does not bless them. Keep your eyes on the Lord, trust him, keep reading and obeying his Word. God will keep his promises.

Ponderings

Praise

Petitions

August 20
Jeremiah 47–48

"O thou sword of the Lord, how long will it be ere thou be quiet? put up thyself into thy scabbard, rest, and be still. How can it be quiet, seeing the Lord hath given it... there hath he appointed it" (Jeremiah 47:6–7).

The Word of God cannot be quieted. It cannot be stamped out. Though many have tried to destroy the Word of God through great persecution of God's people, through mass burnings, and through other attempts to destroy the Bible, it could not be done. God's Word is eternal. Jesus said, "Heaven and earth shall pass away, but my words shall not pass away" (Matthew 24:3). The Word of God is indestructible. As hard as man may try to destroy the Bible, he will always be unsuccessful. Not only is God's Word indestructible, but it is also sure. God will see that his Word accomplishes the purpose for which it was sent. In Isaiah 55:11, the Lord said that his Word "shall not return unto me void, but it shall accomplish that which I please, and it shall prosper in the thing whereto I sent it." The Word of God will not remain silent nor will it ever be destroyed. The words of sages past will one day be forgotten. The tomes of millions of authors will come to naught, but the Word of God will remain in eternity.

Ponderings

Praise

Petitions

August 21
Jeremiah 49

"Thy terribleness hath deceived thee, and the pride of thine heart,… though thou shouldest make thy nest as high as the eagle, I will bring thee down from thence, saith the Lord" (Jeremiah 49:16).

Pride is at the heart of every sin. Pride is selfish and leads to self-destruction. It is pride that causes us to decide that we want to have our own way rather to than follow the Lord's way. Pride causes us to elevate ourselves to a position of being God. Does this sound familiar? As Satan attempted to elevate himself into God's place, it resulted in his fall. When we try to elevate ourselves, the Lord has a way of bringing us down. And the higher we try to go the harder the fall. Proverbs 16:18 states, "Pride goeth before destruction, and an haughty spirit before a fall." Pride always results in a fall. It caused the fall of Satan, the fall of Adam, and it will cause you to fall as well. When you begin to get puffed up in yourself and so full of pride that you rebel against God's Word and God's will, be prepared, God is going to bring you down. As the scripture says, "Humble yourselves therefore under the mighty hand of God, that he may exalt you in due time" (1 Peter 5:6).

Ponderings

Praise

Petitions

August 22
Jeremiah 50

"In those days, and in that time, saith the Lord, the children of Israel shall come, they and the children of Judah together, going and weeping: they shall go, and see the Lord their God" (Jeremiah 50:4).

Jerusalem lay in ruins, Israel was defeated and many of the people had been led away, the captives of King Nebuchadnezzar. This chapter of Jeremiah had to be one of great comfort to the people. They were under the judgment of God because they had turned away from him and served other gods. Even so, the Lord had not forsaken them and desired his people to return and worship him again. Here he is telling his people that there will be a day when Babylon will be destroyed and they would be returning to their homeland. They would come and seek the God of their fathers once again. God is merciful and longsuffering toward us. There may be times, because of our sin, that he will chastise us. The chastisement is not because God is seeking revenge, but because he loves us very much and desires that we walk close to him. God brought his people back. If you are far from him, he will also welcome you back into his loving embrace. He is just waiting for you to come home where you belong.

Ponderings

Praise

Petitions

August 23
Jeremiah 51–52

> "So Jeremiah wrote in a book all the evil that should come upon Babylon, even all these words that are written against Babylon" (Jeremiah 51:60).

As we come to the close of the prophecies of Jeremiah, we have seen the judgment and mercy of the Lord. The judgment came because of sin, primarily the violation of the first and second commandments. "Thou shalt have no other gods before me." And "Thou shalt not make unto thee any graven image" (Exodus 20:3–4). The people of Israel had turned their back on God to serve false gods and idols. God loved his people very much and in his righteous judgment had to chastise them to bring them back to him. Still, he poured out his mercy upon them and brought his people back to their land and to full fellowship and worship. How exciting it must have been for the Babylonian captives, like Daniel, to read the words of Jeremiah and know that God had not forsaken them! Like a caring father who disciplines us, there are times when we must also come under the chastising hand of God. It is because he loves us so much and desires a close relationship with us. Perhaps this is a moment when you need to turn from your false gods and idols and seek the loving face of God. His mercy endures forever, you know.

Ponderings

Praise

Petitions

August 24
Lamentations 1–2

"Let all their wickedness come before thee; and do unto them as thou hast done unto me for all my transgressions: for my sighs are many, and my heart is faint." (Lamentations 1:22).

Sin will never make you happy. Hear the lamentations of Jeremiah as he looks over his beloved city Jerusalem. The city that was once the crown jewel of Israel now lies in a burning heap. What could bring such destruction on this beautiful and glorious city? What would cause the judgment of God to bring such agony and defeat upon her people? The answer is simple—it was sin. As Jeremiah weeps over the fallen city, he remembers how the people had been warned of their destruction. If only they had listened to the God's prophets, if only they had kept their heart right with God, all of this could have been avoided. Why is it that we often believe Satan's lie, that sin will bring us happiness and joy? Jerusalem is a good example of how sin only brings destruction and despair; ultimately, it leads even unto death. Turn from sin and seek to honor the only One who can bring true happiness. Turn from your sin and follow the path that leads into everlasting joy.

Ponderings

Praise

Petitions

August 25
Lamentations 3–5

"This I recall to my mind, therefore have I hope. It is of the Lord's mercies that we are not consumed, because his compassions fail not. They are new every morning; great is thy faithfulness" (Lamentations 3:21–23).

Having seen Jerusalem come under the wrath of God and having been judged for her sin, there is reason for hope for the people of God. That hope is in the unlimited compassion and mercy of God. While God is a righteous judge, he is also full of compassion and mercy for his people. Sin cannot just be excused and swept under the rug. There are always consequences for our transgressions. And while sin must be judged accordingly, God still looks at us with a compassionate and merciful heart. This is exactly the reason why he sent his Son to be the Savior of the world. God desires a relationship with you like he had with Adam in the Garden of Eden before the fall. The relationship we have with God is not because we loved him, but because he loved us first. (1 John 4:10) God's mercy means that while we deserve the punishment of our sin, he would rather forgive our sin and be reconciled to the repentant sinner. The Gospel of Jesus Christ is birthed in the compassion and mercy of God.

Ponderings

Praise

Petitions

August 26
Ezekiel 1–4

"Yet if thou warn the wicked, and he turn not from his wickedness, nor from his wicked way, he shall die in his iniquity; but thou has delivered thy soul" (Ezekiel 3:19).

As disciples of Christ, we have an obligation to tell the good news. We are to warn the lost that judgment is to come if Christ is rejected. If we neglect the Great Commission (Matthew 28:19–20) the consequences are grave and eternal. When we tell others about the saving work of Christ on Calvary and do everything we can to lead souls to Christ, we are obedient to the Great Commission. It is our work to tell and live the Gospel of Christ. When you witness to someone who does not receive the Lord, do not be discouraged. You have done what the Lord has asked you to do. You are only responsible for getting the message out, you are not responsible for the choice people make to receive or reject the Savior. Certainly, we would rather that people receive the Lord and not reject him. However, we cannot force anyone into heaven; it is the Holy Spirit's work to draw the heart of the lost toward the Savior. Just do your part in preaching the Gospel and leave the rest to the Lord.

Ponderings

Praise

Petitions

August 27
Ezekiel 5–8

"And mine eye shall not spare thee, neither will I have pity: but I will recompense thy ways upon thee, and thine abominations shall be in the midst of thee: and ye shall know that I am the Lord" (Ezekiel 7:4).

The Lord is just in all his judgments. There will come a day when we will all stand before him and give an account of our works. Though we like to talk about God's love, mercy, and grace, we cannot ignore his perfect justice. God knows how you are in your public life as well as what you really are in your private life. You may be able to play the game of being a Christian, but God knows your heart. There is no deed or thought that will escape him. God knows you better than you know yourself. He knows your motivations, your passions, and your secret self. When you stand before him, there will be no excuses. It is interesting to note that in the end the one thing that man will know is that Jesus is Lord. Speaking of Jesus, Paul said that, " every knee should bow, of those in heaven, and of those on earth, and of those under the earth, and that every tongue should confess that Jesus Christ is Lord, to the glory of God the Father" (Philippians 2:11). Confess him as Lord now and find grace, or confess him later and face judgment.

Ponderings

Praise

Petitions

August 28
Ezekiel 9–12

"And I will give them one heart, and I will put a new spirit within you; and I will take the stony heart out of their flesh, and will give them an heart of flesh" (Ezekiel 11:19).

Only the Lord can change a man's heart. Man may try to turn over a new leaf or mend his ways. He can go through recovery programs or some other device to change his life, but it is the Lord who changes the very heart of man. God can take a cold stony heart and change it into a heart of flesh. The heart of flesh is a heart that is sensitive to the Word of God and has a desire to please the Lord in everything. This kind of heart change is the result of the work of the Holy Spirit in the new birth. Paul said, "Therefore if any man be in Christ, he is a new creature: old things are passed away; behold all things are become new" (2 Corinthians 5:20). The changed heart is one that has been created new in the individual who has trusted Christ. While man may try to change the exterior behaviors, it is the heart that must be changed. Man can try to change many things, but it takes a work of God to turn a stony heart into a heart of flesh.

Ponderings

Praise

Petitions

August 29
Ezekiel 13–15

"Though these three men, Noah, Daniel, and Job, were in it, they should deliver but their own souls by their righteousness, saith the Lord God" (Ezekiel 14:14).

Every person is responsible for their own relationship with God. The sins of a parent are not past down to their children, nor a husband's sin passed to his wife. Each person will bear the burden of his own sin. That is why we say that Jesus is a *personal Savior*. We cannot remove the blame of our own sin by trying to place it on someone else. Paul said, "For we must all appear before the judgment seat of Christ; that every one may receive the things done in his body, according to that he hath done, whether it be good or bad" (2 Corinthians 5:10). Every person will be judged according to his own sin. Each person is responsible for his own self. This personal responsibility may not remove the consequence of sin on those around us. Look at what happened at Ai (Joshua 7:1–9) because of the sin of one person. When it comes to your personal relationship with God, you stand alone.

Ponderings

Praise

Petitions

August 30
Ezekiel 16–17

"And I will establish my covenant with thee; and thou shalt know that I am the Lord" (Ezekiel 16:62).

Throughout the Old Testament, God would make many covenants with his people. A covenant is an agreement with a promise to accomplish some purpose. The purpose of God's covenants are stated in Leviticus 26:12, "I will walk among you, and will be your God, and ye shall be my people." God desired an ongoing relationship with the people that he had not only created, but had chosen to be his. Every promise that God made and every thing that he brought to pass pointed to this covenant. When Jesus came, the covenant was given to everyone who would receive the gift of his Son. "He came unto his own, and his own received him not. But as many as received him, to them gave he power to become the sons of God, even to them that believe on his name" (John 1:11–12). The covenant would now be a matter of faith in the Son of God. The Lord still desires to be your God and for you to be his people. God's covenant is now passed to you and is based on your faith in the Son of God. Will you receive him by faith or reject him?

Ponderings

Praise

Petitions

August 31
Ezekiel 18–20

"Son of man, speak unto the elders of Israel, and say unto them, Thus saith the Lord God; Are ye come to enquire of me? As I live, saith the Lord God, I will not be enquired of by you" (Ezekiel 20:3).

Some of the elders of Israel had come to Ezekiel to inquire of the Lord. Essentially, they came to have Ezekiel intercede for them by seeking the Lord's favor. However, the Lord would not hear them. Why? The answer was clear; they had forsaken the Lord and turned to idols. They were not interested in serving or obeying the Lord. They wanted the blessing of God and they wanted to continue in their sin. When one comes to God, he must some in full assurance of faith. "But without faith it is impossible to please him: for he that cometh to God must believe that he is, and that he is a rewarder of them that diligently seek him" (Hebrews 11:6). There are many today who try to do the same thing. They want to continue in their sinful lifestyle and yet expect God to bless them. God desires a relationship with his people based on faith and the forgiveness of our sin. When we inquire of the Lord, our first order of business should be the confession of any and all sin.

Ponderings

Praise

Petitions

September 1
Ezekiel 21–22

"And her prophets have daubed them with the untempered morter, seeing vanity, and divining lies unto them, saying Thus saith the Lord God, when the Lord hath not spoken" (Ezekiel 22:28).

We must be careful to search the Word of God. The Apostle John said, "Beloved, do not believe every spirit, but test the spirits, whether they are of God; because many false prophets have gone out into the world" (1 John 4:1). There are many false prophets about us today who would teach us that God has a new message for the church. Or they will attempt to add or take something away from Scripture. They are saying, "Thus saith the Lord God" and then essentially putting words into God's mouth. Like the Berean's of Acts 17, we should receive "the word with all readiness of mind, and searched the scriptures daily, whether those things were so" (Acts 17:11). Everything that we hear, or read should be double-checked in the light of Scripture. Whether it is taught by a pastor, an evangelist, or Sunday school teacher, always compare what they are saying with the Bible. When someone speaks "Thus saith the Lord God," don't just accept what they say at face value; search the Scriptures to see whether those things are so.

Ponderings

Praise

Petitions

September 2
Ezekiel 23–24

> "I the Lord have spoken it: it shall come to pass, and I will do it; I will not go back, neither will I spare, neither will I repent; according to thy ways, and according to thy doing, shall they judge thee, saith the Lord God" (Ezekiel 24:14).

God means what he says. There are many today that try to change or modify what God has said in his Word. They would deny the judgments of God, including hell. His Word is just brushed off as some kind of fairy tale or simply the words of mere men. His laws and commandments are the subject of their scoffing and cynicism. God's Word does not change neither does God go back on his Word. What he says, he will do. "God is not a man, that he should lie; neither the son of man, that he should repent: hath he said, and shall he not do it? or hath he spoken, and shall he not make it good" (Numbers 23:19)? A man may break his promises or go back on his word, but the Lord does not. The promises of God are as good as done. God has never failed in any of his promises and does not intend to. That is why he is worthy of our faith. God is not man and therefore always means what he says. His Word is to be trusted.

Ponderings

Praise

Petitions

September 3
Ezekiel 25–27

"And I will execute great vengeance upon them with furious rebukes; and they shall know that I am the Lord, when I shall lay my vengeance upon them" (Ezekiel 25:17).

The vengeance of God would be poured out on those nations who did not honor him or his people. In this God was keeping a promise he had made to Abraham. "And I will bless them that bless thee, and curse him that curseth thee: and in thee shall all families of the earth be blessed" (Genesis 12:3). The nations that would fall under the vengeance of God had spoken out against or had attacked Jerusalem. By pouring out his vengeance on these nations, God would make his presence known to them, "and they shall know that he is the Lord." In the same way that the Lord would curse these nations, he had also promised a blessing to those who bless Israel. This is why it is important for our nation to honor and show blessing to Israel even today. God is faithful to do what he says. Those who curse Israel will fall under the vengeance of the Lord. However, the Lord will in turn bless those who bless Israel. Either way the power, sovereignty, and presence of God will be known.

Ponderings

Praise

Petitions

September 4
Ezekiel 28–30

"Thou wast perfect in thy ways from the day that thou was created, till iniquity was found in thee" (Ezekiel 28:15).

It is believed that this statement to the King of Tyre goes further than the address to an earthly king. It was a statement made to Lucifer, also called Satan. Lucifer was created and was found in Eden in the early chapters of Genesis; he was created as a beautiful cherub whose covering was that of precious stones. He was equipped to bring praise to the Lord. However, instead, he was lifted with pride to the point of wanting to take God's place on his throne and thereby fell from the glory and presence of God. A common mistake made among many people is that Satan is somehow equal in authority and power with God. He is not. Satan was created as an angelic being. God gave him the ability to choose to worship him and Satan rebelled against God. Satan is not in a power struggle with God. However, he has become the adversary of God. He is also your adversary and will do whatever he can to destroy your relationship with the Lord. He was defeated at the cross and will come to a definite end.

Ponderings

Praise

Petitions

September 5
Ezekiel 31–32

"When I shall make the land of Egypt desolate, and the country shall be destitute of that whereof it was full, when I shall smite all them that dwell therein, then shall they know that I am the Lord" (Ezekiel 32:15).

Egypt and the other heathen nations that surrounded Israel had rejected the Lord and his Word. They had attacked God's people and tried to destroy them. The nations that refused to know the Lord would come to know him though his judgments upon their kings and upon their lands. It is sometimes difficult to understand and accept the judgment of God. However, he is just in all of his ways. For many years, these nations had opportunity to recognize and worship the God of creation. Instead, they worshiped gods that had come from the imaginations of their own hearts. They had "changed the truth of God into a lie, and worshiped and served the creature more than the Creator, who is blessed for ever" (Romans 2:25). In the time when Joseph was in Egypt, they had listened to God's warning about a coming famine and were saved. But, rather than bowing in worship to Joseph's God, they turned to their idols and pagan gods. Now they would know God as their judge.

Ponderings

Praise

Petitions

September 6
Ezekiel 33–35

> "And they come unto thee as the people cometh, and they sit before thee as my people, and they hear thy words, but they will not do them: for with their mouth they shew much love, but their heart goeth after their covetousness" (Ezekiel 33:31).

Sadly, this verse describes many people who go to church today. People get dressed up in their finest clothes, they go to beautiful air-conditioned buildings, and they sit and listen to the preaching of the Word of God week after week. They come in and go out with little evidence in their lives that they ever heard anything that was said. These same people return to their homes and continue in their Sunday rituals without regard to doing or practicing what the Bible says. The next verse says it so plainly, "They hear thy words, but they do them not." Could it be that the real problem is that *they do them not* because they really don't believe them? They like to hear the preacher say the words, but walk away saying "good message, *they* sure needed that," not realizing the real need was in their own lives. What we need are people that have enough faith in the Word of God not only to listen to what the Lord says, but actually to do what he says.

Ponderings

Praise

Petitions

September 7
Ezekiel 36–38

"And ye shall dwell in the land that I gave to your fathers; and ye shall be my people, and I will be your God" (Ezekiel 36:28).

Since the beginning of time, God desired to have a relationship with man. Everything that God had given to man was designed to establish that relationship. When sin entered into the world through Adam, that relationship was broken. God, in his great love for man, tried to reestablish that relationship. The Lord wants to be our God. He wants us to worship and glorify him. He wants to care for us and provide for all our needs. All through the Bible the attempts of God to have this kind of relationship with man is evident. God gave us the Law so that we would know how to properly worship him. When his people rebelled, he chastised them knowing that one day they would return to worship him again. The sin of Adam had to be paid for. Our sin had to be forgiven and we had to be redeemed. In the end, it was only through the death, burial, and resurrection of Jesus Christ that this relationship could be restored. Now, the Lord simply asks us to believe him and received his gift of grace.

Ponderings

Praise

Petitions

September 8
Ezekiel 39–40

> "So will I make my holy name known in the midst of my people Israel; and I will not let them pollute my holy name any more: and the heathen shall know that I am the Lord, the Holy One in Israel" (Ezekiel 39:7).

For a time the people of Israel had forgotten God. They had gone after idols and the gods of other nations. However, God was not going to allow his people to forget him any longer. He caused them to be destroyed as a nation and they were carried away captive to another land. Throughout the captivity, there was a remnant that knew God and had a desire to serve him. Through these few, God restored the nation of Israel and brought the people back to their homeland. It would be an experience that the people of Israel would never forget and consequently would not forget the Lord either. Not only would God be known to his own people, but through the work of God, all nations would know him. There would be no mistaking that through the return of God's people to Israel and the reestablishing of a nation that everyone would know the name of the Lord. They would know him by his judgments upon them and by his mercy toward those who follow him. His name would not be forgotten again.

Ponderings

Praise

Petitions

September 9
Ezekiel 41–43

"And when these days are expired, it shall be, that upon the eighth day, and so forward, the priests shall make your burnt offerings upon the altar, and your peace offerings; and I will accept you, saith the Lord God" (Ezekiel 43:27).

In Ezekiel's day, the Lord required the sacrifice of a ram for the remittance of sin. As the Temple was rebuilt and Temple worship reestablished, God gave Ezekiel very specific instructions concerning the Temple and the offering of a sacrifice for sin. Then he makes this declaration: *I will accept you*. This sacrifice for sin was a foreshadowing of a greater sacrifice for sin. It would be the sacrifice of God's own Son on a Roman cross. The supreme sacrifice of Jesus on the cross would satisfy the judgment of God for eternity. The sacrifice of Jesus would mean the end of the need for the sacrificial lamb. Hebrews 10:10 states, "By the which will we are sanctified through the offering of the body of Jesus Christ once for all." The death of Jesus Christ on Calvary's cross would be enough for every person for all eternity. When we place our faith in the work of Christ on Calvary, God says, "I will accept you."

Ponderings

Praise

Petitions

September 10
Ezekiel 44–46

"Then brought he me the way of the north gate before the house: and I looked, and, behold, the glory of the Lord filled the house of the Lord: and I fell upon my face" (Ezekiel 44:4).

It was a great day for Israel when the Temple was rebuilt following the Babylonian captivity. As Ezekiel stood before the northern gate of the Temple, he witnessed a great event. The glory of the Lord filled the new Temple. God then gave Ezekiel very specific instructions concerning the priests and how they were to worship the Lord in this new house. A similar event happens to a new believer. When a person receives Christ into their lives, they become the very Temple of God. Paul said; "Know ye not that ye are the temple of God, and that the Spirit of God dwelleth in you" (1 Corinthians 3:16)? It is an awesome thought to consider that God inhabits his people. Our worship is not limited to any one given place, like the Temple; we are free to worship God anywhere and at any time. This should not be an excuse to avoid church as we need the fellowship and training of the local assembly. When we realize that we are now the Temple of God, it seems our reaction should be similar to Ezekiel's. We should fall on our faces to worship the God of all creation.

Ponderings

Praise

Petitions

September 11
Ezekiel 47–48

"and the name of the city from that day shall be, The Lord is there." (Ezekiel 48:35b).

Jehovah-shammah, *the Lord is there*. What a great name for a city. Now that Jerusalem and the temple were rebuilt, the people could return to a right relationship with the Lord. God was pleased with the restoration of his people and his city. God put his stamp of approval on the city by giving it a special name, *The Lord is there*. Jerusalem would be the place where God would one day sacrifice his only Son for the redemption of those who would put their faith in him. It would be a special city. The sacrifices and offerings that would be given there would point to a day when there would be a supreme sacrifice for the sins of the world. This sacrifice would lead to another city, the New Jerusalem. It is spoken of in the final pages of the scripture. It will be a beautiful city and like the earthly Jerusalem, it will also bear the name *the Lord is there*. Because of his presence there will be no need for the sun. "And the city had no need of the sun, neither of the moon, to shine in it: for the glory of God did lighten it, and the Lamb is the light thereof" (Revelation 21:23). Oh, what a day it will be when we live in a place called Jehovah-shammah.

Ponderings

Praise

Petitions

September 12
Daniel 1–3

"But there is a God in heaven that revealeth secrets, and maketh known to the king Nebuchadnezzar what shall be in the latter days" (Daniel 2:28).

Young Daniel and his companions had been brought as captives to Babylon and placed in the king's service. They would be educated and groomed in order to be used at the king's disposal. When the day came that the wise men of the king could not interpret or reveal his terrible dream, it was Daniel that God used to bring his message to King Nebuchadnezzar. The message would not only be for him, but would reveal God's plan for many years to come, eventually leading to the coming of the Messiah. Daniel made it clear that Nebuchadnezzar's dream and its interpretation did not come from the training he had received in Nebuchadnezzar's school. The secret message came from God himself. The interpretation that Daniel was to reveal would also come from the Lord. There was no doubt in Nebuchadnezzar's mind that Daniel had been with the Lord. The secret all the wise men could not reveal. All the training they had received was to no avail. When God wants to send a message, there should be no mistaking its source. God had spoken.

Ponderings

Praise

Petitions

September 13
Daniel 4–5

"I thought it good to shew the signs and wonders that the high God hath wrought toward me" (Daniel 4:2).

The fourth chapter of Daniel records the testimony of King Nebuchadnezzar. He was so full of pride in his great kingdom that he thought he was invincible. Through a dream that Daniel interpreted for him the Lord told him how he was going to be brought down. For seven years he would walk around on his hands and knees like the beasts of the field. His hair grew out; his fingernails and toenails grew until they were like bird's claws. His meals would be comprised of grass, eating like an ox. The mighty king of Babylon had been brought to his knees and humiliated. However, the time was appointed that he would be returned to his throne and to his right mind. The King now recounts his experience with the Lord and offers to him his praise and glory. Gone is the pride and arrogance of before. It is amazing how God can change a life. The Lord can take the vilest sinner and make a vessel that will praise and honor him. Nebuchadnezzar learned to praise the Lord the hard way. What will the Lord have to do to bring you to him?

Ponderings

Praise

Petitions

September 14
Daniel 6–8

"…forasmuch as he was faithful, neither was there any error or fault found in him." (Daniel 6:4b).

Daniel was faithful. When he was asked to eat at the king's table, he refused. When he and his companions were asked to bow down to the king's idol, they refused. When laws were made in an attempt to keep him from prayer, they were made of no effect. Daniel always remained faithful to the Lord. Taken captive to a foreign land and placed into the King's service, it would have been easy for Daniel to go with the flow and compromise himself with the philosophies and behaviors of this new world. Yet, the Bible records that Daniel remained faithful to his God. We live in an age of weak and selfish Christians, who at the first sign of criticism or threat, deny their faith, and join up with the *in* crowd. Oh that God would help us to be like Daniel. The Scripture states, "Moreover it is required in stewards, that a man be found faithful" (1 Corinthians 4:2). To be faithful means that our trust in God is unshakable. It means that no matter how hard it gets or whatever persecution comes, we will not deny our God. No greater comment can be said about a person than that throughout his life, he remained faithful.

Ponderings

Praise

Petitions

September 15
Daniel 9–12

> "Yea, whiles I was speaking in prayer, even the man Gabriel, whom I had seen in the vision at the beginning, being caused to fly swiftly, touched me about the time of the evening oblation" (Daniel 9:21).

Daniel was praying, confessing the sin of Israel as well as his own sin. In the midst of his prayer he sensed a touch. It was Gabriel, the messenger angel of God. Daniel's prayer was being answered and Daniel would soon know what God had planned for his people. The first message that Gabriel had for Daniel was very personal in nature, "thou art greatly beloved" (Daniel 9:23). He then went on to explain to Daniel about some of the visions that he had previously seen. These visions were prophecies that were pointing to the greatest event that would happen in all of human history; the time that the Messiah would come and give his life for the salvation of those who would place their faith in the Lord. Not only did Gabriel give him some indicators that would signal the Messiah's coming, but Daniel was also given the time frame in which he would come. It is easy for us to look back and see that these prophecies were fulfilled. Imagine how exciting it was for Daniel to know that they would be occurring according to God's Word delivered by a special messenger!

Ponderings

Praise

Petitions

September 16
Hosea 1–4

"Afterward shall the children of Israel return, and seek the Lord their God, and David their king; and shall fear the Lord and his goodness in the latter days" (Hosea 3:5).

God called on Hosea to illustrate his relationship with the children of Israel in a very unusual way. The people who once served and honored the Lord had turned their backs on him and began serving and worshiping Baal and other idols. God likened this to that of a harlot or an unfaithful wife. God knew that this turning away would only be for a while and that one day his people would return to him. In Hosea 1:10, God reminds the children of Israel of the covenant relationship he had with them. And though they had turned their backs on him, he would wait until they would seek him again. There may be times in our own lives when it seems we turn away from God. Be assured that the Lord has not left you nor has he forsaken you. He may chastise you and take you through some trials with the intent of bringing you back to himself. Our relationship to God is very important and should not be taken lightly or for granted. God loves you very much and desires to walk with you closely every day.

Ponderings

Praise

Petitions

September 17
Hosea 5–9

"For I desired mercy, and not sacrifice; and the knowledge of God more than burnt offerings" (Hosea 6:6).

The people of Israel had grown so accustomed to doing sacrifices and offerings that they had lost their significance. God was more interested in having a relationship with his people than he was in all the rituals they were performing. In much the same way the performance of Christian duties has also become little more than a system of rituals. We go to church, we sing our hymns, we say our prayers, give our offerings, we sit through a sermon, and go home never having an experience of true worship. God did not create man to see him perform meaningless rituals. God created man so that he could have a relationship with him. God wanted us to have a *knowledge* of him. Can you say that you know the Lord? Do you recognize his voice? Does he answer you when you pray? Do you talk to the Lord like he is your best friend, or do you recite empty prayers that have lost their meaning? God wants you to know him in a very personal way. He is more interested in you than in your empty religious rituals.

Ponderings

Praise

Petitions

September 18
Hosea 10–14

"I will heal their backsliding, I will love them freely: for mine anger is turned away from him" (Hosea 14:4).

The overriding theme of the writings of Hosea is the Lord's plea for his people to return to him. The people had forsaken the Lord and served the gods of the land. However, God still loved his people very much and longed for them to return to him. There are many who have backslidden from the Lord, many who have forsaken the Lord and are chasing after the gods of this world. There are many who used to go to church, who used to teach a Sunday school class, who used to have a close relationship with the Lord. You may have forsaken the Lord, but he has not forsaken you. He longs to walk close to you again. If you will just come to him, confess, and repent of your sin, God is gracious and merciful and will heal your backsliding. God will patiently wait with open arms for you to return to him. His love is not diminished by sin, for his love is everlasting. "Turn to the Lord; say unto him, Take away all iniquity and receive us graciously" (Hosea 14:2). Turn to him today; he is patiently waiting for you.

Ponderings

_____
_____
_____

Praise

_____
_____
_____

Petitions

_____
_____
_____

September 19
Joel 1–3

"Fear not, O land; be glad and rejoice: for the Lord will do great things" (Joel 2:21).

No matter what circumstance you are in, you can count on this, "the Lord will do great things." There is nothing that is impossible with the Lord. There is no reason for the believer to go around in despair and depression, for we serve a God who can and will do great things. God is able to do things that we are not even aware of. The promise of his Word is "call unto me and I will answer thee and show you great and mighty things that ye know not of" (Jeremiah 33:3). When it seems that you are at the end of your rope and you cannot go on any further, just hang on, God will do something great for you. The problem is we do not expect great things from God nor do we request great things from God. In our minds we often limit God's capability and willingness to help us. Look what God did for the children of Israel. They were held in captivity, their homeland was destroyed, and yet God brought them back home again and the Temple and Jerusalem were rebuilt with their captor's help. In the words of a great missionary *attempt great things for God, expect great things from God.* God is able to do great things for you.

Ponderings

Praise

Petitions

September 20
Amos 1–4

> "Therefore thus will I do unto thee, O Israel: and because I will do this unto thee, prepare to meet thy God, O Israel" (Amos 4:12).

The judgment of God was about to come upon the people of Israel. Though they were God's chosen people, they had turned their backs on the Lord and were no longer serving him. God was going to punish them in order to bring them back to himself. God was not being mean to them or wanting to hurt them for no reason. The very fact the Lord sent Amos to warn them of the coming judgment is indicative of the fact that the Lord would rather that they would just return to him. Through Amos, God was trying to warn them so that they would have an opportunity to change their ways. There is coming a day when we will all stand before the judgment seat of God. The Bible is clear that "it is appointed for men to die once, but after this the judgment" (Hebrews 9:27). Are you prepared to meet thy God? To be prepared you must have received Jesus Christ as your personal Lord and Savior. Certainly judgment is coming, but those who know the Lord will stand before him justified. "There is therefore now no condemnation to those who are in Christ Jesus" (Romans 8:1).

Ponderings

Praise

Petitions

September 21
Amos 5–9

"For thus saith the Lord unto the house of Israel, Seek ye me, and ye shall live" (Amos 5:4).

God has promised that those who diligently seek him will find him. God is not playing hide and seek with you. It is possible to seek the Lord in every situation and at any time. Jeremiah said, "And ye shall seek me, and find me, when ye shall search for me with all your heart" (Jeremiah 29:13). The Lord is available to all who will come and seek him. The Lord is very near. In times of trouble he can be found. In times of distress and misery, he can be found. In times of praise and worship, the Lord can be found. The problem is that often we are not seeking the Lord at all. We try to stumble through life without so much as even giving the Lord a thought. Jesus taught us that rather than seeking the things of the world we should first of all seek after the Lord. "But seek ye first the kingdom of God, and his righteousness; and all these things shall be added unto you" (Matthew 6:33). Seek the Lord in all things and you will find him. That's a promise!

Ponderings

Praise

Petitions

September 22
Obadiah and Jonah

"So the people of Nineveh believed God, and proclaimed a fast, and put on sackcloth, from the greatest of them even to the least of them" (Jonah 3:5).

Nineveh was a great and wicked city. God called Jonah to go and preach to the people there. His message was one of impending judgment, if the people did not turn from their wickedness and repent of their sin. Of course, it took some miraculous events to get a reluctant Jonah to Nineveh. However, when he was finally obedient to God's call and preached to that city, there was one of the greatest revivals ever recorded in history. The people believed God and began to fast in sackcloth and ashes. There was a great sorrow and lamentation over their sin. The judgment of God was turned away from them. There were over 120,000 people in Nineveh that got right with the Lord through the preaching of Jonah; you would think that he would rejoice over such a victory. Instead he was disappointed that God did not judge the city. God had poured out his grace on this wicked people. How often have we carried grudges and felt that the wrath of God should fall on someone who has offended us. We should be thankful that God is the one who is "… a gracious God, and merciful, slow to anger, and of great kindness" (Jonah 4:2b).

Ponderings

Praise

Petitions

September 23
Micah 1–4

"Then shall they cry unto the Lord, but he will not hear them: he will even hide his face from them at that time, as they have behaved themselves ill in their doings" (Micah 3:4).

God has promised to answer our prayer. "Call unto me, and I will answer thee, and shew thee great and mighty things, which thou knowest not" (Jeremiah 33:3). However, there is a condition under which the Lord's ear might be closed to our cry. As it was in the times of Micah, the Lord will not hear us if we insist on continuing to live in sin. To call on the Lord, you must recognize his sovereignty, authority, and his will. Isaiah said, "But your iniquities have separated between you and your God, and your sins have hid his face from you, that he will not hear" (Isaiah 59:2). God is certainly willing to answer our prayer, but we must come with a clean heart and pure motives. God is not going to enable someone to continue in their sin. It is in this situation that our first prayer should be the confession of our sin in repentance. When it seems that God is not answering prayer, perhaps it is time to take inventory of ourselves and see that we are walking with him in righteousness and holiness.

Ponderings

Praise

Petitions

September 24
Micah 5–7

"He hath shewed thee, O man, what is good; and what doth the Lord require of thee, but to do justly, and to love mercy, and to walk humbly with thy God?" (Micah 6:8).

What does the Lord require of us? First, the Scripture says, *to do justly*. This means that we are to do right. In all of our actions and attitudes we are to do what is right not just convenient. We are saved *unto righteousness*. The sinful lifestyle we had in the past should be put away and our new objective should be to seek out what is right and do it. Secondly, the Lord requires that we *love mercy*. When we are wronged or hurt in some way, our natural response is to seek revenge or some kind of retribution. Instead we are to seek mercy and kindness. The greatest example of this is shown is God's mercy toward us every day. "It is of the Lord's mercies that we are not consumed, because his compassions fail not. They are new every morning: great is thy faithfulness" (Lamentation 3:22–23). The last thing that the Lord requires is that we *walk humbly* with him. "God resisteth the proud, but giveth grace unto the humble" (James 4:6).

Ponderings

Praise

Petitions

September 25
Nahum 1–3

"The Lord is good, a strong hold in the day of trouble; and he knoweth them that trust in him" (Nahum 1:7).

The Lord is good and his desire for you is good. He has a great plan for your life and if you follow the Lord each day, you will see just how good he is. When the going gets rough and it seems that there is no answer or solution to your troubles, it is vital that you cling as close to the Lord as you can. He has promised never to leave you nor forsake you. And even in the hard times he is near. The Lord does not abandon us in the hard times, but goes through them with us. He is like an anchor that holds fast and does not allow us to drift aimlessly. It is in the day of trouble that we must trust him the most. Call on the Lord and he will give you the wisdom and direction that you need from day to day. When everything around seems to be falling apart, you can depend on the Lord and his help. He is *a stronghold in the day of trouble*. As you trust him, he will show you the way. He already knows all that you might be going through and he also knows what the outcome will be. Though the going might be tough, just hang on, for God has good things ahead for you.

Ponderings

Praise

Petitions

September 26
Habakkuk 1–3

"Thou art of purer eyes than to behold evil, and canst not look on iniquity" (Habakkuk 1:13).

God is holy and cannot allow sin even into his presence. When sin entered into the world, it caused man to be eternally separated from God. "But your iniquities have separated between you and your God, and your sins have hid his face from you, that he will not hear" (Isaiah 59:2). In order for us to be holy enough to enter into God's presence, we must be as holy as he is. The only way this is possible is to somehow exchange our unholiness for his holiness. When Jesus died on the cross, he took upon himself all of our sin and did just that. He took our sin upon himself and gave us his righteousness. Having received the righteousness of Christ through faith in him, we are allowed into the very presence of a Holy God. Notice there is no way you can earn this holiness. It is offered by the grace of God through faith. "For by grace are ye saved through faith; and that not of yourselves: it is the gift of God" (Ephesians 2:8).

Ponderings

Praise

Petitions

September 27
Zephaniah 1–3

> "Hold thy peace at the presence of the Lord God: for the day of the Lord is at hand: for the Lord hath prepared a sacrifice, he hath bid his guests" (Zephaniah 1:7).

There is always a consequence to every sin. There is a temporal consequence as the immediate result of sin, such as the pain and misery that sin can cause. There is also the guilt and hurt that is the result of sin. There is also an eternal consequence to sin, which is death. "The wages of sin is death" (Romans 3:23). In order for our sin to be forgiven the price of sin must be paid. God himself provided the payment for our sin in the sacrifice of his Son on Calvary's cross. The death of Jesus Christ was the supreme sacrifice that would take away all of our sin. God loved us so much that he sacrificed his own Son so that we could be saved. He now extends to us the invitation to come and receive the payment for our sin. "And the Spirit and the bride say, Come. And let him that heareth say, Come. And let him that is athirst come. And whosoever will, let him take the water of life freely" (Revelation 22:17).

Ponderings

Praise

Petitions

September 28
Haggai 1–2

"Now therefore thus saith the Lord of hosts; Consider your ways" (Haggai 1:5).

It is good to occasionally sit back, take an honest look at ourselves, and consider our ways. Our number one objective in life should be to glorify the Lord and love him supremely. Are the things you are doing in your life glorifying him? Does the Lord have the preeminence in your life? Take a look at every aspect of your life. Are you spending time with the Lord every day reading his Word and talking to him in prayer? Are you being faithful to your local assembly? Are you being a faithful witness at your workplace and in your neighborhood? It may be that after considering your ways you will find issues that need some adjustment. Our schedules and activities often crowd out the Lord in such a subtle way that we do not realize what is happening to us. Perhaps there are some things that you are doing that are robbing your time with the Lord or are damaging your testimony. The remedy is simple. Confess and repent of your sin, and make a few changes so that God has his rightful place in your life. Perhaps there are some things that need to be eliminated from your life so that you can glorify the Lord fully.

Ponderings

Praise

Petitions

September 29
Zechariah 1–5

"Therefore say thou unto them, Thus saith the Lord of hosts; Turn ye unto me, saith the Lord of hosts, and I will turn unto you, saith the Lord of hosts" (Zechariah 1:3).

It has been said, "If you feel far from God, guess who moved." When a person has turned away from the Lord like Israel did, the Lord will wait until that individual turns to him. In the meantime, the Lord may execute his chastising hand in order to bring one back into fellowship with him. By the wooing of the Holy Spirit or by the conviction of sin, the Lord will do whatever has to be done to bring that child home again. Like the father of the prodigal son, he will wait and welcome the wandering child home. When we confess and repent of our sin, the heavenly Father is willing to forgive us our sin and restore us to fellowship with him. "If we confess our sins, he is faithful and just to forgive us our sins, and to cleanse us from all unrighteousness" (1 John 1:9). God's desire is not to punish us, but to bring us into full fellowship with him. That is why he would rather that we be reconciled unto him. Turn to him and he will turn to you.

Ponderings

Praise

Petitions

September 30
Zechariah 6–10

"Thus speaketh the Lord of hosts, saying, Execute true judgment, and shew mercy and compassions every man to his brother: And oppress not the widow, nor the fatherless, the stranger, nor the poor; and let none of you imagine evil against his brother in your heart" (Zechariah 7:9–10).

When we are offended in some way, often our first response is to "get even" or to retaliate. It is human nature to strike back at an offender. As we mull over the offense committed against us, we begin to plan and scheme at how we will get someone back for what they did to us. However, the Lord says that we are to show "mercy and compassion" and not "imagine evil" against our brother. It is best to take the offense to the Lord first and allow him to work out his will in the matter. Paul said that we should "Bless them which persecute you: bless, and curse not" (Romans 12:14). When we try to take matters into our own hands by seeking revenge or retaliation, we only make a bigger mess of things thus making the offense worse than it was in the first place. Rather than seeking revenge, seek reconciliation by showing mercy and compassion to the offender.

Ponderings

Praise

Petitions

October 1
Zechariah 11–14

"And it shall come to pass, that every one that is left of all the nations which came against Jerusalem shall even go up from year to year to worship the King, the Lord of hosts, and to keep the feast of tabernacles" (Zechariah 14:16).

There is coming a day when every nation, every tongue, and every race of people will come before the Lord and worship him as the King of Kings. "That at the name of Jesus every knee should bow, of things in heaven, and things in earth, and things under the earth; And that every tongue should confess that Jesus Christ is Lord, to the glory of God the Father" (Philippians 2:10–11). All the nations of the earth will recognize the Lord for who he is. All of the gods of this earth will pale into nonexistence. There will be no unbended knee or silent tongue as everyone recognizes that *Jesus Christ is Lord, to the glory of God the Father.* The great thing is that you do not have to wait to honor Christ as Lord, you can do that now. When we say that he is the Lord of our life, we are recognizing that we completely belong to him. Recognize that Christ is the Lord of your life and get a head start on worshiping him into eternity.

Ponderings

Praise

Petitions

October 2
Malachi 1–4

"Bring ye all the tithes into the storehouse, that there may be meat in mine house, and prove me now herewith, saith the Lord of hosts, if I will not open you the windows of heaven, and pour you out a blessing, that there shall not be room enough to receive it" (Malachi 3:10).

It has been said, *"You can't out give God."* This is true as God has promised to bless those who bring their tithes and offerings into the storehouse. While the purpose of our giving should be to glorify the Lord, God has shown himself faithful to those who give a tenth of their earnings to him. The blessing of giving comes in many forms. It may not be in financial gain. The blessing may be in the form of good health or allowing us to continue to work for our earnings. The blessing may be in the form of an extended use of appliances and machines that we use every day. Whatever the case, you can be sure that God blesses those who give unselfishly to him. Bringing the tithe into the storehouse is a means of showing our love and commitment to the Lord. It is also a form of worship. The money we give represents a segment of our life. Give your tithe and allow the blessing of God to flow into your life.

Ponderings

Praise

Petitions

October 3
Matthew 1–4

"Behold, a virgin shall be with child, and shall bring forth a son, and they shall call his name Emmanuel, which being interpreted is, God with us" (Matthew 1:23).

Emmanuel, God with us. Imagine the Creator of all the Universe took upon himself the form of a man and came to this earth to dwell among men! Make no mistake about it, the Scripture is clear. Jesus is God in the flesh and came to this earth to live a perfect life, to die a death we could not die, and to pay a price that we could not pay. He left the throne of glory to descend to a people who would reject him and eventually kill him. The Almighty took upon himself the form of a servant. Why would God who is thrice holy do such a thing for sinful man? It was because of his love for each one of us. "For God so loved the world, that he gave his only begotten Son, that whosoever believeth in him should not perish, but have everlasting life" (John 3:16). God so loved the world that he was willing to pay the ultimate price for our sin. "But God commendeth his love toward us, in that, while we were yet sinners, Christ died for us" (Romans 5:8). The only way he could pay such a price was to become *Emmanuel*, God with us.

Ponderings

Praise

Petitions

October 4
Matthew 5–6

"But seek ye first the kingdom of God, and his righteousness; and all these things shall be added unto you" (Matthew 6:33).

Much of our life is spent attempting the acquisition of things. Generally it is the basic things we need such as food, clothing, and shelter. Once those things are in hand we begin to pursue the things we want. As for the basic necessities of life, Jesus taught us that there is an even more important pursuit; the pursuit of God and his righteousness. The Lord knows we have need of the things that keep us alive and safe. We are to totally depend on him for those things. Our time and attention should be given to seeking God and his righteousness. Earlier, Jesus told the crowd on this mountainside that "except your righteousness shall exceed the righteousness of the scribes and Pharisees, ye shall in no case enter into the kingdom of heaven" (Matthew 5:20). How is this possible? It is only possible by giving up our sin and accepting the righteousness of Christ. The key is this; seek Jesus first in all things even the basic necessities of life.

Ponderings

Praise

Petitions

October 5
Matthew 7–9

"But the men marveled, saying, What manner of man is this, that even the winds and the sea obey him!" (Matthew 8:27).

To the disciples, Jesus seemed to be like any other ordinary man. When a storm descended over the Sea of Galilee, Jesus was taking a nap in the boat. Then the warning rang out! "Help us, we are going to perish!" Jesus told the storm and the sea to calm down then rebuked the disciples for their lack of faith. How silent those few moments must have been as the sea became so very still! The violent storm had obeyed the voice of the Savior and turned to a quiet calm. To Jesus this was not so unusual, for he had made the sea and the wind. To the disciples it was an incredible event leaving them to wonder who this man could be that was in the boat with them. When the storms of life seem to violently shake up the boat, we can turn to the One who can miraculously calm the storm. "What manner of man is this?" the disciples asked. It is the man of Galilee who had come to take upon himself the form of a servant, eventually saving us from more than just a storm, but also from the curse of sin that was upon all mankind. He was Jesus, the Son of God.

Ponderings

Praise

Petitions

October 6
Matthew 10–11

"Come unto me, all ye that labour and are heavy laden, and I will give you rest." (Matthew 11:28).

The invitation has been issued, *come unto me*. All of mankind suffers under the weight of sin. Sin in turn produces guilt and all manner of suffering. The burden that we carry cannot be removed by escapism or in the pursuit of the pleasures of this world. That weight of sin can only be removed by bringing it to the Savior and giving it to him. Jesus bore the burden of our sin on himself when he died on that old rugged cross. 1 Peter 2:24 reminds us that Jesus was the one "Who his own self bare our sins in his own body on the tree, that we, being dead to sins, should live unto righteousness: by whose stripes ye were healed." Jesus now invites us to come and bring all our sin to him. He promises to lift the burden and give us rest. Not only is the rest we receive from the burden of our sin, it is also an eternal rest in a place that he is preparing for those who trust him. The whole world groans under the weight of Adam's sin. Come to Jesus today, bring him all of your burdens, and find a rest that is reserved for the people of God.

Ponderings

Praise

Petitions

October 7
Matthew 12–13

"All these things spake Jesus unto the multitude in parables; and without a parable spake he not unto them:" (Matthew 13:34).

It has been said that a parable is *an earthly story with a heavenly meaning.* Jesus taught us heavenly truths by giving us illustrations of real life situations. Often his parables were comparisons to eternal things so that the people could have a clearer understanding of them. Jesus used situations that were common to the people of his day, such as, farming, business, and other daily routines of life. The teaching of eternal truths using parables were also the fulfillment of the Old Testament, specifically Psalms 78:2, which states, "I will open my mouth in a parable: I will utter dark sayings of old." The parables that Jesus told were intended to give a clearer understanding of heaven, hell, the Kingdom of God, and other eternal matters. Often the people did not understand what Jesus was saying and he would have to explain the comparisons that he had made in parables. Jesus was the Master Teacher and left us a good example of ways to explain the Gospel to those who do not know the Lord. Perhaps we would do well to learn these parables so that we too could use them in our own attempts at winning souls for the kingdom of God.

Ponderings

Praise

Petitions

October 8
Matthew 14–17

"For what is a man profited, if he shall gain the whole world, and lose his own soul? or what shall a man give in exchange for his soul?" (Matthew 16:26).

A man will spend a lifetime attempting to acquire the goods and riches of this world, giving little attention to the eternal destiny of his soul. There is nothing in this world that a person can take with him into eternity. As the old preacher said, *I've never seen a hearst pulling a U-haul.* The riches of this world will have no value in eternity. The gold that man tries to gain in this life will be no more than pavement on the streets of heaven. It is usually not until a man's life comes to its expected end that one will give any thoughts to God and eternity. Then hoping against hope, one somehow expects that he has done enough good to merit God's mercy and grace. The question of eternity and our relationship with God must be settled now, while there is still time. Make up your mind now to accept Jesus as the Lord of your life and give him first place in everything. Rather than pursuing the riches of this world our time should be spent in pursing the *Kingdom of God and his righteousness*. Eternity depends on it.

Ponderings

Praise

Petitions

October 9
Matthew 18–20

"For the Son of man is come to save that which is lost" (Matthew 18:11).

The purpose of Jesus' coming to this earth has been debated for centuries. Some say he was simply a good teacher who was very wise and there is much we can learn from his teaching. Others claim that he was a social revolutionary who changed the course of human history by his teaching and example of love for his fellow man. Still, other's say that he was no more than a renegade preacher who gained an audience by slight of hand and trickery and then preached to the poor. But, make no mistake about it; Jesus came for one reason, to save the lost. Who are the lost? It is every person that is born on this earth. Every person carries the curse of Adam's sin and thus needs to be saved from the curse of that sin which is death. It is a wonder that the reason for the coming of the Son of Man is so misunderstood. Jesus said it himself, "For the Son of man is come to seek and to save that which was lost" (Luke 19:10). Jesus came to this world for one reason and that is to save us from our sin. Every person must come to Jesus to be saved from sin. After all, that is why he came—to save the lost.

Ponderings

Praise

Petitions

October 10
Matthew 21-22

> "Jesus said unto him, Thou shalt love the Lord thy God with all thy heart, and with all thy soul, and with all thy mind. This is the first and great commandment" (Matthew 22:37-38).

When a lawyer asked Jesus which commandment is the greatest in the law, he was not really looking for an answer. His only purpose was to tempt the Savior into some kind of great debate. The answer left the man speechless. Who on this earth has ever been able to completely obey this law? While we should attempt to love the Lord with all that we have, we are so often drawn away by the things that are in the world. To love the Lord above everything would certainly be shown in how we live. Does your attendance in church show your love for the Lord or does it show your love for something else? What about your giving, or the choices you make in the use of your time? Our love of God is not shown only in what we say, but in what we do. To love him with all our heart, soul, and mind would mean that everything else in this world should pale into insignificance. Our very life would show how much we love the Lord. What do your priorities show about your love for the Lord?

Ponderings

Praise

Petitions

October 11
Matthew 23–24

"But of that day and hour knoweth no man, no, not the angels of heaven, but my Father only" (Matthew 24:36).

Jesus promised that he would return to this earth one day. For generations people have tried to predict when this great event would happen. One Christmas Eve a group of mistaken people gathered on the rooftop of a home in the mid-west expecting that Jesus would return for them before sunrise. How embarrassing it was for them as they climbed down from that roof on Christmas day! Many preachers and evangelists in their attempt to convince people of the coming of Christ have tried to set deadlines and timetables for his return only to be found in error. The time of Jesus' return is not for us to know or even attempt to predict; only the Father knows. It is more important for you to be prepared for that day. Later in this same chapter, Jesus said, "Therefore, be ye also ready: for in such an hour as ye think not the Son of man cometh" (Matthew 24:44). It would seem that Jesus will come when we least expect him. Every day could be the day of his coming. It could even be today. Will you be ready?

Ponderings

Praise

Petitions

October 12
Matthew 25–26

"Watch and pray, that ye enter not into temptation: the spirit indeed is willing, but the flesh is weak" (Matthew 26:41).

We must be ever vigilant against the temptations that would lead us to sin. We must guard against the enemy who will throw things into our path in an effort to cause us to stumble. We cannot always blame temptation as the work of the devil. We must guard against the flesh as it is weak. James 1:14 states," But every man is tempted, when he is drawn away of his own lust, and enticed." Though our spirit may be willing to take a stand against the sin that would come in to our lives, *the flesh is weak*. Not only must we guard against temptation, we must constantly be in touch with the Lord through prayer. Through prayer we can maintain a constant walk with the Lord, as Paul said, "Pray without ceasing" (1 Thessalonians 5:17). We are encouraged to pray about everything all the time. Pray as you drive around doing those daily errands. Pray in what is often called *down times*, when you have those few moments alone. To avoid falling into sin through temptation we must be ever watching and ever praying.

Ponderings

Praise

Petitions

October 13
Matthew 27–28

"And Jesus came and spake unto them, saying, All power is given unto me in heaven and in earth. Go ye therefore, and teach all nations, baptizing them in the name of the Father, and of the Son, and of the Holy Ghost: teaching them to observe all things whatsoever I have commanded you: and lo, I am with you always, even unto the end of the world. Amen "(Matthew 28:18–20).

This passage of Scripture is known to many as the *Great Commission*. It is the command of Jesus to go out into *all the world* and tell everyone about him. We are not to keep the Gospel to ourselves but to go into the entire world and give it away. We are to put our efforts, our finances, and our attention to spreading the Gospel to everyone. Not only are we to take the Gospel to all nations, we are to lead them to obedience to the Lord in baptism, and then, teach everything that Jesus taught us. The *Great Commission* is a great undertaking and should not be taken lightly. Millions are dying in their sin while many Christians sit in padded pews in beautiful buildings. What are you doing to see that the Gospel is taken around the world? You can give, you can pray; and yes, you can even go.

Ponderings

Praise

Petitions

October 14
Mark 1–3

"And he healed many that were sick of divers diseases, and cast out many devils; and suffered not the devils to speak, because they knew him" (Mark 1:34).

As Jesus, the Great Physician, traveled throughout the land he healed many people who were sick with all manner of diseases. There was no malady that was beyond his touch. The lepers were made clean of their scabs and rotting flesh. Those with withered limbs were made completely whole. The blind were given their sight and the lame were made to walk again. The miracles of Jesus were always complete and immediate. When a lame man was told to get up and walk, it was not necessary for him to go through rehabilitation or wait to gain his strength; he simply got up and began to walk. Jesus would also cast out the demons that had taken possesssion of individuals. When Jesus cast out demons, it did not require any coaxing or pleading on his part. They knew who Jesus was and would obey his every command. Those demons knew that they had no chance against the Creator, the Almighty God of heaven and earth. Jesus is still the same today; he can heal all diseases, and demons still tremble at the mention of his name.

Ponderings

Praise

Petitions

October 15
Mark 4–5

"And they come to Jesus, and see him that was possesssed with the devil, and had the legion, sitting and clothed, and in his right mind; and they were afraid" (Mark 5:15).

What a curious sight it must have been to see this man living among the tombs. There were incisions all over his body where he had cut himself repeatedly. Some had tried to help him by tying him up so that he could not hurt himself or be a threat to others. However, somehow he was always able to get loose. The silence of the night would be broken by his fierce cries. Most just ignored him, others pitied him; some just shook their heads in confusion. Then he met Jesus. The problem was not one of psychology, sociology, or physiology. It was a problem of possesssion. This man had been taken over by a whole legion of devils. Jesus knew what to do. He sent all that legion of devils into a herd of swine. Such an event must have upset the pork market in that region as over 2000 head of pigs jumped into the sea. The amazing thing is that when the people came and saw this former maniac sitting on the seashore, now *clothed and in his right mind*, they were afraid. What was the cause of their fear? Was it Jesus, demons, or a man changed by the power of God?

Ponderings

Praise

Petitions

October 16
Mark 6–7

"And he said unto them, come ye yourselves apart into a desert place, and rest a while: for there were many coming and going, and they had no leisure so much as to eat" (Mark 6:31).

Our lives have become so busy. It would seem with all the modern conveniences that we would have more time to slow down and give time for rest. However, we find that the opposite is true. The easier we try to make our lives the busier we get. Jesus and the disciples had been so busy with ministry that they hardly had time to even eat. So Jesus declared a time of rest. They escaped into the quiet place where there would be no demand on their time or energies. Rest is so important that God even established a day to rest. "Six days shall work be done: but the seventh day is the Sabbath of rest, an holy convocation; ye shall do no work therein: it is the Sabbath of the Lord in all your dwellings" (Leviticus 23:3). We often think that the time we take to rest is wasted time. However, without rest a person will become so weary and worn that he can do no work for the glory of God. Rest does not just happen; you must plan for a time of rest. Plan to give yourself a time to just rest…Jesus did.

Ponderings

Praise

Petitions

October 17
Mark 8–9

"And when he had called the people unto him with his disciples also, he said unto them, Whosoever will come after me, let him deny himself, and take up his cross, and follow me" (Mark 8:34).

To follow Jesus we must be willing to give him first place in everything. This begins with the denying of self. If Jesus is to be the Lord of our life, we must obey his every Word. This means that we surrender ourselves to his will and not our own. His plan for our life now becomes our plan. All of our selfish ambitions must be given over to a commitment of searching and obeying God's will. It sounds like a drastic measure, and it is; but in reality we are not giving up anything, we are finding the best that God has for us. A cross represented authority over life and death. In order to take up our cross, we give Jesus complete authority over our lives, even unto death. Jesus did no less for us. Finally, we are to follow him. This requires that we are in constant communication and fellowship with him. To follow Jesus every day we must remain close to him, constantly seeking his will and direction for our lives. Are you willing to do what is necessary to be a disciple?

Ponderings

Praise

Petitions

October 18
Mark 10–11

"And Jesus looking upon them saith, With men it is impossible, but not with God: for with God all things are possible" (Mark 10:27).

There is no person who is so far away from God that he cannot be saved. The statement that Jesus made was not one of the general ability of God. It was in response to a question the disciples asked concerning the salvation of one who had great wealth. They asked, "Who then can be saved?" Jesus had been telling them how difficult it was for a rich man to be saved. Notice that Jesus did not say it was impossible, but that it was *hard*. A rich man tends to feel self secure in his riches and has no need for God. Remember the rich man who looked at all he had and needed to build more barns to store it all. He sat back and said to himself, "Soul, thou hast much goods laid up for many years; take thine ease, eat, drink, and be merry." Then the Lord said to him. "Thou fool, this night thy soul shall be required of thee: then whose shall those things be, which thou hast provided? So is he that layeth up treasure for himself, and is not rich toward God" (Luke 12:19–22). It may be difficult for a rich man to trust the Lord for salvation, but it is not impossible.

Ponderings

Praise

Petitions

October 19
Mark 12–13

"And have ye not read this scripture; the stone which the builders rejected is become the head of the corner:" (Mark 12:10).

Jesus quoted to his detractors a prophecy from Psalms 118:22; "The stone which the builders refused is become the head stone of the corner." The corner stone was the most important in the construction of a building. It would have to be a stone that was perfect in every way. Its corners would have to be perfectly square and it sides perfectly straight. It is representative of Christ. The cornerstone would be used as the guide for the placement of every other stone in the building. If the cornerstone was not completely perfect, then the building would not come together properly. The truth of this prophecy was fulfilled in the rejection of Jesus Christ by the Jews. Rejected by the builders, Jesus became the cornerstone. He is the perfect One against whom our lives should be aligned. When we are in synchronization with him, our lives come together according to his perfect plan. The Cornerstone, what a beautiful picture of the One who is perfect against whom we can construct our lives.

Ponderings

Praise

Petitions

October 20
Mark 14

"She hath done what she could: she is come aforehand to anoint my body to the burying" (Mark 14:8).

As Jesus was waiting on supper at Simon the leper's house a humble woman walks into the room unnoticed. She quietly slips around the conversing men who are engrossed in their guest. They carefully listen to his every word. Suddenly there is the sound of something being broken and the room fills with a sweet aroma. Then they see her, she is pouring out the contents of the beautiful broken box onto the Savior's head. It was a nice gesture indeed, but why such an expensive product? It could have been sold for a good price and the money given to the poor. The men's hearts begin to swell up with anger at the apparent waste. Then Jesus, knowing their hearts speaks up. "Leave her alone, she hath done a good thing, She hath done what she could." That is all Jesus asks of us—to do what we can. We can't all do everything, but we can do what we are able to do. Not everyone can sing a beautiful song, not everyone can deliver a stirring message. Not everyone can build with precision, but we can all do what we are able to do for the Master.

Ponderings

Praise

Petitions

October 21
Mark 15–16

"And when the centurion, which stood over against him, saw that he so cried out, and gave up the ghost, he said, Truly this man was the Son of God" (Mark 15:39).

Had he seen everything? This centurion had been assigned to carry out the arrest and execution of the Nazarene called Jesus. Had he been there on that predawn morning when they found Jesus in a garden praying with his followers? Had he been there with those who mocked his authority as *King of the Jews?* We are not certain of how much of the arrest and trial of Jesus this centurion had witnessed. We do know that he was a witness to his crucifixion. He saw when they placed the cross beam of his execution cross on his shoulders and was made to carry it though the streets of Jerusalem. He heard the sounds of the spikes being hammered through his hands and his feet. He heard the words that were uttered from his parched lips. "Father, forgive them for they know not what they do." He saw those who stood by, some weeping, and some casting insults. He saw the sky turn black and felt the earth rumble beneath his feet. He saw the Savior exhale his last breath and came to one conclusion: *Truly this man was the Son of God.*

Ponderings

Praise

Petitions

October 22
Luke 1–2

"For with God nothing shall be impossible" (Luke 1:37).

"How shall this be, seeing I know not a man?" asked Mary. How is it that God can come upon a young maiden and bring from her a child born of the Holy Spirit? How is it that the immortal can come into contact with the mortal? The conception and birth of the Son of God would be nothing short of a miracle. Even through cousin Elizabeth, God would bring a miracle child into the world. By human measure and standards these births could not have happened, and yet with God *nothing shall be impossible.* The Lord is a God of the impossible. If he could cause such a miracle in a young maiden to bring the Savior into the world, imagine what he can do in your life. Our prayers should not be confined to human capabilities, as the Lord can do anything. He brought a whole universe into existence by simply speaking it to be so. Each day he makes a sunset that is new and perfectly beautiful. Often we place our human limitations on the One who can do the impossible. The Bible records many instances of how the Lord can do what seems to us impossible. That's why we call them miracles.

Ponderings

Praise

Petitions

October 23
Luke 3–4

"And they were astonished at his doctrine: for his word was with power" (Luke 4:32).

Imagine hearing the voice of Jesus proclaiming the truth of the ages. As his voice rang out people would sit up and take notice for he spoke with the power that brought the Universe into existence. When a delegation from the Pharisees was sent down to investigate what this preacher was all about, they returned with the report that "Never man spake like this man" (John 7:46). The people were used to hearing the monotone, unauthoritive voices of the scribes and priests who would speak in the synagogues; but when Jesus spoke, they knew something was different. He spoke with authority as though he had written the words himself. He spoke with a power the people could not only hear but could feel deep in their soul. They knew that when he spoke, his words were true and not fabricated. That same power is still found in the Word of God. Listen to his voice in every Word as you allow him to speak directly to your heart. There is a power in the Word of God that is like no other power. It has the power to change a life, or to soothe a troubled soul. In the Word of God, Jesus still speaks and speaks with power.

Ponderings

Praise

Petitions

October 24
Luke 5–6

"And the whole multitude sought to touch him: for there went virtue out of him, and healed them all." (Luke 6:19).

When someone comes seeking Jesus to meet a need in their life, that need is always met. Every person who seeks him finds him and finds that he is all-sufficient to meet every need. Every person who came to Jesus for healing was healed. No one was ever turned away. The leper with the stench and horror of rotting flesh was made whole. The lame who stumbled to his feet was made to walk. The blind who knew of his passing by the sound of the crowds that were around him were made to see. When Jesus healed someone, their healing was immediate and complete. There was no need for rehabilitation or physical therapy. The man who was lame would jump to his feet rejoicing in his ability to walk. The healings were also permanent. You would not find the people Jesus healed seeking a return visit to be healed again. When Jesus passed through a crowd there was not one who would be turned away without being healed. As Jesus passed by, every need would be met for Jesus *healed them all*.

Ponderings

Praise

Petitions

October 25
Luke 7–8

"And it came to pass afterward, that he went throughout every city and village, preaching and shewing the glad tidings of the kingdom of God: and the twelve were with him," (Luke 8:1).

As Jesus lived and walked on this earth, he never stayed in one place for very long. He had a message to deliver and the best way to do this was to keep moving from city to city and village to village. His message was urgent for it meant the salvation of every person who would hear and believe. His message was one of *glad tidings of the Kingdom of God*. He had come to deliver good news. That news was that every person who was born of Adam's race could be reconciled to God by having their sin forgiven. Jesus was more than a healer, he was more than just a good teacher; he was the Son of God who had come to take away the sin of the world. There is still urgency in getting the message out to the whole world, and the best method of delivering that message is still one city or one village at a time. Even though we have vehicles to distribute the message to the masses, the best way is to find a single city and there proclaim the *good tidings of the Kingdom of God*.

Ponderings

Praise

Petitions

October 26
Luke 9–10

"And Jesus said unto him, No man, having put his hand to the plough, and looking back, is fit for the kingdom of God" (Luke 9:62).

It has been said that one should *try* Jesus to see if he can make the difference in a person's life. The offer is made as though one could *try* Jesus like someone might try on a shirt or a new dress. When one comes to Jesus, it should be for more than just a trial run. The commitment must be complete. When Jesus invites us to come to him, it is not for just a trial, it is for eternity. Jesus used the illustration of someone at the plough intent on breaking up the sod ahead and not on what had been broken up behind. When a person confesses that Jesus is to be Lord of his life, it is a commitment that should be for eternity. To look back suggests that the commitment that was made was just superficial and not genuine. Too many say an empty prayer without committing their lives in making Jesus Lord of their life. When he is Lord, we obey his every command and follow him without looking back. Jesus said that if we are just along for a trial run without total commitment to him, *we are not fit for the kingdom of God.* Which way are you looking?

Ponderings

Praise

Petitions

October 27
Luke 11–12

"And he said unto them, Take heed, and beware of covetousness: for a man's life consisteth not in the abundance of the things which he possessseth" (Luke 12:15).

In our modern society it seems that a man's worth is directly connected to his wealth. The media is filled with the news of those who have been blessed with an abundance of possesssions. It was also true in Jesus' day. The wealthy are given special honors and privileges and are held in great esteem by those who are less fortunate. But Jesus gave us first a caution concerning the accumulation of wealth through covetousness and then gave us a different perspective on life. The desire for more and more stuff results in a sin called covetousness. It is the desire for the possesssions of someone else. It is a warning to those who envy the wealthy as well as a warning to those who would give their entire lives to the accumulations of things. Jesus went on to point out that a man's life does not consist of the things he possessses, but rather in the pursuit of being rich toward God. Instead of chasing after the things of the world, we should seek the kingdom of God. (See verses 12:21 and 12:31)

Ponderings

Praise

Petitions

October 28
Luke 13–15

> "It was meet that we should make merry, and be glad: for this thy brother was dead, and is alive again; and was lost, and is found" (Luke 15:32).

The salvation of a soul should always be cause for rejoicing. When someone repents of their sin and turns to the Lord, we should rejoice with them and receive them into fellowship. How shameful it is when a new believer is scorned or turned away because of his past life. Certainly there may be issues of recompense; remember Zacchaeus who returned the money he had taken from his clients under false pretense. (See Luke 19:1–10) However, the recompense should have no bearing on our forgiveness or whether or not we rejoice with those who come to the Lord. The Bible says that "there is joy in the presence of the angels of God over one sinner that repenteth" (Luke 15:10). If the angels rejoice over one that repents, what keeps us from also rejoicing? A soul that was dead has found life in Christ. The soul that was lost has been found. This should be cause for us to rejoice along with the angels in heaven. "And my soul shall be joyful in the Lord: it shall rejoice in his salvation" (Psalms 35:9).

Ponderings

Praise

Petitions

October 29
Luke 16–18

"And he spake this parable unto certain which trusted in themselves that they were righteous, and despised others:" (Luke 18:9).

Two men went into the Temple to pray. One of them was dressed in the finest of religious fashion. The other also dressed in the best business attire of his day. On the outside one could not see much difference in them, but in their hearts there was a great difference. The first stood before the Lord and gave him an account of all the good things he had done for God. *I fast twice in the week, I give tithes of all that I possesss,* he says. The other man does not so much as even lift his eyes toward heaven and has only one request, *God be merciful to me a sinner.* The first feels he is righteous and just in all of his good doings and deserves God's recognition and blessing. The other cries out to God for mercy knowing that he does not deserve anything. In the final summary of these two worshipers, Jesus says that it was the second man who went away justified in the eyes of the Lord. God is not interested in what we accomplish for him; he is interested in what he can accomplish in us. The one who lifted himself up was put down; the one who was humbled before God was raised to heavenly heights.

Ponderings

Praise

Petitions

October 30
Luke 19–20

"And when he was come near, he beheld the city, and wept over it" (Luke 19:41).

For a little over three years Jesus had walked the streets of the city of Jerusalem. He healed those who were sick; he made the lame to walk and the blind to see. He had gone into the Temple and chased the moneychangers and merchants away who had tried to turn the *house of prayer* into a market place. He had preached to them the gospel of the Kingdom of God. Now, as Jesus looks over the city and sees the emptiness of those who had rejected him, a tear trickles from his eye. There are only two times that the Scripture mentions Jesus weeping. One is just before he raised Lazarus from the dead; the other is here as he gazes over this beloved city. His heart is broken as he knows that it would just be a few hours before he will pay the price for every man's sin, and yet he is being rejected by his own people. "He came unto his own, and his own received him not" (John 1:11). It is hard to understand how people can reject the Son of God, especially those who had seen and heard him. It is difficult to understand how people can reject the One who can give them eternal life even today. It gives one cause for weeping.

Ponderings

Praise

Petitions

October 31
Luke 21–22

"And they asked him, saying, Master, but when shall these things be? and what sign will there be when these things shall come to pass?" (Luke 21:7).

Jesus had been talking about the destruction of Jerusalem and the Temple. He had also been talking about his return to this earth one day. So, the disciples asked him when these things would happen and for what signs they should be watching. Jesus went on to tell them of global events that would precede his coming. It seems we live in a day of *sign seekers*. There are prophecy conferences throughout the nation. Many of the books on the bestseller lists deal with the *last days* and the coming of Christ. The seeking of signs have occupied much of our time. It is certainly exciting to see the culmination of the ages approaching right before our eyes; however, we must be careful that we don't get so occupied looking for signs that we are distracted from the main thing that Jesus told us to do. "Go ye into all the world and preach the Gospel to every creature" (Mark 16:15). Granted, the Gospel can be preached through the teaching of the Scriptures concerning Bible prophecy. Perhaps we should be more concerned with preaching the Gospel than looking for signs.

Ponderings

Praise

Petitions

November 1
Luke 23–24

"And he said unto them the third time, Why, what evil hath he done? I have found no cause of death in him: I will therefore chastise him, and let him go" (Luke 23:22).

Having questioned Jesus thoroughly, Pilate found no good cause to have Jesus put to death. He had even sent him to Herod of Galilee who also found no cause to execute Jesus. They could not find a reason for his execution because Jesus had done no wrong; he had only confronted the religious leaders with their own hypocrisy. Even those who were around Jesus at his crucifixion bore testimony of his sinlessness. One of the thieves that was crucified with him said that though they were being punished justly "this man hath done nothing amiss" (Luke 23:41). One of the Roman soldiers who assisted in the crucifixion of Jesus observed, "Certainly this was a righteous man" (Luke 23:47). Later Peter would also testify that Jesus "had done no sin, neither was guile found in his mouth" (1 Peter 2:22). There was no reason for Jesus to die a criminal's death except for one, to bring salvation to those who would believe in him.

Ponderings

Praise

Petitions

November 2
John 1–2

"He was in the world, and the world was made by him, and the world knew him not" (John 1:10).

The Creator walked among his creation. The one who made the earth would walk upon its ground and get his feet dirty. He who made the water would get thirsty and need a drink. He who made all things would know the pangs of hunger and want for a piece of bread. He had come into the world he had made. When he began to meet the people he had made, he was rejected. The world did not know who he was. Oh, they knew he would be someone great, perhaps a liberator from the Roman oppression or a great teacher among the Rabbis. But, they did not know him as the Creator of the world or the Savior of their souls. As Jesus began his ministry he began with his own people, the children of Israel. They rejected him. "He came unto his own and his own received him not" (John 1:11). He made himself available to all who would receive him. And those who would receive him, he welcomed into the family of God. "But as many as received him, to them gave he the power to become the sons of God, even to them that believe on his name" (John 1:12).

Ponderings

Praise

Petitions

November 3
John 3–4

"He that believeth on the Son hath everlasting life: and he that believeth not the Son shall not see life; but the wrath of God abideth on him" (John 3:36).

The choice is clear; believe on the Son of God and you will live forever or refuse to believe him and suffer the wrath of God. To believe on him means that one must totally rely on him for salvation. There must be no dependence on one's self or in any other to bring eternal life. The person that chooses to believe in the work of Jesus on Calvary's cross will receive life everlasting in ages to come and the abundant life while on this earth. When one chooses to reject Christ he falls into the hands of a righteous judge who has already condemned the sinner to death. It would seem that the choice is an easy one to make and yet people refuse to accept God's gift of salvation every day. Like the man who rejected Christ for the wealth of this world they go away *sorrowful* not understanding that true joy and satisfaction comes in knowing Christ (Matthew 19:22). God once placed this choice before the people of Israel, a choice between life or death, a blessing or a curse; then the Lord told them what choice to make. He told them to *choose life* (Deuteronomy 30:19). So, what is your choice?

Ponderings

Praise

Petitions

November 4
John 5–6

"Then Simon Peter answered him, Lord, to whom shall we go? thou hast the words of eternal life" (John 6:68).

As Jesus worked his way through the hills and valleys of Galilee, he healed many diseases and fed the multitudes. Such miracles did not go unnoticed by the populace as many began to follow him. But Jesus knew their hearts and that the people had just come to see a show or be fed by his miraculous hand. When Jesus revealed that he knew what was in them, many left and did not return (John 6:64–66). Now looking to his twelve disciples, he asked them, "Will you also go away" (John 6:67). Then Simon Peter declared his loyalty and life to the Savior. "To whom shall we go? thou hast the words of eternal life." Peter knew that Jesus was, without question, the Son of God. There was no other place to go to find eternal life. It would be sometime later that Peter would stand on the steps of the Temple declaring to his brethren "Neither is there salvation in any other: for there is none other name under heaven given among men, whereby we must be saved" (Acts 4:12). Jesus is the only way to eternal life, there is no other.

Ponderings

Praise

Petitions

November 5
John 7–8

> "Jesus said unto them, Verily, verily, I say unto you, Before Abraham was, I am." (John 8:58).

There was no doubt in the minds of the Pharisees who Jesus was claiming to be. So much so, that as soon as the words of truth came out of his mouth the Pharisees began to cast stones at Jesus for the crime of blasphemy. Jesus made it clear that he is God. In his answer to their question, "Whom makest thou thyself," Jesus made it also clear that he was the Son of God. The language that he used is very interesting indeed, for Jesus did not say that before Abraham I was, or used to be, but he used the little phrase *I AM*. At first glance it is an indication of his eternal being. He always was and always will be. God is eternal. But upon a closer examination we also see that he used a name that was familiar to the Jews. When Moses stood before the burning bush in the third chapter of Exodus, he asked the Lord who he should say sent him. "And God said unto Moses, I AM THAT I AM: and he said, Thus shalt thou say unto the children of Israel, I AM hath sent me unto you" (Exodus 3:14). The Pharisees understood clearly who Jesus was claiming to be, Almighty God.

Ponderings

Praise

Petitions

November 6
John 9–10

"I am the good shepherd, and know my sheep, and am known of mine" (John 10:14).

Jesus is the Great Shepherd. What a description of the One who loved us so much that he was willing to lay down his life for us! Our Great Shepherd leads and guards over us in order to meet our every need. David outlined the work of the Great Shepherd in his little psalm, the Twenty-third Psalm. The Great Shepherd sees to it that we have everything that we need. He leads us to the still water; he takes us to the place were the pastures are lush and green. He knows us in a very personal way. Every individual in his flock is important. Like the shepherd of Luke 15 when one is wayward, he will seek it out until he finds it and returns it to the fold. When the Shepherd calls, the sheep who know their Shepherd's voice follow him to a place of safety. He protects his sheep from danger. As the sheep are brought into the fold at the close of day, he carefully accounts for each one and then literary lies down in the doorway to protect his sheep from the predators of the night. Our Great Shepherd also provides eternal life for his sheep. When the Shepherd calls, do you recognize his voice?

Ponderings
___
___
___

Praise
___
___
___

Petitions
___
___
___

November 7
John 11–12

"And there were certain Greeks among them that came up to worship at the feast: The same came therefore to Philip, which was of Bethsaida of Galilee, and desired him, saying, Sir, we would see Jesus" (John 12:20–21).

We do not know if these Greeks had ever seen or heard of Jesus before. It is possible that they had seen him when he entered Jerusalem in the triumphant entry. We do know that they were seeking for some spiritual meaning in their lives. They had come to Jerusalem to worship. They obviously had rejected the polytheism of their native land and were searching for the one true God. When they found Philip, they had but one desire, "Sir, we would see Jesus." Exactly what they expected from Jesus the Scripture does not say, but their enquiry is a reminder to us that many are seeking for the Savior. Many desire to see Jesus and him alone. They are tired of empty religion and meaningless rituals. They are looking for the One who can give eternal life. Philip and Andrew took the Greeks to see Jesus. Our task is to bring every person we know to meet him also. Do the seekers see Jesus in your life? Are they inquiring of you, "Sirs, we would see Jesus"?

Ponderings

Praise

Petitions

November 8
John 13–15

"By this shall all men know that ye are my disciples, if ye have love one to another" (John 13:35).

How do the people of the world know that we are followers of Jesus Christ? Some show their faith by wearing T-shirts with Christian messages or passages of Scripture. Others show their faith in their jewelry by wearing crucifixes or crosses. Many will display their faith by putting bumper stickers on their cars or hanging Christian symbols from their rear view mirror. In their homes they put up plaques and pictures depicting Christian messages. While all of these things are good, there is one way that is often ignored or forgotten. Jesus said that people would know we are his followers by the way Christians love each other. What example of love have we given to the world? Churches that split over insignificant matters and Christians at each other's throat over disagreements seem to be the norm. The best way to show our Christianity is by showing others the love that Christ showed to us. It was a love that was self-sacrificing and unconditional. Our Christianity is shown in how we love, not only in the material things we display.

Ponderings

Praise

Petitions

November 9
John 16–17

"These words spake Jesus, and lifted up his eyes to heaven" (John 17:1).

Listen in on an intimate conversation as the Son of God speaks to his heavenly Father. It is Jesus praying for you. This is truly *the Lord's Prayer*. Jesus is only a few hours from being crucified for the sin of the world. He bows before the Father to intercede for you and to communicate that his mission is nearing its completion. He prays that you will have a fullness of joy (vs. 13), that you would be kept from evil (vs. 15), and that you should be sanctified or set apart from the world by the truth of the Word of God (vs. 17). This is an unusual glimpse into the prayer life of Jesus. We often read how Jesus would come apart from his busy life to spend time with his Father in prayer. John who recorded these words would have been close enough to hear them and recorded them for us under the inspiration of the Holy Spirit. Jesus closes his prayer by declaring that God's name and love has been revealed to the world. He prayed that the same love the Father had for the Son would also be in us and that his abiding presence would continue into eternity.

Ponderings

Praise

Petitions

November 10
John 18–19

> "Then came Jesus forth wearing the crown of thorns, and the purple robe. And Pilate saith unto them, Behold the man!" (John 19:5).

Here stands Jesus, convicted as a criminal and sentenced to die by crucifixion. Here is a man who had done only good on the earth his entire life. He healed the blind, made the lame to walk, and had made the unclean leper whole and clean. He forgave the sin of a prostitute and put to shame the self-righteousness of the Pharisees. He welcomed the little children and fed the multitudes. What had he done to deserve such an end? See him there crowned with the sin of the world. His crown of thorns represented the curse that was placed upon all the earth at the fall of Adam. He is draped in a purple robe to represent his authority as King of the Jews. The crowd begins to jeer and cast insults at him they called for his immediate execution. Jesus, the Son of God stands before the world condemned to die a sinner's death, and yet he would die for the very ones who were arranging his death. On the cross he cried out to the Father, "Forgive them for they know not what they do" (Luke 23:34). Jesus, who did no sin died for the sin of every person born of Adam's race. Behold the man!

Ponderings

Praise

Petitions

November 11
John 20–21

"The said Jesus to them again, Peace be unto you: as the Father hath sent me, even so send I you" (John 20:21).

Just as God sent his Son to the earth, Jesus sent out the saints in a similar fashion. Both were sent with a purpose, to bring salvation to people who are lost and need to be saved. Jesus came to bring salvation; in the same way we are to bring salvation through the preaching of the Gospel. God sent his Son to the earth because of his great love for mankind. It is with that same compassion that we are to go to bear the Good News to every person. Jesus was sent with a vision, a vision that would lead him to a cruel Roman cross where he gave his life. Can we do any less than to give our lives in the work of the Lord? God sent his Son to a people who would reject him; we should not be surprised when we are rejected for preaching the Word of God. God sent his Son to make disciples out of ungodly people. That should be our cause as well, to turn ungodly people into committed followers of Jesus Christ. In our work for the Lord, Jesus should always be our example. For as the Father sent him, even so were you sent to do his will.

Ponderings

Praise

Petitions

November 12
Acts 1–3

"And they continued stedfastly in the apostles' doctrine and fellowship, and in breaking of bread, and in prayers" (Acts 2:42).

Here we see the ministries of the early church. Notice that before anything was accomplished we find the early church engaged in a prayer meeting (Acts 1:14). After being filled with the Holy Spirit, the next was the ministry of evangelism. There were 3000 souls saved at this impromptu meeting. Once the church was established and growing, there was yet much to be done in obedience to the Great Commission. So, they continued in the *apostle's doctrine.* This involved the teaching of God's word and the training of new believers. Every day (Acts 5:42) there were Bible studies and training sessions in the Temple and in the homes of the people. There was also much *fellowship.* This is missing in many of our churches today. Believers need time to spend together sharing about life's experiences and encouraging one another. The *breaking of bread* spoken of was the celebration of the Lord's Supper, just as Jesus had told them to do to remember his death till he comes again. Finally, we see the church returning to a ministry of prayer. The life and ministry of the church begins and ends with prayer.

Ponderings

Praise

Petitions

November 13
Acts 4–5

"Then Peter and the other apostles answered and said, We ought to obey God rather than men" (Acts 5:29).

The apostles had received two orders, one from the Lord and one from the Sanhedrin who had arrested them for preaching in Jerusalem. After threatening them "they called them, and commanded them not to speak at all nor teach in the name of Jesus" (Acts 4:18). After being arrested for disobeying this order they were put in prison. However, they did not remain there. In the night an angel came and opened the door to let them out and give them another order, "Go, stand and speak in the temple to the people all the words of this life" (Acts 5:20). Peter and the other apostles were once again arrested and brought in to answer to the council. It was not difficult for them to choose whom they would obey, as they told the council, "We ought to obey God rather then men." Though their choice was an easy one, the consequences were not so easy. After beating them, the council set them free. They left "rejoicing that they were counted worthy to suffer shame for his name" (Acts 4:41).

Ponderings

Praise

Petitions

November 14
Acts 6–7

"But we will give ourselves continually to prayer, and to the ministry of the word" (Acts 6:4).

The apostles found themselves busy with the daily distribution of food to the widows and others in need. However, there arose a problem in that they were not getting around to everyone. Not only that, but the daily distribution of food was taking the apostles away from their most important ministries, those of prayer, teaching, and preaching the Word of God. The solution was to appoint other people who would be servants of the church. They established some standards (Acts 6:3) and chose out seven men to take care of this ministry. These servants became known as *deacons*. The deacons were to serve in the daily ministry of physical labor, in this case serving food. Notice that they were not given any authority in the church other than to serve in such a way as to give the church leaders time to pursue their ministries of prayer and Bible study. Somewhere we have lost the original purpose of deacons. They are not to be in charge of running the church; they are simply servants of the church. In what way could you help your Pastor so that he can give more time to prayer and Bible Study?

Ponderings

Praise

Petitions

November 15
Acts 8–9

"Therefore they that were scattered abroad went every where preaching the word." (Acts 8:4).

The new church at Jerusalem certainly had her share of problems. The Jewish leaders were now persecuting the church severely. Saints were being arrested and some even killed for their faith. While the apostles were able to stay in Jerusalem many had to flee into the regions around the city. When these people went out, they took the Gospel with them. So the persecution resulted in aiding the spread of the Gospel. When people left town to get away from the persecution, they went preaching the Word to every one with whom they came in contact. While the persecutors were trying to stamp out the Gospel they were only spreading it further. Often when we are faced with some trial or dilemma, it seems that there can be no good come of it. And then we find that God was using this circumstance in our lives to do something for his glory. Paul said, "And we know that all things work together for good to them that love God, to them who are the called according to his purpose" (Romans 8:28). When the going gets rough, just follow the Lord, there may be good things ahead.

Ponderings

_____
_____
_____

Praise

_____
_____
_____

Petitions

_____
_____
_____

November 16
Acts 10–11

"And the apostles and brethren that were in Judea heard that the Gentiles had also received the world of God" (Acts 11:1).

When Peter preached the Gospel at the house of Cornelius, a Gentile, it caused not a small stirring among the Jewish believers. After all, the Gospel was preached among the Jews, how was it possible that an unclean Gentile could be saved. As far as they were concerned, God had no love or compassion toward Gentiles. Jesus had come to them and up until this time the Gospel had mostly been preached among the Jews. What a shock it was to their thinking that even Gentiles could be saved! But that was the reality. The Gospel of Jesus Christ was not reserved for only one people. When Jesus died, he died for the sins of the whole world. When Jesus told them to go and preach, he said, "Go ye into all the world and preach the Gospel to every creature" (Mark 16:15). No one was to be excluded from God's gift of salvation. He wants every person to know how much he loves them and that he sent Jesus to die for their sin as well. God sees us all the same, as lost sinners in need of a Savior.

Ponderings

Praise

Petitions

November 17
Acts 12–13

"Peter therefore was kept in prison: but prayer was made without ceasing of the church unto God for him" (Acts 12:5).

When Peter was put into prison because Herod *saw that it pleased the Jews*, the people of the church did the only thing they knew to do—pray. Even while they were gathered at Mary's house crying out to the Lord, God was answering their prayer. An angel appeared at the prison and escorted Peter past all the guards and through the open gates. When Peter went to the prayer meeting and knocked on the door, he was left standing on the front porch as Rhoda went to tell the others. At first they did not believe her. Isn't it amazing how often we pray for God to do some miracle on our behalf and when the miracle comes we refuse to accept it in unbelief! When we pray, we should not be so surprised to find that God had already been working to answer our prayer. He knows what we need even before we ask him, and often he is already preparing an answer to our prayer before we even ask. Why should we be so surprised when God answers our prayers? After all, he promised!

Ponderings

Praise

Petitions

November 18
Acts 14–15

"But we believe that through the grace of the Lord Jesus Christ we shall be saved, even as they" (Acts 15:11).

It did not take long for there to arise a group of people who would try to add works to the grace of God and thus distort the Gospel of Jesus Christ. In this case it was the Pharisees who were steeped in their holiness and self-righteousness. They decided that faith was not enough, and that in order for one to be saved one also had to be circumcised and obey the Law of Moses. There was a big meeting at the Church in Jerusalem to discuss the matter. They came to the conclusion that salvation was a gift from God and did not need to be earned by any kind of additional works. They sent out leaders encouraging people to be respectful of some of the Jewish traditions, but that salvation was by God's grace. Later Paul would write to the church at Ephesus, "For by grace are ye saved through faith; and that not of yourselves: it is the gift of God: Not of works, lest any man should boast" (Ephesians 2:8–9). There is nothing in this world you can do to earn your salvation. It is God's gift of love to everyone who will place their faith in his Son.

Ponderings

Praise

Petitions

November 19
Acts 16–17

"And the times of this ignorance God winked at; but now commendeth all men every where to repent:" (Acts 17:30).

As Paul walked through the markets of Athens, he saw on every corner and in every place idols that represented the gods of Greece. This motivated him even more to preach the Gospel of the true and living God. When the philosophers and thinkers of Athens heard him speak of one who had risen from the dead, it piqued their interest; and they inquired of him to tell them more. Paul used this opportunity to declare unto them the Lord Jesus Christ. As he looked around, he noticed an idol with the inscription *to the unknown God*. He told the Athenians that this was the God of creation and that he is not worshiped in *temples made with hands*. He told them how that if they would just seek him, they would find him. And there on Mars hill Paul led many of his listeners to the Lord. Of course, there were some who mocked him and rejected the Gospel; others wanted to hear more. How many there are today who worship at the altar of an *unknown god!* We must keep telling them how God loves them and sent his Son to die for their sin.

Ponderings

Praise

Petitions

November 20
Acts 18–19

"Many of them also which used curious arts brought their books together, and burned them before all men" (Acts 19:19).

Ephesus was a city filled with idols and all manner of false gods and magicians. When Paul brought the Gospel to Ephesus, there was a great change that began to take place in the lives of the people who lived there. The inhabitants of Ephesus were accustomed to seeing magicians and wizards ply their arts by performing what appeared to be miracles, but they could not do anything that compared to the miracles of God that were wrought by Paul's presence. As people began to believe on the Lord Jesus Christ, they began to confess their false practices. Many even brought their books of evil enchantments and burned them before all the people. It was a statement of repentance from their former lives and a testimony of their commitment to Jesus Christ. The cost was great; the Scripture says that the worth of the books were *fifty thousand pieces of silver* which could be estimated to be worth about six million dollars. What a testimony to a complete commitment to following the Lord Jesus Christ!

Ponderings

Praise

Petitions

November 21
Acts 20–21

> "But none of these things move me, neither count I my life dear unto myself, so that I might finish my course with joy, and the ministry, which I have received of the Lord Jesus, to testify the gospel of the grace of God" (Acts 20:24).

How important is it for us to see that the Gospel of Jesus Christ is preached to every person? How important is your own ministry of witnessing? To Paul it was more important than his own suffering, imprisonment, and even his own life. He was so committed to preaching the Gospel of Christ and carrying out the ministry that God had given him that his own suffering was of little consequence. In a day of padded pews and air-conditioned buildings it would seem that suffering for the Gospel's sake is the farthest thing from our minds. Many churches have completely suspended their visitation and outreach ministries finding that it is difficult to get people to even come to a Worship Service. Many churches have simply become entertainment centers with little regard for the Great Commission or obedience to the Word of God. How important is reaching people for the Lord to you? It should be the most important.

Ponderings

Praise

Petitions

November 22
Acts 22–23

"And the night following the Lord stood by him, and said, Be of good cheer, Paul: for as thou hast testified of me in Jerusalem, so must thou bear witness also at Rome" (Acts 23:11).

Before he ascended into heaven, Jesus gave the disciples both a command and a promise. He said, "Go ye therefore, and teach all nations, baptizing them in the name of the Father, and of the Son, and of the Holy Ghost: Teaching them to observe all things whatsoever I have commanded you: and, lo, I am with you alway, even unto the end of the world" (Matthew 28:19–20). Now while Paul awaited his fate in a Roman prison cell, he found that he was not there alone, for the Lord was with him. In that prison cell the Lord encouraged Paul, "Be of good cheer." God was not finished with Paul just yet and had a plan laid out for him to preach the Word of God in Rome just as he had in Jerusalem. As followers of Jesus, we are assured of his presence with us wherever we go. He is always there with us. He also has a plan for us, which includes taking the Gospel to someone who needs the Lord. The promise of God's presence and his command to make disciples has never been rescinded. Now go.

Ponderings

Praise

Petitions

November 23
Acts 24–26

> "And after certain days when Felix came with his wife Drusilla, which was a Jewess, he sent for Paul, and heard him concerning the faith in Christ" (Acts 24:24).

After Paul's encounter with the Lord on his way to Damascus, God sent Ananias to baptize and disciple him. At first, Ananias did not want to do it because of Paul's reputation of persecution against the believers in Jerusalem. However, God told Ananias of his plan to use Paul to preach the Gospel in many places. "But the Lord said unto him, Go thy way: for he is a chosen vessel unto me, to bear my name before the Gentiles, and kings, and the children of Israel" (Acts 9:15). Paul had preached to the *children of Israel* in Jerusalem, he had also preached to *Gentiles* in the regions of Asia. Now, we find Paul standing before kings and other potentates proclaiming the name of Christ just as the Lord said he would do. From the time that Paul was saved, God had a plan for his life that would eventually take him all the way to Rome. In these final chapters of Acts we can see God's plan unfolding. God has a plan for you as well. A plan that may take you to places you never imagined.

Ponderings

Praise

Petitions

November 24
Acts 27–28

"Preaching the kingdom of God, and teaching those things which concern the Lord Jesus Christ, with all confidence, no man forbidding him" (Acts 28:31).

Paul never lost sight of what God had called him do to. He continued to teach and preach Jesus Christ and never quit. How many there be today that claim they *used* to serve the Lord in some capacity! *I used to be a Sunday school teacher*, or *I used to be a pastor,* are words often spoken by people who for some reason had quit the ministry. The Great Commission has never been annulled. No matter what our circumstances or situation we should always keep on preaching and *teaching those things that concern the Lord Jesus Christ.* Paul could have quit when he was beaten and left for dead at Iconium. He could have quit when he was arrested at Jerusalem. He could have given up when he was shipwrecked on his way to Rome. Paul never got to a place were he would say *I used to preach the Gospel*. No matter why you may have given up, get back into the ministry of the Gospel. Though you may be discouraged and downhearted, don't give up. Keep on keeping on for the sake of the Gospel of Christ. After all, he did not give up on you.

Ponderings

Praise

Petitions

November 25
Romans 1–3

"For I am not ashamed of the gospel of Christ: for it is the power of God unto salvation to everyone that believeth; to the Jew first, and also to the Greek" (Romans 1:16).

When the name of God is blasphemed in your presence or the subject of Christianity comes up in a conversation, do you take a stand for the Lord or are you embarrassed for people to know that you claim to be a Christian? For too long believers have been silent when they should have spoken up for the name of Christ. It is not always the popular position to assume in a world that is increasingly denying the Word of God. However, no matter how unpopular it is or how uncomfortable you feel, there are times when you must take your stand for the Gospel and for the Word of God. It was a dangerous position to take in Paul's day. Often believers were arrested, put in jail, and even killed for their stand for the Gospel. Remember what Jesus said? "Whosoever therefore shall confess me before men, him will I confess also before my Father which is in heaven. But whosoever shall deny me before men, him will I also deny before my Father which is in heaven" (Matthew 10:32–33). Don't be ashamed of the Gospel of Christ. Take your stand!

Ponderings

Praise

Petitions

November 26
Romans 4–7

"I find then a law, that, when I would do good, evil is present with me" (Romans 7:21).

After committing some grievous sin, how often have we heard, *I knew better, but I did it anyway?* It is indicative of the ongoing battle we have with sin. Can you relate to Paul when he confessed, "For that which I do, I allow not: for what I would, that do I not; but what I hate, that do I?" So often the very sinful things we want to remove from our lives are the same things we continue doing. So, how do we overcome these besetting sins? Paul goes on to say that victory can be had *through Jesus Christ our Lord.* (vs. 25) There is a way to have victory over sin; by yielding ourselves daily to God's will and obeying his Word. Romans 6:16 holds the answer to victory over sin. "Know ye not, that to whom ye yield yourselves servants to obey, his servants ye are to whom ye obey; whether of sin unto death, or of obedience unto righteousness?" Obedience is not always easy because it requires a daily effort and commitment of submission to the Word (and will) of God. Victory over sin can only be achieved by a close daily walk with the Lord. Who will you serve today?

Ponderings

Praise

Petitions

November 27
Romans 8–10

"Who shall separate us from the love of Christ? shall tribulation, or distress or persecution, or famine, or nakedness, or peril, or sword?" (Romans 8:35).

The question is asked, *Who (or what) shall separate us from the love of Christ?* The question could be taken in one of two ways. First, what shall keep us from loving Christ, or secondly, what shall keep Christ from loving us? From the context of this passage it is clear that the latter is the correct understanding of this question. (See vs. 38–39) The simple answer to the question is *nothing;* there is nothing that keeps the Lord from loving us. Not even our sin or disobedience keeps the Lord's love from us. Jeremiah said, "The Lord hath appeared of old unto me, saying, Yea, I have loved thee with an everlasting love: therefore with lovingkindness have I drawn thee" (Jeremiah 31:3). God's love for mankind is unconditional; there is nothing we have to do to earn his love, and there is nothing that will keep him from loving us. His love is also eternal; there will never come a time when he will stop loving us. Of this you can always be assured, God loves you, and he always will.

Ponderings

Praise

Petitions

November 28
Romans 11-14

"But why doest thou judge they brother? or why dost thou set at nought thy brother? for we shall all stand before the judgment seat of Christ" (Romans 14:10).

Passing judgment on fellow believers in Christ has become a favorite pastime of many Christians. It would seem that they have found *true* righteousness and have appointed themselves the judges of what everyone else is doing. The temptation to judge comes from selfishness and self-righteousness. Often our judgments come from envy or jealousy. However, we must remember that when we set ourselves up as a judge, we are attempting to take God's place on the throne. God knows all, including the hearts of every individual. He knows the motivations and the intents of our hearts. There is One who judges and that is the Lord. In this passage of Scripture, Paul goes on to say that "…every one of us shall give account of himself to God" (Romans 14:12). Rather than being so concerned with what others are doing, we should even be more concerned with what we are doing. When we stand before God, we will not give account of others, but only of ourselves.

Ponderings

Praise

Petitions

November 29
Romans 15–16

"For whatsoever things were written aforetime were written for our learning, that we through patience and comfort of the scriptures might have hope" (Romans 15:4).

The books of the Old Testament were written so that we could learn about God and what he expects of us. The accounts of Genesis through Deuteronomy tell us of God's attributes and how he deals with people. The books of history tell us of the failure of human governments and unfolds God's plan of redemption. The poetic books give us words of wisdom as well as songs of praise and worship. The books of prophecy not only give us insights into the future, but also contain God's message to his people. It is in the pages of the Old Testament that we obtain hope by learning and understanding the works of God. In 1 Corinthians 10:11, Paul said that the miracles that happened to the people of the Old Testament "… happened unto them for ensamples: and they are written for our admonition, upon whom the ends of the world are come." The books of the Old Testament should not be written off as *irrelevant*. They are very relevant for our learning and admonition.

Ponderings

Praise

Petitions

November 30
1 Corinthians 1–4

"But as it is written, Eye hath not seen, nor ear heard, neither have entered into the heart of man, the things which God hath prepared for them that love him" (1 Corinthians 2:9).

The mental images we have of heaven are made up of our imagination. We try to imagine what waits for us in eternity. We are told in Scripture of streets of gold, a crystal sea, various gems, and precious stones. Yet, we are still left to our imagination in trying to get a glimpse of its actual appearance. No human, other than Jesus, has been able to paint a picture for us. The things that await us in heaven are so far beyond our imagination that they have not even *entered into the heart of man*. We imagine heaven to be a wonderful and beautiful place, a place were there is perfect peace and absolute holiness. However, we have not even scratched the surface when it comes to understanding what heaven is really like. God has prepared such a fantastic place for us that we cannot even imagine its magnitude or beauty. It will be more than our finite minds can even comprehend. The things that God has prepared for us will only be revealed when we reach that heavenly shore.

Ponderings
___
___
___

Praise
___
___
___

Petitions
___
___
___

December 1
1 Corinthians 5–9

"What? Know ye not that your body is the temple of the Holy Ghost which is in you, which ye have of God, and ye are not your own?" (1 Corinthians 6:19).

Soon after the children of Israel had left Egypt they arrived at Mount Sinai. There God gave to Moses the Law governing their behavior and worship. It was at Mt. Sinai that God also told Moses how to construct and furnish a building called the Tabernacle. It would later be reconstructed as a permanent place in Jerusalem and called the Temple. It would be the place where God would meet with his people. The word *temple* comes from a Greek word that means *dwelling place*. It would become the *dwelling place* of God. When Jesus died on the cross something remarkable happened. God's dwelling place would no long be the Temple in Jerusalem, but in the body of each person who received Jesus Christ into their lives. As believers in Christ, we have become the Temple of God. In 1 Corinthians 3:16 Paul said it this way: "Know ye not that ye are the temple of God, and that the Spirit of God dwelleth in you?" Imagine, you are now the *dwelling place* of God. Are you taking care of God's *dwelling place*?

Ponderings

Praise

Petitions

December 2
1 Corinthians 10–13

"There hath no temptation taken you but such as is common to man: but God is faithful, who will not suffer you to be tempted above that ye are able; but will with the temptation also make a way to escape, that ye may be able to bear it" (1 Corinthians 10:13).

Every individual faces temptations of some kind. Temptation can come from several sources. Often the devil will tempt people to sin. He knows our weaknesses and will tempt us to sin at our weakest point. Temptation also comes from our own natural desires or lusts. James said, "But every man is tempted, when he is drawn away of his own lust, and enticed" (James 1:14). In whatever way we are tempted there are a few things that we can count on. First, the temptation WILL come. No one is free of temptation. That does not mean that we have to give in to the temptation. The temptation itself is not sin; it is when we act on the temptation that it becomes sin. Secondly, there is always a way out. Often when temptation comes we are looking for a way in rather than a way out. However, the escape is not far away. Finally, there will never be a temptation that confronts you that is more than you can bear; God promised.

Ponderings

Praise

Petitions

December 3
1 Corinthians 14–16

"Therefore, my beloved brethren, be ye steadfast, unmovable, always abounding in the work of the Lord, forasmuch as ye know that your labour is not in vain in the Lord" (1 Corinthians 15:58).

Because of the resurrection of Jesus Christ we have been given victory over death and sin. Therefore Paul encourages us to do or be three things. First we are to be steadfast. To be *steadfast* means that we are to be *fixed on a spot*, never to be moved. We are to be firmly planted and rooted in the Lord Jesus Christ and in his Word. Secondly we are to be *unmovable*, unmovable like the tree that is planted by rivers of water. Nothing in this world should be able to move us in our resolve to serve the Lord faithfully and fully. Finally, Paul says that we are to abound *in the work of the Lord*. To abound means to excel or to do more than is expected of us. The work of the Lord is found in fulfilling the Great Commission; preaching the Gospel to *every creature*. We are to excel in the work of the Lord knowing that our labour is *not in vain*. Though we may not see immediate results, we have the promise that our work will count for something in the Kingdom of God.

Ponderings

Praise

Petitions

December 4
2 Corinthians 1–4

"Who comforteth us in all our tribulation, that we may be able to comfort them which are in any trouble, by the comfort wherewith we ourselves are comforted of God" (2 Corinthians 1:4).

The word *comfort* in this verse comes from the Greek word *parakaleo* or *paraklesis*, which means to *call to one's side*. It is the same word that Jesus used when he described the Holy Spirit as the *Comforter* (John 14:16). It speaks of one who comes along side another with the intent to help or encourage. We often go through trials for various reasons. Sometimes the trials we experience strengthen our faith, other times our trials bring us to a greater level of maturity. (See James 1:1–5) Whatever the reason, all of the trials we experience in this life give us a capability to comfort or encourage others who are going trough the same trials. The comfort ultimately comes from the indwelling Holy Spirit, but there are times when another believer can benefit from hearing about the trials that you have gone through and how God brought you through them. Learn to encourage others by sharing the victories you have had in your own trials in life.

Ponderings

Praise

Petitions

December 5
2 Corinthians 5–9

"Therefore if any man be in Christ, he is a new creature: old things are passed away; behold, all things are become new" (2 Corinthians 5:17).

Jesus Christ makes all the difference in the world to those who have placed their faith in him. Part of the miracle of the New Birth is the change in the life of a person who received Christ into their lives. Jesus can take an alcoholic and make him sober. He can take the drug addict and make him clean. When a person truly gives their life to the Lord, they are never the same again. Sometimes the change is dramatic and quite obvious, other times the change might be more subtle. In the testimony of most believers is the story of their life before Christ and how he changed them to what they are today. Trusting Christ is more than turning over a new leaf, it is a complete change in our thoughts, motives, and direction. Christ gives us new life, new hope, and a new home. Our life is now in and for him. We no longer live for ourselves but to please the Lord. Our hope is no longer in our own abilities, but in what the Lord can do through us. Our home is no longer in this world, but in heavenly places. Yes! Christ makes all the difference.

Ponderings

Praise

Petitions

December 6
2 Corinthians 10–13

"Examine yourselves, whether ye be in the faith; prove your own selves. Know ye not your own selves, how that Jesus Christ is in you, except ye be reprobates?" (2 Corinthians 13:5).

From time to time it is beneficial for the believer to take a self-examination. It is especially important when it applies to personal salvation and the presence of sin. Take some time to review in your mind your own salvation experience. It might even be a good idea to write it out. Think of the time when you bowed before the Lord under the conviction of your own sin, asked his forgiveness, and invited him into your life. Reviewing or *proving* your salvation experience gives you an assurance of your salvation. Look at the Scriptures that you were shown when you were saved and let them speak to your heart once again. It is also a good idea to examine your heart concerning the presence of sin. David prayed, "Search me, O God, and know my heart: try me, and know my thoughts: And see if there be any wicked way in me, and lead me in the way everlasting" (Psalms 139:23–24). As God reveals the sin that is in your life, be quick to confess it and make it right with the Lord.

Ponderings

Praise

Petitions

December 7
Galatians 1–3

"But though we, or an angel from heaven, preach any other gospel unto you than that which we have preached unto you, let him be accursed" (Galatians 1:8).

The words of Paul are very strong and forceful in this verse. As in Paul's day there are those around who have perverted the Gospel of Christ. Usually this perversion is in the form of either adding something to the Gospel such as works, or removing something from the Gospel, such as faith. Some had come to Galatia teaching that in order to be saved, one must keep the law. This was adding works to the Gospel. In 1 Corinthians 15:13-4 Paul explained just exactly what the Gospel was. He said, "For I delivered to you first of all that which I also received: that Christ died for our sins according to the Scriptures, and that he was buried, and that he rose again the third day according to the Scriptures." He also stated that the Gospel had to be accepted on the basis of faith and not by the *works of the Law.* "Knowing that a man is not justified by the works of the law, but by the faith of Jesus Christ, even we have believed in Jesus Christ, that we might be justified by the faith of Christ" (Galatians 2:16a). Let him who preaches any other Gospel *be accursed.*

Ponderings

Praise

Petitions

December 8
Galatians 4–6

"Brethren, If a man be overtaken in a fault, ye which are spiritual, restore such an one in the spirit of meekness; considering thyself, lest thou also be tempted" (Galatians 6:1).

When a fellow believer falls into some kind of sin, many are quick to condemn, criticize, and judge. Why is it that when a brother has fallen, it is the Christians that are the first to condemn him? We are often admonished in Scripture about judging our brother and yet many do it anyway. Rather than passing judgment on one who has fallen we should be attempting to restore them into fellowship with the Lord and ourselves. Remember what happened when the Pharisees brought a woman to Jesus that was taken in adultery (John 8:1–11). Jesus said to them "he that is without sin among you, let him first cast a stone at her" (John 8:7b). Our attempt at restoration should not be with any self-righteousness or pride, but in a spirit of humility. Recognize that no one is exempt from temptation and all are likely to fall into the same sin. Our intention toward a brother who has sinned should be restoration; after all it could be ourselves who are in need of help and restoration.

Ponderings

Praise

Petitions

December 9
Ephesians 1–6

"And be ye kind one to another, tenderhearted, forgiving one another, even as God for Christ's sake hath forgiven you" (Ephesians 4:32).

How many Christians live at odds with each other because they are not willing to forgive? Something is said and feelings are hurt, and rather than responding with forgiveness, we grow bitter, angry, and resentful. Our response to a person should not be based on their behavior toward us, but on how the Lord responded to us and our sin. Romans 5:8 states, "But God commendeth his love toward us, in that, while we were yet sinners, Christ died for us." Did you catch that little phrase, "While we were yet sinners?" God did not wait until we loved him to send Jesus to pay for our sin. His love was so great toward us that he made the first move in sending his own Son to die for us. "We love him, because he first loved us" (1 John 4:19). God loved us first even when we were not deserving of his love. Now he expects us to love others like he loved us, and in that love forgive others even as he forgave us. Since we are forgiven of our sin, we are free to forgive those who have offended us. Who do you need to forgive?

Ponderings

Praise

Petitions

December 10
Philippians 1–4

"Be careful for nothing; but in everything by prayer and supplication with thanksgiving let your requests be made known unto God" (Philippians 4:6).

There is no reason for a believer to be anxious, nervous, or to be overcome with worry when we have such a promise from the Lord. God knows everything that comes into our lives and cares greatly about what happens to us. When situations arise that would cause us anxiety and worry, we are to take them to the Lord. Certainly he knows our need before we even ask; however, when we take our cares to him we have a confidence that he hears our prayer and supplication and is sufficient to meet every need. Just in the act of taking our cares to him we are showing our faithfulness in the Lord. When we make our requests known to him, we are also demonstrating our dependence on the Lord. Notice that when we bring our needs to him it is to be with an attitude of appreciation. We come with a thankful heart knowing that God will hear and answer our prayer. As we pray, there is a peace that comes over us in knowing that God is in control. The worry and anxiety are gone and replaced with the peace of God.

Ponderings

Praise

Petitions

December 11
Colossians 1–4

"And he is the head of the body, the church: who is the beginning, the firstborn from the dead; that in all things he might have the preeminence" (Colossians 1:18).

For Jesus to have the *preeminence* means that he has first place. If Jesus is truly the Lord of your life, then he must have the first place in everything. When you are faced with making a major decision, you must ask yourself, "What would Jesus do?" He must be first in every aspect of our lives. In our finances he should receive the *first fruits*. In the choices we make we must consider how this choice is obedient to the Word of God and how it will honor the Lord Jesus Christ. The natural thing to do is to put ourselves first and consider how we are affected by our choices. When Jesus has first place, many of our choices are already made. Attending worship at your local assembly should not be a choice you have to make every week. If Jesus is first, the choice is already made. Is Jesus first in your relationships? What about how you spend you time, and your money? What about your choices in entertainment? Jesus must come first in everything.

Ponderings

Praise

Petitions

December 12
1 Thessalonians 1–5

"Wherefore comfort one another with these words" (1 Thessalonians 4:18).

The words that outline the events surrounding the Rapture (the catching away of the saints) should be comforting words to every believer. They remind us of when the Lord will come to take us out of this world of sin and sorrow. What a day that will be when Jesus comes to take those who believe in him to be with him fulfilling his promise! (John 14:3) This event will mark the end of our time on earth and begin the closing days of time as we know it. It is comforting to know that such a day will come. However, for those who have rejected the Gospel of Christ these words should strike terror in their hearts. For it also marks the beginning of the Great Tribulation, seven years of worldwide terror, destruction, and judgment. Before the Tribulation begins, the Christians will be taken off of this earth. After the Rapture, those who are left will suffer greatly under the leadership of the Antichrist spoken of in Revelation. Whether or not you are taken in the Rapture depends on what you have done with Jesus Christ. 1 Thessalonians 4:14 holds the key, "For If we believe that Jesus died and rose again, even so them also which sleep in Jesus will God bring with him."

Ponderings

Praise

Petitions

December 13
2 Thessalonians 1–3

"Finally, brethren, pray for us, that the word of the Lord may have free course, and be glorified, even as it is with you:" (2 Thessalonians 3:1).

Paul knew the importance of prayer and was not ashamed to ask the brethren at Thessalonica to pray for him and his ministry. Many a missionary will stand before a congregation and request prayer, and their request is often received as insignificant. When missionaries ask you to pray, it is not a light request; they need you to pray for them. Many pray for missionaries in such generalities that their prayers seem empty. When you pray for missionaries who are laboring in their respective fields, learn to pray specifically for them by name. Take note of their prayer letters and of their particular needs, and requests, and then pray specifically for that need. Also pray consistently for them. "Pray without ceasing" (1 Thessalonians 5:17). Pray for your missionaries every day and for the events and activities in which they will have a part. Pray for their families. Pray that the seed of the Word of God will be planted in fertile soil. When Paul requested prayer, it was not a light request. Your missionaries need you to pray for them.

Ponderings

Praise

Petitions

December 14
1 Timothy 1–6

"Let no man despise thy youth; but be thou an example of the believers, in word, in conversation, in charity, in spirit, in faith, in purity" (1 Timothy 4:12).

Timothy was a young man whom Paul was mentoring for the ministry. In this little epistle, Paul is teaching him how to oversee the affairs of the local church. The purpose of his letter can be found in chapter 3, verse 15; "But if I tarry long, that thou mayest know how thou oughtest to behave thyself in the house of God, which is the church of the living God, the pillar and ground of the truth." Paul encourages him not to allow anyone to look down on or *despise* his youth. The best way to show his qualification as a leader is to be an example to those around him. He would not convince people of his position by fancy words or superior intellect. His best method of preaching the Gospel and teaching the believers would be by his own example. The best pastors are those who show the Christian life in how they live and not so much by what they say in the pulpit. The same is true for anyone who is in Christian leadership. Allow Christ to be seen in you and others will learn from your example.

Ponderings

Praise

Petitions

December 15
2 Timothy 1–4

> "Nevertheless the foundation of God standeth sure, having this seal, The Lord knoweth them that are his. And Let every one that nameth the name of Christ depart from iniquity" (2 Timothy 2:19).

Those who have genuinely put their faith in Christ can be assured of this; God knows *them that are his.* Jesus said it this way, "My sheep hear my voice, and I know them, and they follow me" (John 10:27). Being confident that the Lord knows his own gives believers an assurance that they are in God's hand and that God knows all about their trials and burdens. Believers are encouraged to bring all their cares to the Lord. "Casting all your care upon him; for he careth for you" (1 Peter 5:7). God knows those who are his and cares about what happens in their lives. He has a great plan for each one and his desire for his own is to bring blessing into their lives. Knowing that they are in God's care, Christians are then to live free from the sin that had enslaved them. If they are to grow to be like Jesus, they must remove all sin from their lives and avoid even the appearance of being involved in sinful behavior.

Ponderings

Praise

Petitions

December 16
Titus and Philemon

"This is a faithful saying, and these things I will that thou affirm constantly, that they which have believed in God might be careful to maintain good works. These things are good and profitable unto men" (Titus 3:8).

There is no question that we are saved by the grace of God. "For by grace are ye saved through faith" (Ephesians 2:8). The merits of our own works amount to a pile of filthy rags when it comes to our salvation. However, we must not throw away good works at the expense of grace. Ephesians 2:10 states, "For we are his workmanship, created in Christ Jesus unto good works, which God hath before ordained that we should walk in them." God intended for us to show our salvation by our good works. We were not saved to continue in sin, but to live a life that is full of godliness and righteousness. Jesus said, "Let your light so shine before men, that they may see your good works, and glorify your Father which is in heaven" (Matthew 5:16). It is our good works through which the light shines. In order for people to see Jesus in us, they must see our good works. Yes, we are saved by grace, but we must let our *light shine* so that others can see Christ in us and in turn glorify the Lord.

Ponderings

Praise

Petitions

December 17
Hebrews 1–4

"Wherefore, holy brethren, partakers of the heavenly calling, consider the Apostle and High Priest of our profession, Christ Jesus" (Hebrews 3:1).

Did you ever think of Jesus as an *Apostle*? An apostle is a messenger sent with a particular message. Jesus is the *Apostle* of God. He came to this earth with the message of God. That message was one of love and reconciliation. Jesus not only brought the message, he was that message. God so loved the world that he sent his Son to demonstrate that love. "But God commendeth his love toward us, in that, while we were yet sinners, Christ died for us" (Romans 5:8). He was not only God's *Apostle*, but he was also our *High Priest*. The High Priest was a mediator between God and man. He would minister the atonement at the altar for the forgiveness of man's sin. As our High Priest, Jesus had to know what it was to be man. "For we have not an high priest which cannot be touched with the feeling of our infirmities; but was in all points tempted like as we are, yet without sin" (Hebrews 4:15). Jesus became our High Priest in order to bring us to God.

Ponderings

Praise

Petitions

December 18
Hebrews 5–8

"For when for the time ye ought to be teachers, ye have need that one teach you again which be the first principles of the oracles of God; and are become such as have need of milk, and not of strong meat" (Hebrews 5:12).

Churches are filled with people who have been believers for many years. While they should have grown to the point that they could be teaching others, they are still babes in Christ in need of milk. There are two problems that have created this predicament. First, many who come to the Lord for salvation do not follow him in discipleship. They do not have a personal habit of Bible study and prayer. They go to church; they give; and they sit in a pew and soak up the messages without ever searching the Scriptures for themselves. The second problem also comes from a lack of good discipleship training. Many of our churches have become evangelistic centers only. There is no clear in-depth teaching of the Word of God. People are not being equipped to do the work of the ministry in teaching new believers. Don't allow yourself to become one of these grown-up baby Christians. Study the Word on your own and teach someone else how to follow the Lord along with you.

Ponderings

Praise

Petitions

December 19
Hebrews 9–10

"For then must he often have suffered since the foundation of the world: but now once in the end of the world hath he appeared to put away sin by the sacrifice of himself" (Hebrews 9:26).

Every year the high priest was to enter the Holy of Holies in order to offer a sacrifice known as the atonement. He would shed the blood of an innocent lamb for the remission of the sins of the people. He would also confess their iniquity while placing his hands upon a goat, thus placing all their sin upon it. That goat was taken out into the wilderness and released, signifying the removing of the sin of the people. When Jesus died on the cross, he became the final atoning sacrifice. He took upon himself all of our sin and shed his innocent blood for us. No longer would the high priest have to offer atonement again. The supreme sacrifice of Jesus on the cross would be sufficient to take away the sins of the whole world. "Herein is love, not that we loved God, but that he loved us, and sent his Son to be the propitiation (atoning sacrifice) for our sins" (1 John 4:10). Jesus is our sacrificial lamb.

Ponderings

Praise

Petitions

December 20
Hebrews 11–13

"But without faith it is impossible to please him; for he that cometh to God must believe that he is, and that he is a rewarder of them that diligently seek him" (Hebrews 11:6).

Man tries many ways to please God. He may try rituals and ceremonies that often become empty and meaningless. He may try to please God through donations to the church or para-church organizations. Others think they will please God by showing up in a church service once a week. Others think they can please God through tireless labor doing *God's work*. All of these things are good in and of themselves; however, there is one thing missing. *Without faith it is impossible to please him.* It is our faith that pleases God. We can participate in ceremonies, give everything we have to the Lord's work, and it is all meaningless without faith. Faith is defined for us in the first verse of Hebrews 11. "Now faith is the substance of things hoped for, the evidence of things not seen." The one thing that God desires from us most is to simply trust him. To please the Lord, you must have a complete trust in him and in his Word.

Ponderings

Praise

Petitions

December 21
James 1–5

"But every man is tempted, when he is drawn away of his own lust, and enticed. Then when lust hath conceived, it bringeth forth sin, and sin, when it is finished, bringeth forth death" (James 1:14–15).

Man has become a master of blaming his sin on other things than himself. Many will place the blame of their sin on the devil; others place the blame on the situation. Still others will blame their sin on family members or even God. Man's sin comes from within himself. From the time of Adam's fall in the Garden of Eden, man has a tendency towards sin. James explains that sin is usually because of man's *lust*. Though the word *lust* is often connected with sexual desires it actually applies to all the desires that are in a person's heart. Our sin comes from our own uncontrolled appetites. It is when we allow these desires to take control of our lives that we cross over into sin. The real issue here is, who is in control? Rather than following our heart's desires we should be seeking God's righteousness and bringing ourselves into obedience to God's Word and will. When we follow our own will, the end results are disastrous.

Ponderings

Praise

Petitions

December 22
1 Peter 1–5

"Wherefore, let them that suffer according to the will of God commit the keeping of their souls to him in well doing, as unto a faithful Creator" (1 Peter 4:19).

There comes a time in every believer's life when he will experience suffering. It may come in the form of attacks by Satan or even by the brethren. It may come in the form of physical disease or other ailments. Sometimes the suffering is the result of financial setbacks. Whatever the cause may be, there should only be one response, commit yourself fully to the Lord, *the faithful Creator*. We should not be surprised when a time of trial or suffering comes into our lives. Our example of suffering is Jesus. "For even hereunto were ye called: because Christ also suffered for us, leaving us an example, that ye should follow his steps" (1 Peter 2:21). This passage goes on to say that when Jesus suffered insults and threats that he *reviled not again* nor did he return the threats. His course of action was to "commit himself to him who judges righteously." Are you suffering through some trial? Your best course of action is to follow in the footsteps of the Savior and commit your suffering to the Lord.

Ponderings

Praise

Petitions

December 23
2 Peter 1–3

"The Lord is not slack concerning his promise, as some men count slackness; but is longsuffering to us-ward, not willing that any should perish, but that all should come to repentance" (2 Peter 3:9).

There has never been a promise that God has made that he did not keep. He promised that if we would put our faith in his Son, who died for us, that we would not "perish, but have everlasting life" (John 3:16b). It is God's will and purpose for every person to come to a saving knowledge of Jesus Christ. God wants everyone to be saved. The Scriptures tell us that "God so loved the world that he gave his only begotten son" (John 3:16a). There is not one person that God does not love and desire to enter into eternal fellowship with him. When Jesus died on the cross, it was not just for a select few, but for every person who would come to him, repent of their sin, and ask him to come into their lives. Jesus said, "For God sent not his Son into the world to condemn the world; but that the world through him might be saved" (John 3:17). If you have never accepted Christ as your own personal Savior, it is God's will that you come to him today.

Ponderings

Praise

Petitions

December 24
1 John 1–5

"These things have I written unto you that believe on the name of the Son of God; that ye may know that ye have eternal life, and that ye may believe on the name of the Son of God" (1 John 5:13).

When a person has placed their faith in the Lord Jesus Christ, they can be assured of their salvation. There is no reason that a believer should wonder about or question their salvation. Salvation is not a guessing game. It is not a question of whether I have been good enough to enter heaven's gates. Our salvation is not dependent on our works or good deeds. It is entirely dependent on what we have done with Jesus Christ. Those who have put their faith in him can know that they have eternal life. For the believer, salvation is a certainty not a question mark. Jesus told a great Jewish scholar who had asked him about eternal life, "That whosoever believeth in him (Jesus) should not perish, but have eternal life" (John 3:15). This man would have had many good works in his life, but they would not be enough. He still had to *believe* on the Lord Jesus Christ. You can know you have eternal life when you put your faith in the Lord.

Ponderings

Praise

Petitions

December 25
2, 3 John, Jude

"Beloved, when I gave all diligence to write unto you of the common salvation, it was needful for me to write unto you, and exhort you that ye should earnestly contend for the faith which was once delivered unto the saints" (Jude 3).

As we come into the last days, there should be no surprise at the rise of those who would mock our faith. There are many false prophets and teachers among us. Many of them expound their false doctrines through television and radio and many there be that flock to them. We should not allow them to continue in their false teachings unchallenged. Everything that you hear must be measured against the Scripture. To stand in defense for the fundamentals of the Scripture is to *contend for the faith*. There are too many people who accept what they hear from preachers and evangelists without checking to see that they are preaching the truth. Jesus warned that in the last days. "…there shall arise false Christs, and false prophets, and shall shew great signs and wonders; insomuch that, if it were possible, they shall deceive the very elect" (Matthew 24:24). Beware of false prophets, study the Scripture, and *contend for the faith*.

Ponderings

Praise

Petitions

December 26
Revelation 1–4

"The Revelation of Jesus Christ, which God gave unto him, to shew unto his servants things which must shortly come to pass; and he sent and signified it by his angel unto his servant John" (Revelation 1:1).

The final book of the Bible is the Revelation of Jesus Christ in the last days. There is much interest in this last book of the Bible as it holds the secrets of the future. Through his servant, the Apostle John, God reveals what will come in the last days and gives us a glimpse of what it will be like in eternity. This is the only book that promises a blessing to its readers, "Blessed is he that readeth" (Revelation 1:3). The blessings are held in store for the believers who read of their gathering around the throne with the heavenly angels to sing the praise and glory of the King of Kings and Lord of Lords. In reading revelation the believer finds hope and an assurance of his presence in eternity. He also learns of his final victory as the Savior returns for the final defeat of the enemy riding on a white horse. (Revelation 19) It must have been difficult for John to try to explain the things that he saw, yet he revealed to us the Son of God in all of his coming glory.

Ponderings

Praise

Petitions

December 27
Revelation 5–7

"For the great day of his wrath is come; and who shall be able to stand?" (Revelation 6:17).

We often hear about God's love and his grace, but little is spoken of his wrath. The Psalmist said, "Who knoweth the power of thine anger? even according to thy fear, so is thy wrath" (Psalms 90:11). The day of God's wrath will come against those who have rejected the Lord Jesus Christ. "Who shall be able to stand" against the terrible wrath of the Lord? The answer is given to us in Romans 5:8–9: "But God commendeth his love toward us, in that, while we were yet sinners, Christ died for us. Much more then, being now justified by his blood, we shall be saved from wrath through him." The only way to escape the wrath of God is through the shed blood of his Son. Through the death of Jesus Christ we are made right (justified) with God and his wrath is taken from us. John said it way, "He that believeth on the Son hath everlasting life: and he that believeth not the Son shall not see life; but the wrath of God abideth on him" (John 3:36). So, who shall be able to stand in the *day of his wrath?* Only those who have placed their faith in the Lord Jesus Christ shall be able to stand in that day.

Ponderings

Praise

Petitions

December 28
Revelation 8–11

"And the seventh angel sounded; and there were great voices in heaven, saying, The kingdoms of this world are become the kingdoms of our Lord, and of his Christ; and he shall reign for ever and ever" (Revelation 11:15).

All governments of human origin and design are destined to fail. However, the Kingdom of God is eternal and will never fail. An eternal kingdom requires an eternal King and his name is Jesus. From eternity past it was determined that he would have an eternal Kingdom. Isaiah prophesied, "Of the increase of his government and peace there shall be no end, upon the throne of David, and upon his kingdom, to order it, and to establish it with judgment and with justice from henceforth even for ever. The zeal of the Lord of hosts will perform this" (Isaiah 9:7). The subjects of the Lord's eternal kingdom will be composed of those who in their lifetime placed their faith in him. Our aim on this earth should be to seek this Kingdom above all else. Jesus said, "But seek ye first the kingdom of God, and his righteousness; and all these things shall be added unto you" (Matthew 6:33). Seek an eternal kingdom that has an eternal King.

Ponderings

Praise

Petitions

December 29
Revelation 12–15

"And they sing the song of Moses the servant of God, and the song of the Lamb, saying Great and marvelous are thy works, Lord God Almighty; just and true are thy ways, thou King of saints" (Revelation 15:3).

In eternity the saints will sing a glorious song. The title of this song is "The Song of Moses the Servant of God and the Song of the Lamb." While we don't have the melody of this hymn, we do have the words that we will be singing. They are words of praise to the *King of saints*. The song seeks to glorify the Lord for his *great and marvelous* works. His ways are declared *just and true*. As the song comes to a close, we will sing of his holiness. This song will not just be sung by a select few, but all nations will come to worship at the throne of God. It is a pleasant thought when you consider the glorious manner in which the Lord will be worshiped in eternity. But, why wait when you can worship him now, and worship him for all the same reasons? The God who will be praised for his works, his ways, and his holiness can be worshiped now. He is worthy of all our praise in time as well as eternity. "Give unto the Lord the glory due unto his name; worship the Lord in the beauty of holiness" (Psalms 29:2).

Ponderings

Praise

Petitions

December 30
Revelation 16–19

"And he saith unto me, Write, Blessed are they which are called unto the marriage supper of the Lamb. And he saith unto me, These are the true sayings of God" (Revelation 19:9).

Near the end of the Tribulation period there is going to be a great gathering of Christ and his saints. It is called the *marriage supper of the lamb*. Jesus will be united forever with his bride, the Church. The saints of God will be arrayed in *fine linen, clean and white* which is the *righteousness of the saints*. Those who are genuinely born again will be invited to this great supper. There will be much rejoicing and gladness at this supper (Revelation 19:7). The bridegroom will be honored and worshiped for redeeming his bride. Supper usually implies fellowship in the Scripture. The marriage supper of the Lamb will also be a time when the Son of God will fellowship with those who had placed their faith in him. It was for this reason that God sent his Son to die on an old rugged cross. John said earlier in his little epistle, "Truly our fellowship is with the Father, and with his Son Jesus Christ" (1 John 1:3b). What a great day it will be when we at last sit down to fellowship with our Blessed Redeemer!

Ponderings

Praise

Petitions

December 31
Revelation 20–22

"And the Spirit and the bride say, Come. And let him that heareth say, Come. And let him that is athirst come. And whosoever will, let him take the water of life freely" (Revelation 22:17).

All through the Scripture the invitation is given, "Come!" In the Old Testament the Lord said, "Incline your ear, and come unto me: hear, and your soul shall live; and I will make an everlasting covenant with you, even the sure mercies of David" (Isaiah 55:3). In the New Testament Jesus issued the invitation this way, "Come unto me, all ye that labour and are heavy laden and I will give you rest" (Matthew 11:28). The invitation is open to all those who will come and put their faith in the Lord Jesus Christ. It is God's desire that we come to him to find forgiveness of sin so that we can have complete fellowship with him. He desires a relationship with us that is based on trust and the work of his Son on the Cross. God is waiting for you to come to him. When you do, he will welcome you with open arms and forgiveness. He will not turn anyone away. The invitation is still open, won't you come to him today? There will come a day when the invitation will be closed forever. Don't wait!

Ponderings

Praise

Petitions

listen|imagine|view|experience

AUDIO BOOK DOWNLOAD INCLUDED WITH THIS BOOK!

In your hands you hold a complete digital entertainment package. Besides purchasing the paper version of this book, this book includes a free download of the audio version of this book. Simply use the code listed below when visiting our website. Once downloaded to your computer, you can listen to the book through your computer's speakers, burn it to an audio CD or save the file to your portable music device (such as Apple's popular iPod) and listen on the go!

How to get your free audio book digital download:

1. Visit www.tatepublishing.com and click on the e|LIVE logo on the home page.
2. Enter the following coupon code:
   500a-6fff-3e5e-ecba-14f5-b248-d14b-d214.
   Download the audio book from your e|LIVE digital locker and begin enjoying your new digital entertainment package today!